Maurice Pellisson

Roman Life in Pliny's Time

Maurice Pellisson

Roman Life in Pliny's Time

ISBN/EAN: 9783337043087

Printed in Europe, USA, Canada, Australia, Japan

Cover: Foto ©ninafisch / pixelio.de

More available books at **www.hansebooks.com**

ROMAN LIFE

IN

PLINY'S TIME

By

MAURICE PELLISON

Translated from the French by
MAUD WILKINSON

With an Introduction by
FRANK JUSTUS MILLER
Professor in The University of Chicago

PHILADELPHIA
GEORGE W. JACOBS & CO.
103-105 South Fifteenth Street

CONTENTS.

ILLUSTRATIONS.

INTRODUCTION.

THE story of growth from a group of unconnected hill-top settlements upon the Tiber to a political organization with world-wide dominion seems hardly to belong to sober history. Great national development has mostly come from the union of nations already existing, or from the powerful impetus contributed by parent nations to colonial stocks. But the Roman Empire was unique in this. It sprung from a single city which, though it extended its sway over the whole known world, never ceased to be not alone the seat of government, but the government itself. Rome was the nation. From her forum radiated to every land those military roads, the highways of commerce and dominion, that made her rule a vital thing wherever her conquering legions found their way. This masterful city not only absorbed all real power, but gathered up all the learning, the art, the customs and religions of the nations and made them her own ; until to be a Roman came to mean to be a citizen of the world, and Roman citizenship was a coveted prize to be attained at any cost of blood or treasure.

This wide dominion was attained by gradual and natural growth, extending over hundreds of years. The separate settlements on the hill-tops by the Tiber early joined for self-defense in one community, with common cause and common government. Because of this union they were able to master one by one all the isolated communities by which they were surrounded, and gradually, after many hard-fought wars, their sway extended over Italy. Soon Rome had occasion to champion the cause of Italy against foreign invasions, and Carthage, her nearest and greatest rival, was subdued in three great wars. In the course of these struggles, Sicily, Sardinia, and Corsica, together with Northern Africa and Spain, were added to Roman territory, the first extension of dominion beyond the bounds of Italy. In these struggles also for the first time Rome learned and the world learned that Roman arms were the match for the strongest foreign foe. The impetus of conquest extended next to Greece, and that proud land, which was full grown in civilizing arts when Rome was in her infancy, became a Roman province. Still farther east the Roman boundary was pushed until it included Asia Minor, and, at least in nominal sway, vast tracts of Asia. Meanwhile, in the north and west, Gaul, Germany, and Britain were subdued. No land was too barren or remote to escape her notice. If its people were wealthy they attracted her greed of gain ; if poor but brave, her greed of conquest.

The conquest of Greece.

This vast and heterogeneous domain was welded together into one composite whole by a wise provincial and colonial policy. Each conquered land was organized into a Roman province, with limited home rule, often under the nominal sway of some trusted native prince, but really tributary to Rome ; under Roman governors and Roman fiscal agents golden streams of wealth were kept constantly flowing to the imperial city. Rome's power was further strengthened at remote points by her colonial system, which planted colonies of her own citizens, largely veteran soldiers, in the newly conquered lands ; in this way Rome distributed her very self throughout the world.

Rome's wise colonial policy.

How was this mighty growth accomplished ? What

elements in the Roman race predestined her to wide dominion, and made her the favored nation of the earth? Right answers to these questions would reveal all that is most vital in the national history. For the history of a nation, as of a man, is but the account of the working out of those forces which lie at the basis of national and individual life.

The causes of Rome's greatness.

First among these constructive elements in Roman life was Roman character. This was made up of those virtues which are easily recognized to be distinctly Roman. There was "dignitas" that dignity or self-respect which made every citizen of Rome a king, added gravity to life, and forbade flippant trifling with person or with fame. So sacred was the Roman dignity that comedy and satire, which thrive on personalities, were forced to veil their wit and moderate their sneers. Roman literature, considered not alone for what it is, but especially for what it is not, is itself a standing proof of this strong sense of self-respect in the Roman character. Closely allied to this virtue were "iustitia" and "constantia," that righteousness of judgment and firmness of execution which enabled the first Brutus to forget paternal love and condemn his own sons for their sin against the state; which led Regulus to brave the utmost tortures of Carthage that he might keep a Roman's oath; which made the Roman arms invulnerable against outnumbering foes. It was such virtues as these in the character of the early Romans that laid the foundations of Rome's future greatness. These virtues were enhanced by the simple, hardy life of those earlier times, when men like Cincinnatus guided plowshare and state alike; when Cato toiled in cleansing now his rocky fields and now the Roman senate; when Manius Curius spurned Samnite gold that he might rule the Samnites.

Roman character.

Such qualities in her citizens predestine any nation to dominion.

A second prominent element in Roman national life was her combined spirit of conservatism and progress. This spirit was manifested in the tenacity with which the Romans held to established manners, customs, religion, law, government, every activity of life which assumed a fixed outward form.   Ancestral customs, like ancestors themselves, were held in reverence.   If changes came, it was only after evils inherent in the old had become unbearable.   In such a society no sudden revolution is possible ; customs endure until they become national ; the Roman *toga* becomes the symbol of Roman citizenship ; the eagles of Rome the emblems of victory and dominion ; life, persistent in its manifestations, becomes embedded in the very language ; and the state itself, the government, endures from generation to generation, changing with the needs of advancing civilization, but free from destructive upheavals.   This spirit of resistance to the new was most strikingly attested by the bitter struggle which the old religion maintained to the last against the fresh and irresistible power of the young Christianity.

But Rome's conservatism did not prevent her accepting, from any source, whatever promised any real advantage.   Her receptive and digestive powers were enormous, she borrowed and imitated freely from every hand, and every nation subdued by Rome left a material impress upon Roman civilization.   While statecraft, law, and war, together with the development of domestic economy and life, were all her own, her literature, religion, philosophy, and arts were deeply influenced by addition and imitation from many outside sources, especially from the Greeks.   Such a cosmopolitan culture, joined to native strength, contributed much to Rome's preëminence.

Great weight must also be given in considering the elements of Rome's greatness, to her amazing genius for law and statecraft. These, as has just been said, were all her own. So keen was her legal instinct, so wise her legislation, and so sound the development of her constitution, that Rome may justly be said to have laid the foundations of law and order for the whole civilized world. This 'genius was closely related to the Roman characteristic of justice which proceeded with such calmness of judgment and clearness of vision with reference to right. It was related to Roman conservatism also, in that the presumption was always in favor of established law or custom, and every advance was the result of growth. None but the Roman genius could have established a home government that should endure with little change for so many centuries ; none could have maintained even if it could have acquired so vast and unwieldy an empire. At a time when transportation was at best very slow, when communication of any sort with distant regions was exceedingly difficult, even the limited world of that time was vastly larger than the complete world of to-day. And yet, in spite of this, Rome's great domain was ordered and controlled in every detail by Roman law. Not only her civic power but even the influence of her very fashions was felt in the remotest province ; the barbarous Briton vied with Mede and Parthian in learning Roman arts and manners ; those who began by proudly refusing to learn the Roman language, ended by striving for distinction in eloquence ; and, as has been already said, to acquire the *toga* of citizenship was the provincial's highest ambition.

But Rome had also a marked genius for war. Even if the traditional Romulus be rejected with his military establishment and government of Rome, certain it is that the military and civil development of the nation went hand in hand from the first. That very popular assembly which had all real political power, the *comitia centuriata*, was organized on a purely military basis. "The whole people, patricians and plebeians, were divided into five classes according to a property qualification, and each of these five classes was subdivided into a certain number of voting units. In addition to these there were eighteen centuries of knights and four centuries of musicians, smiths, and carpenters. The people, in fact, were here looked upon as an army and divided into fighting bodies. The one hundred and seventy centuries of the five classes were all infantry; the cavalry was formed of the eighteen centuries of knights." Founded upon a military basis, Rome long continued a nation of warriors, whose every citizen by virtue of his franchise was a soldier. The Roman peasantry, like the English yeomanry, were designed by nature for perfect soldiers. Hardy sons of the soil, they became inured by their daily life to all the hardships that war could bring; while their constant struggles both in Rome's defense and for the extension of her power made them a nation of veterans. It was in this "hard school of war" that the true Roman "virtus," or manhood, according to their sturdy ideals, was developed, a virtue which scorned peril, and looked upon a life of hardship as ideal. These were the soldiers who formed the famous legions of Rome, those thunderbolts of war which were well nigh irresistible on countless battlefields. Nor were there worthy generals wanting to a worthy army. In the long line of military heroes that the world has known, high rank has always been awarded to the Scipios, the Fabii, the Cæsars, the Pompeys, the Agricolas of Rome. These men were not merely leaders on the field ; they were masters of the art of war, and established principles of military strategy which have been the objects of the study of the world's great captains since their day. It was such soldier-statesmen as these that first acquired empire, and then placed it upon stable foundations.

Closely linked with Rome's military prowess, as an element of progress, was her mighty "swing of conquest." This has a powerful effect whether considered subjectively or objectively. On the one hand, the consciousness of power begotten of long success produces a belief in one's own invincibility which compels victory ; while, on the other hand, the very name and reputation of success serve as an advance guard which subdues enemies without a blow. So it was with Rome. The consciousness of power nerved her arm to the blows of battle, and the prestige of the Roman name not infrequently obviated the necessity of battle and won her bloodless victories.

But not war and government alone, but letters also had an important part in Rome's development. Her first contact with Greece, which came early in the advance of her conquest, started a train of Hellenizing influence in Roman society which never ceased. Though much more slowly and imperceptibly, still none the less surely and completely did Greece master her conqueror. In all matters pertaining to literature, philosophy, and the arts, she was the acknowledged leader. Roman poetic form was fashioned upon her faultless meters ; Roman drama followed her plots ; Roman oratory was based upon her models ; Roman

philosophy was but a recapitulation of her wisdom.   But
letters, even if exotic, found in Italy congenial soil.   In
the interval of battling for existence and conquest that
followed her long struggles with Carthage, Rome found
time to think of finer things ; and in this interval old
Ennius sang the annals of Rome's greatness ; while the
rude farces that had entertained the populace gave way
to Latin versions of the Greek comedians.   From these
beginnings Roman letters grew in polish, dignity, and
grace, until the climax was reached in the full burst of
Roman song in the golden period of the Augustan Age.

The Augustan age.

In this age of peace and freedom from distractions of
every kind the gentle arts reached their highest development.   Never before were men of letters so honored
and fostered by the leaders of the state ; never before
had there been such inspiration for the poetic fancy as
was now furnished by the power and glory and the ever-
increasing beauty of Rome.

And yet Rome fell.   Notwithstanding the slow and
safely conservative nature of her growth, which should
have given strength even to colossal size ; in spite
of those sterling elements in the Roman character
which should have insured a sound national heart ;
in spite of that progressive spirit which caught and
assimilated all elements of good from every source ;

Rome's dominion destined to decay.

in spite of that genius for government which set itself
the task of organizing the whole world into one mighty
state, and almost realized the superb dream of unifying
all mankind ; in spite of a military organization embedded in the very foundations of the state, whose legions
were the most perfect weapons of warfare that the world
had known ; in spite of that generous æsthetic development which refined and glorified this material strength
and splendor ;—in spite of all this, Rome fell.   Not all

at once, for no nation ever fell in one abrupt ruin, but in a ruin no less complete because gradual, extending over centuries of time. While she was still in the height of her glory there were already plainly discernible those elements of disintegration which were destined to undermine her power and parcel out her vast domain among the nations of the earth.

What were these elements of decay? They are to be found chiefly in the perversions of the very elements which fed her strength. Because of the greatness and splendor of Rome vast numbers of citizens were attracted from the farms and towns of Italy, where had been bred the strong bone and sinew of the state. Here in the city, vast numbers were pauperized by the largesses of food and public entertainment furnished by the state, and grew into an ever-increasing menace to the moral health of the body politic. The national spirit of acquisition inevitably bred a spirit of greed in individuals, and all society became absorbed in the pursuit of wealth. Wealth poured in in vast streams, to be followed by ever-increasing luxury. Great tracts of land were now diverted from useful to ornamental purposes. Small farms were replaced by great estates, and the entire class of farmers, the sturdy peasantry of older Rome, disappeared. While from Greece came the refining and elevating influences of literature and art, there came in the train of these many elements of moral degradation. The simple old national religion of Rome, comparatively spiritual and pure, was invaded and superseded by the debasing divinities that held their court on Mt. Olympus, and by the still more bestial gods of Egypt and the Orient. Meanwhile, as Rome became more cosmopolitan, simpler fashions of life were replaced by elegance and luxury, the enervating influences of which struck at the home, the very heart of society. Governors were not exempt from the national greed of gain, and pillaged the provinces which they were set to govern until the name of Rome became a synonym for oppression and an object of hate. The very armies were no longer composed of citizen soldiers, but of aliens, who fought, not for fatherland but for their daily wage. Ambitious leaders struggled for the mastery and no blood or treasure was sacred that stood in the way of their success.

The relation of private life of citizens to the history of a state.

Such is the background for the study of Roman manners at the end of the first century of the Christian era, a picture with its high lights of strength and growth, and with its dark shades of weakness and decay. In a study of the national structure, it is difficult to realize that the state was built of men, and that these men had all the ordinary human interests that absorb so large a part of life in the present day. The ensuing chapters will assist in this realization as they describe the every-day life of the people. Such a study as the following chapters contain will be of value not only as it increases the reader's store of facts, but chiefly as it leads to a clearer comprehension of the fact that all history is the history of men, and that the life of a state is the composite of the lives of all its citizens.

FRANK J. MILLER.

The University of Chicago,
June 1, 1897.

ROMAN LIFE IN PLINY'S TIME.

CHAPTER I.

EDUCATION.

THE age of the Antonines was characterized by a number of transformations in the manners of the Romans. One of the most interesting of these was that which took place in the attitude of fathers toward their children. This might almost be compared with the domestic revolution upon which M. Legouvé remarks in his studies on education in the nineteenth century.

> Children [says he] occupy to-day a much more important position in the family. Their parents live more with them ; they live more for them ; they attend more to their health, watch more over their education, think more about their well-being, listen more to their opinions. The children have almost become the principal personages of the house ; and a witty man expressed the spirit of this fact in a single phrase, when he said, "Their highnesses the children" (*Messieurs les enfants*).

If some moralist, contemporary of Trajan or of Marcus Aurelius, had had the leisure and the desire to study the domestic life of a Roman family, he would have been struck by a very similar change. At Rome the rights of a father of a family over his children were unlimited. The new-born child was laid at his feet. If he wished to recognize it, he stooped and took it in his arms. If he turned away from it, the child was carried out of the house and exposed in the street. When it did not die of hunger and cold, it belonged to any one who was willing to burden himself with it, and became his slave. The father always held over his son the right of life and death. Doubtless but few used this terrible right. We know, however, that Augustus, suspecting his daughter Julia of adultery, did not hesitate to have her child killed. The philosopher Seneca, who has written so much that is eloquent and noble, finds it very natural, and quite reasonable, that crippled and deformed children should be drowned ; and Cicero, who loved so fondly his dear Tullia, said brutally in the Tusculan disputations :

> If a young child dies, the survivors ought to bear his loss with equanimity ; if an infant in the cradle dies, they ought not even to utter a complaint.

Under the republic, at the dawn of the empire, there was, as we see, quite an absence of any tender feeling for childhood. It was in vain that Terence had, in some of his writings, delightfully expressed and recommended this sentiment.

Manners grew milder under the Antonines. The philosopher Favorinus, in pathetic language, besought mothers to nurse their own children.

> Is it not [he said to mothers] an outrage against nature, is it not being only half a mother, to reject one's child just after having given it life? Is it consistent to nourish with one's blood, in one's body, some unknown thing, and then to refuse to nourish it with one's milk, when one sees it alive, and when it is a human being ?

Plutarch, about the same time, wrote a treatise on education. The pages of this book are full of affection for childhood. Care should be taken, according to Plutarch, not to require too much of young children ; they should be refreshed by wholesome recreation, for "rest is the sauce of labor." The father, who must put the finishing touch upon the education of his son, should freely exercise indulgence, remembering that the boy is to be won to follow liberal studies by "exhortations and rational motives, and on no account to be forced thereto by whipping." This was a precept which the fathers of the time of Plautus did not understand, or at any rate practiced but little. They gave their children over to masters, who, when one of their pupils made a mistake in a single syllable of his lesson, made "his skin as spotted as his nurse's gown." Good fathers, according to Plutarch, will refrain from such harshness. "They may occasionally," he says, "loosen the reins and allow their children to take some liberties they are inclined to, and again, when it is fit, manage them with a straighter bridle. But chiefly should they bear their errors without passion if it may be."

Indulgence to be exercised by fathers.

If we wish to measure the progress which the Romans had made toward a milder treatment of their children, it will be sufficient to call to mind the family picture of Marcus Aurelius, which M. Boissier has drawn for us from the correspondence of Fronto with the emperor.

Marcus Aurelius in his family.

However young the children are, their ailments are the anxiety of Marcus Aurelius. How sadly he speaks of the croup from which his daughters are suffering, and the obstinate cough of his "dear little Antoninus"! This charming little brood, as he calls it, occupies him almost as much as the empire. Any one who talks to him about it is sure to please him, and Fronto does not fail, when he writes to him, to send a greeting "to the little ladies," and kisses for "their little fat feet and their pretty little hands."

This progress was not limited to the family circle; it was strengthened by public institutions. Formerly, abandoned children, as we have seen, became the slaves of those who picked them up; often they were treated with kindness and regarded as adopted children; but

Abandoned children.

often, too, they fell into the hands of horrible traffick-
ers, the *comprachicos* of antiquity, speculators in public
misery, who mutilated them in order to make beggars
of them.

Come [cries a rhetorician, addressing one of these wretched
dealers in the sufferings of children], bring on all those corpses,
which can scarcely drag themselves along ; show us your troop
of the blind, the lame, and the famished.   Take me into your
den ; I wish to see this workshop of human calamities, this
morgue of children.

To Trajan belongs the honor of having been among
the first to put a check upon this hideous business.   In
his correspondence with Pliny we find him interested in
organizing public aid for abandoned children, and from
his tone in speaking of the importance of this matter,
we feel that it lay near to his heart.

But all progress is necessarily at first accompanied by
difficulties and excesses.   Tenderness for children was
often developed at the expense of the wholesome maxims which had formerly been observed in the process of
their education ; and often affection degenerated into
mere compliance with their whims, and proper indulgence into weakness.   The writers of the first century
after Christ mourn this enfeeblement of paternal authority.   In their concert of lamentations, the voice of Quintilian is heard the loudest :

Would that we ourselves did not corrupt the morals of our
children ! We enervate their very infancy with luxuries. That
delicacy of education, which we call fondness, weakens all the
powers both of body and mind. . . . . We form the palate
of our children before we form their pronunciation. They
grow up in sedan-chairs ; if they touch the ground, they hang
by the hands of attendants supporting them on each side.
We are delighted if they utter anything immodest. Expressions which would not be tolerated even from the effemi-

nate youths of Alexandria, we bear from them with a smile and a kiss. Nor is this wonderful : we have taught them ; they have heard such language from ourselves. They see our mistresses, our male objects of affection ; every dining-room rings with impure songs ; things shameful to be told are objects of sight. From such practices springs habit, and afterward nature. The unfortunate children learn their vices before they know that they are vices.

It is against such excesses that Juvenal wrote his Fourteenth Satire : *Juvenal's warning.*

> So Nature prompts ; drawn by her secret tie,
> We view a parent's deeds with reverent eye ;
> With fatal haste, alas ! the example take,
> And love the sin, for the dear sinner's sake.
>
> . . . .
>
> O fatal guides ! this reason should suffice
> To win you from the slippery route of vice,
> This powerful reason ; lest your sons pursue
> The guilty track, thus plainly marked by you !
> For youth is facile, and its yielding will
> Receives, with fatal ease, the imprint of ill.
>
> . . . .
>
> Swift from the roof where youth, Fuscinus, dwell,
> Immodest rites, immodest sounds expel ;
> The place is sacred ; far, far hence, remove,
> Ye venal votaries of illicit love !
> Ye dangerous knaves, who pander to be fed,
> And sell yourselves to infamy for bread !
> Reverence to children, as to heaven, is due.

Admirable words ! They express the true principles of early education—to love your child, that he may not cease to be lovable and happy, but to respect him also, remembering that to-morrow he will become a man and a citizen.

It was at this epoch, when questions of education were receiving the attention of noble minds, that public instruction was first provided for. While in Greece *Public instruction.*

legislators had always been active in establishing schools, at Rome the state had taken no responsibility in the matter of education. Polybius and Cicero expressed much surprise at this negligence. But under the Antonines the emperors interested themselves in the establishment of schools. Vespasian was the first to give pay to the Greek and Latin rhetoricians. He allowed Quintilian a salary equivalent to about $5,000 in our money. M. Boissier says, in his work entitled "The Religion of the Romans from Augustus to the Antonines":

The biographer of Hadrian tells us that this emperor bestowed honors and riches upon professors in every branch of learning, and that when he found that they were incapable of discharging their duties, he dismissed them from their chairs after having paid them well. He established at Rome, in the capitol itself, a sort of university or academy, called the Athenæum, where people flocked to hear the orators and poets of renown. Antoninus Pius granted many privileges to the philosophers and rhetoricians of all the provinces, and provided them with salaries. Finally, Marcus Aurelius established and endowed four chairs of philosophy in Athens. Each of the four masters who filled these chairs was to teach the principles of a different school of philosophy, and each master received a salary of 10,000 drachmæ [about $1,000] from the public treasury.

This movement at Rome, encouraged by the emperors, soon extended to the smaller towns. Pliny, who was so much interested in intellectual matters, exerted himself to the utmost to found a public school at Comum, his native town. He did not think it beneath him, although a renowned man of letters, an illustrious advocate, an official orator, to spend his time seeking teachers for his young fellow-townsmen. What is more, he besought even Tacitus to aid him in his attempts, so keen was the interest which he felt in this enterprise. Moreover, the enthusiasm which he exhibited in this undertaking was not of a purely Platonic character, for he contributed money toward the carrying on of the work.

Now I have no children myself at present [he said to an inhabitant of Comum], and I will willingly contribute to a design so beneficial to my country, which I look upon in the light of a child, or a parent, a third part of any sum you may think proper to raise for this purpose. I would take upon myself the whole expense, were I not apprehensive of my benefaction being hereafter abused and perverted to private ends, as I have observed to be the case in several places where teachers are engaged at the public expense. The only way of meeting this evil is to leave the choosing of the professors solely in the hands of the parents, whose obligation to make a proper choice will be enforced by the necessity of having to pay toward the professors' salaries.

Pliny's contribution.

YOUNG ROMAN BOY.   Rome.

Schools thus founded were not open only for those whom fortune had favored with wealth. So strong was the conviction that education is beneficial, that efforts were made to help those who, on account of limited means,

Assistance for students of limited means.

would otherwise be unable to attend school. Trajan was the first to establish funds to be expended in the education of poor but promising young persons. And Pliny followed at Comum the example which the emperor set in the capital. Student aid funds, we see, are of ancient and illustrious origin.

Public or private instruction.

From this time the respective advantages of private and of public education were discussed by the thinkers of the day. Quintilian devoted a chapter to this subject, and being in the question both judge and pleader he decided emphatically in favor of <u>public instruction.</u> Many parents, however, wished to keep their children near them ; and such parents often took the greatest pains to cultivate the minds of their sons and to give them all possible advantages for acquiring knowledge. Pliny, as we learn from his letters, was several times commissioned to choose tutors for the children of his friends, and he was much impressed with the seriousness of his responsibility, and evidently felt honored that parents should trust him with a matter of such grave importance in their eyes.

Quintilian's conception of education.

What, then, was the nature of this education whose progress had become the object of general attention? The first books of Quintilian give us valuable information on this subject.

Nurses.

Quintilian held that education should begin from the cradle. For this reason he thought that nurses should be cultivated women. But Quintilian, carried away by his subject, is not always free from exaggeration. Doubtless parents thought his advice hard to follow, and probably the instruction of children began at about the age of seven.

The alphabet.

The alphabet was the first thing to be learned. As long ago as this, care was taken to make study attractive, and the little learner was furnished with ornamented ivory letters, which he enjoyed using, and which he regarded as toys. Next came writing. The writing masters, who were as skilful as those of our day, would place in the hands of their pupils tablets, where, in the wax, grooves were traced to guide the pencil of the beginner. The models set to be copied were chosen with care, and contained maxims of morality rather than idle phrases. When these first steps were accomplished, the child was passed on to the grammarians. It seems that the study of grammar, which we so justly regard as important, was not held in very high esteem by the Romans of this time. This may

Writing.

Grammar.

Boy Fishing. Museum of Naples.

probably be accounted for by the manner in which the subject was then taught. For, if we may trust Quintilian, the instruction given in grammar was not free from pedantry and was characterized by much subtlety. As soon as the child understood *the art of speaking correctly* and knew how *to explain the poets* (these were the two results which the study of grammar sought), he was taught the principles of reading aloud,

Reading aloud.

by which, says Quintilian, "a boy may know when to take breath, where to divide a verse, where the sense is concluded, where it begins, when the voice is to be raised or lowered, what is to be uttered with any particular inflection of sound, or what is to be pronounced with greater slowness or rapidity, with greater animation or gentleness than other passages."

So the principles in the art of reading aloud which M. Legouvé teaches were taught long ago in the Roman schools.

When the child becomes a youth, more advanced studies are entered upon—philosophy, music, and rhetoric, which comprises oratory. Quintilian holds that these three branches should be carried on simultaneously:

Rhetoric, philosophy, and music.

Ought we to attend to the teacher of grammar only, and then to the teacher of geometry only, and cease to think, during the second course, of what we learned in the first? Should we then transfer ourselves to the musician, our previous studies being still allowed to escape us ? . . . Why, then, do we not give similar counsel to husbandmen, that they should not cultivate at the same time their fields and their vineyards, their olives and other trees, and that they should not bestow attention at once on their meadows, their cattle, their gardens, and their beehives?

But do not be misled by this variety of subjects into supposing that the Roman schools, like ours, prepared men to be specialists, that they turned out geometricians or musicians. No, these various sciences were taught only for the sake of the more perfect acquisition of the art which crowned them all—the art of oratory.

Object of the Roman education.

Although the empire had succeeded in quieting the forum, and in excluding eloquence from the domain of politics, the art of public speaking continued to be cultivated as much as ever at Rome. This was due to

the influence of tradition and to inherited taste. Under
the republic, when eloquence was the gate to every
sphere of distinction, the young Romans trained themselves in oratory by listening, at the forum, day after
day, to some important politician or some illustrious
advocate, and they completed their preparation in the
privacy of their own houses, by an exercise called
declamation. They would invent, for instance, a difficult law case, or perhaps imagine some political question, worthy of exciting the passion of an assembly,
and alone, in the quiet of a secluded study, they would
seek for ingenious arguments or stirring appeals.

But under the empire the public square became silent,
the debates of the court dwindled into insignificance.
No matter ; the young men continued to prepare themselves for struggles which could no longer exist, and
declamation, which formerly was only a means, became
an end in itself. What seems surprising at first thought
is that political subjects were most eagerly selected for
treatment, and seemed most attractive to the rhetorical
professors of the day as exercises for their pupils. Juvenal, at forty years of age, was perhaps still, with a
great array of antitheses and apostrophes, advising
Sulla to lay down his power ; tyrants long ago pros-
trate were being executed by entire classes of students
in speeches as brilliant as harmless. Men were glad to
revive from the past occasions for expressing the sentiments which they were forced to stifle in regard to the
present. They found this a certain relief in the extreme
servitude to which they felt themselves subjected by
some of the emperors. And the rulers themselves understood, without doubt, that it was for their own
advantage to allow the young men to spend thus their
noble impetuosity ; for we find no example of a school

of oratory being closed, or the professors persecuted by governmental authority. The princes thought that practical experience would impress its own lesson upon these heated imaginations, and that life, in teaching these great scholars to endure life, would cool their ardor for things long past and their noble rage over forgotten wrongs. Skeptics, moreover, were not wanting to laugh at these oratorical triumphs won in the obscurity of the classroom, to make fun of these college conspirators, and to point out the artificial and puerile character of these impromptu speeches, which required fifteen days of preparation, of these orations which were supposed to be addressed to a nation, but which had for hearers only beardless youths and a poor stick of a pedant.

> What madmen [said Petronius] are these declaimers, who cry out, "These wounds I received in defense of the public liberty. This eye was lost in your service! Give me some helpful hand to lead me to my children, for my severed hams can no longer support me." In my opinion, the reason why young people are made such blockheads in the schools is that they neither hear nor see any of those things which belong to the common usage of life.

The criticism is keen and discriminating. But after all, if these students and their teachers were wrong sometimes in living aloof from the spirit of their age, they were often right in so doing.

"In studying antiquity," said Livy, "my soul becomes ancient." So with some of these professors and learners—the imaginary resurrection of the past enriched their minds. Pliny speaks of a certain Isæus, who all his life had been a rhetorician, adding:

> I know no class of men more single-hearted, more genuine, more excellent than this class.

Marcus Aurelius wrote to Fronto:

I send you my decree of to-day, and my reflection of yesterday. But [he said to him also] you do not cease to set me in the way of truth, and to open my eyes. You teach me what envy, duplicity, and hypocrisy may lurk in a tyrant's heart, and how many great lords have never experienced sentiments of affection.

Fronto all his life corresponded with the emperor, who always heeded his counsels, and often even asked for them. It might truly be said that Fronto exercised an influence over the spirit and the character of the best ruler which the empire had known. Was not that a beautiful triumph for a professor of rhetoric?

The study of rhetoric or oratory, which crowned and completed the education of a young Roman, had, we must own, more than one ridiculous aspect. But it had also its redeeming advantages, since it furnished an opportunity for expressing the claims of justice and for declaring rights too often scorned. Unfortunately, most young men, after entering into life, took at once the humorous view of their drill in oratory and lost sight of the considerations that made the ridiculous aspects of their study excusable, and even touching. Some, Persius for instance, placed themselves under the guidance of a philosopher, who developed in their souls the first germs of a high morality. In his Fifth Satire Persius tells us:

> When first I laid the purple by, and free,
> Yet trembling at my new-felt liberty,
> Approached the hearth, and on the Lares hung
> The *bulla*, from my willing neck unstrung;
> When gay associates, sporting at my side,
> And the white boss, displayed with conscious pride,
> Gave me, unchecked, the haunts of vice to trace,
> And throw my wandering eyes on every face;

> When life's perplexing maze before me lay,
> And error, heedless of the better way,
> To straggling paths, far from the route of truth,
> Woo'd, with blind confidence, my timorous youth,
> I fled to you, Cornutus, pleased to rest
> My hopes and fears on your Socratic breast,
> Nor did you, gentle sage, the charge decline ;
> Then, dextrous to beguile, your steady line
> Reclaimed, I know not by what winning force,
> My morals, warped from virtue's straighter course ;
> While reason pressed incumbent on my soul,
> That struggled to receive the strong control,
> And took, like wax, tempered by plastic skill,
> The form your hand imposed, and bears it still !

Cornutus.

Very few, however, after escaping from rhetoric, found the refuge and the harbor of philosophy. These young people of seventeen years, who, at the festival of the Liberalia, had deposited before the Lares of their homes the emblems of childhood, the *toga prætexta*, and the *bulla* worn about the neck, who had put on the straight tunic and the *toga virilis*, who had been conducted by parent or guardian to the record-office of the capitol to be enrolled upon the list of citizens—these youths, so suddenly transformed into men, did not dream of being frightened at their new liberty and of committing it into the hands of a Cornutus. "Life's perplexing maze," which lay before the poet Persius, did not long perplex the majority of the Roman youths. Is there any need of stating what course they chose? Their goal was languid pleasure, riches speedily acquired, and power easily won. But must we conclude that this choice was the fruit of the education which they had received from their teachers? Was it not rather due to the influence of the society into which the youths entered? What of the family example, that powerful and decisive example, the thought of which inspired Juvenal

The low morality of Roman youths.

The influence of society.

with one of his finest satires—should this count for nothing?

After a careful consideration, we have formed the opinion that even in the time of the Antonines, when there was an interruption in the decadence of Roman society, the underlying tendencies were more powerful than the outward attempts at morality; that many a father, while his son was a child, adopted measures to make a good man out of him, but afterward, by his conduct and his counsels, killed the germs which he had previously tried to nourish. And, in short, it seems to us that although suitable instructors were provided for the child, for the youth there were no guides, because his natural educators abandoned their duty. *Moral tendencies under the Antonines.*

We have attempted to follow the Roman boy up to his entrance into life. It is not so easy to present a picture of the early years of the girl who is to become one day his companion. The information which the ancient writers have left us concerning women is scanty and far from satisfactory. Let us try, however, to make the most of it. *Unsatisfactory information in regard to a girl's early life.*

A girl has just been born. The anxiety of the mother is expressed by a thousand precautions, a thousand superstitious practices. Amulets are hung about the neck of the child, to preserve her from accidents and from suffering. Prayers are offered in the temples to the gods, that the child may be blessed with beauty. When intelligence begins to dawn in her young mind, her nurse or governess is at hand to narrate to her those marvelous stories which, from the earliest times, have fascinated and terrified children — stories about ghosts and specters, about the Lamiæ, the Gorgon, hobgoblins, and about Gelo, the witch, the kidnapper *Her infancy.*

of children, known at Lesbos from the time of Sappho.

Soon it becomes necessary to arrange for the educa-tion of the little girl.   The first thing is to teach her to perform the duties belonging to her sex—especially to weave and to spin.   These manual employments con-stituted an essen-tial part of every good education, even in the most aristocratic fami-lies.   We learn from Suetonius that A u g u s t u s wore no clothes e x c e p t t h o s e m a d e b y t h e w o m e n of his f a m i l y — h i s d a u g h t e r s, his g r a n d d a u g h t e r s, his wife, or his sister. The in-scriptions u p o n the tombs of the high-born ladies of the empire rarely fail to record among their merits that they could spin wool.   As for mental culture, the young girls of middle rank received it in the public schools, in company with the boys.   Martial tells us of a teacher who is the terror of his pupils of both sexes.   The French revolutionists, who were full of the spirit of classic antiquity, remembered, no

Her manual training.

Her intellectual education.

A POMPEIIAN COURT.
From a painting by L. Bazzani.

doubt, this method of coeducation which the Romans practiced. Condorcet, in the proposal which he presented to the Legislative Assembly for the organization of a national system of education, suggested that boys and girls should be taught the same things together in the same schools.

At Rome the mental training of the women consisted especially in the reading of the poets, in the study of music, and in dancing lessons, or training in poise and carriage, such as is given to-day in boarding-schools for young ladies. The families of rank were not satisfied with this. From the end of the republic, as we shall show later, women occupied an important place in the social world. They had obtained for themselves an influence which, under the empire, was felt sometimes in politics. It was natural, then, that a mother should aspire to make her daughter one of those persons, distinguished for their brilliancy, who establish the tone in social circles, and who sometimes issue commands to the world. So patrician girls, brought up at home, often received a very complete education. This fact may be inferred from the following letter of Pliny :

Girls are prepared for social life.

I write this to you in the deepest sorrow. The youngest daughter of my friend Fundanus is dead ! I have never seen a more cheerful and more lovable girl, or one who better deserved to have enjoyed a long, I had almost said an immortal, life ! She was scarcely fourteen, and yet there was in her a wisdom far beyond her years, a matronly gravity united with girlish sweetness and virgin bashfulness. With what an endearing fondness did she hang on her father's neck ! How affectionately and modestly she used to greet us, his friends ! With what a tender and deferential regard she used to treat her nurses, tutors, teachers, each in their respective offices ! What an eager, industrious, intelligent reader she was ! She took few amusements, and those with caution. How self-controlled, how patient, how brave she was, under her last

The daughter of Fundanus.

illness ! She complied with all the directions of her physicians ; she spoke cheerful, comforting words to her sister and her father ; and when all her bodily strength was exhausted, the vigor of her mind sustained her. That indeed continued even to her last moments, unbroken by the pain of a long illness or the terrors of approaching death ; and it is a reflection which makes us miss her, and grieve that she has gone from us, the more.

A fortunate disposition could not have availed to give so many good qualities to a young girl who was almost a child. We must agree that only an excellent education, added to natural tendencies, could have rendered a person so accomplished. Moreover, a Roman youth, finding in the daughter of Fundanus so many attractions joined to such intellect and virtue, was on the point of making her his wife. The Roman girls, in fact, completed their education at about the age of fourteen, when they were ready for marriage.

We shall next speak of their condition after leaving the paternal home to enter the home of a husband.

CHAPTER II.

WOMEN AND MARRIAGE.

AMONG the Romans sentiment had no place in the arrangement of a marriage. The excessively delicate and refined Madelon would have been ill contented with the management of love affairs in Rome.

> The idea [exclaims Madelon, in Molière's play, "Les Précieuses Ridicules"] of coming pointblank to conjugal union, of only making love in making the marriage contract, of jumping to the end of the romance at once! I tell you, father, there can be nothing more tradesmanlike than such a proceeding. The very thought of such a thing makes me sick.

But the Roman maidens were not over-refined, and they did not require, like Madelon, that their future husbands should "know how to utter sentiments that were sweet, tender, and passionate."

Under the republic people married for the sake of having children. Parents usually had a good many, and were probably happy. Under the empire the object of marriage was different. Then people entered into matrimony because they wished to establish a house, to have a recognized position, to settle down in life. The choice of a husband or of a wife was determined solely by considerations of convenience, of rank, and of fortune. There was in all this nothing romantic, and the novelists and ballad-makers, whose business it is to marry the lover and the innocent girl, in spite of the opposition of a savage father and the plots of an odious rival, would have been reduced to silence at Rome.

The marriageable age.

The early age at which girls were married did not allow them time to have a preference. They were too young to choose. Law fixed the marriageable age at twelve years, and custom made it fourteen. When a girl passed her nineteenth year she was no longer considered, under ordinary circumstances, eligible for marriage.

Parents are the match-makers.

Parents, we see, were the ones to arrange

FAUSTINA, WIFE OF MARCUS AURELIUS.
Museum of Naples.

for the marriage of a daughter. It was their place to pick out her future husband, usually a man of at least thirty years. We know of no examples of resistance to the paternal will. And law confirmed the proverb "Silence gives consent."

"The daughter," said Ulpian, a celebrated Roman jurist, "who does not object, is regarded as consenting." And he adds, "She has, moreover, no right to resist her father, unless he tries to give her a dishonored or deformed husband."

Ulpian's testimony.

In this delicate matter, what motives influenced the parents? What qualities did they seek in a son-in-law? Pliny shall tell us. His friend, Junius Mauricus, had requested him to suggest a suitable match for the daughter of a brother, Rusticus Arulenus. Let us see how Pliny performs his commission :

You desire me to look out a proper husband for your niece. . . . I should be long in determining a choice were I not acquainted with Minucius Acilianus, who seems formed for our purpose. . . . He is a native of Brixia, one of those provinces in Italy which still retain much of the old modesty, frugal simplicity, and even rusticity of manner. He is the son of Minucius Macrinus, whose humble desires were satisfied with standing at the head of the equestrian order ; for though he was nominated by Vespasian in the number of those whom that prince dignified with the prætorian office, yet, with an inflexible greatness of mind, he resolutely preferred an honorable repose to the ambitions, shall I call them, or exalted pursuits in which we public men are engaged. His grandmother on his mother's side is Serrana Procula, of Patavium ; you are no stranger to the character of its citizens ; yet Serrana is looked upon, even among these correct people, as an exemplary instance of strict virtue. . . . In short, you will find nothing throughout his family unworthy of yours. Minucius himself has plenty of vivacity, as well as application, together with a most amiable and becoming modesty. He has already, with considerable credit, passed through the offices of quæstor, tribune, and prætor ; so that you will be spared the trouble of soliciting for him those honorable employments. He has a fine, well-bred countenance, with a ruddy, healthy complexion, while his whole person is elegant and comely, and his mien graceful and senatorian—advantages, I think, by no means to be slighted, and which I consider as the proper tribute to virgin innocence. I think I may add that his father is very rich. When I contemplate the character of those who require a husband of my choosing, I know it is unnecessary to mention wealth ; but when I reflect upon the prevailing manners of the age, and even the laws of Rome, which rank· a man according to his possessions, it certainly claims *some* regard ; and, indeed, in establishments of this nature, where children and many other· circumstances are to be duly weighed, it is an article that well deserves to be taken into the account.

Good moral character, noble family, a career brilliantly commenced, attractive personality, large fortune —all these qualifications, according to Pliny, were united in Minucius Acilianus. He was a suitor that could be recommended without hesitation, and the daughter of Rusticus Arulenus would have been hard to please if she had not liked him. Doubtless many young girls had to put up with less ; doubtless many families did not find, nor perhaps even seek, sons-in-law as accomplished as Minucius Acilianus. But we have attempted to speak only of the aristocracy. For we have scarcely any information in regard to the domestic life of the lower classes.

Advantage of beauty to a girl.

What we know of the education of girls indicates the intellectual and moral qualities desired in them by those who sought them in marriage. It is evident that beauty was one of the chief attractions to a suitor, since, according to Juvenal, it was the first thing a mother desired for her child.

> When'er the fane of Venus meets her eye,
> The anxious mother breathes a secret sigh
> For handsome boys ; but asks, with bolder prayer,
> That all her girls be exquisitely fair.

Health sacrificed to beauty.

Nor did a mother neglect to set off a daughter's beauty by every art in her power. If a daughter was a coquette the mother would help her to make her form more slender and to dress as becoming as possible. From the time of Terence great value was set upon beauty, and even the health of a girl was exposed for its sake.

> The girl isn't like our girls [says a character in Terence's " Eunuch "], whom their mothers are anxious to have with shoulders kept down and chests well girthed, that they may be slender. If one is a little inclined to plumpness, they declare that she's training for a boxer, and stint her food ; although their constitutions are good, by their treatment they make them as slight as bulrushes.

But the most important equipment for a girl was her lowry. The Romans were a people above everything else practical, and they had very little disinterestedness. When Lucretius, that admirable poet whose thought is so high and noble, counsels young men to avoid illicit love, to what motive does he appeal? He touches lightly upon the dangers of those sad passions, suggesting that they ruin the health, degrade the mind, and destroy self-respect, but he dwells with special emphasis upon the fact that young men waste their fortunes by self-indulgence.

Importance of a dowry.

> And all the wealth their good sires toiled to gain
>   Changes to head-gear, and rich anadem,
> And Cean robes with trailing sweep of train,
>   And feasts, and goblets thick with many a gem.

A young man of serious mind avoided expensive women ; but that was not all—he sought women who might bring him wealth. In the time of the ancient virtues, there was a tendency in this direction. Even then, the dowry took the place of beauty, of youth, of birth, or of honor itself. "If only she has a dowry," says one of Plautus's characters, "she has no vice."

In the refined and corrupt civilization of the first two centuries of the empire, considerations of self-interest, it is easy to believe, were no less powerful. Girls without dowry frightened away eligible young men. Pliny was not ignorant of this when he generously made a present of fifty thousand sesterces (about $2,125) to his friend Quintilian's daughter. The following is the letter which accompanied the gift :

Pliny's gift to Quintilian's daughter.

Though your desires, I know, are extremely moderate, and though you have brought up your daughter as became a daughter of yours and the granddaughter of Tutilius, yet as she is going to be married to a person of such distinction as

Nonius Celer, whose civil employment necessarily imposes upon him a certain style of living, her wardrobe and establishment should be enlarged according to the rank of her husband ; circumstances which, though they do not augment our real dignity, yet certainly adorn and grace it. But as I am sensible the wealth of your revenue is not equal to the wealth of your mind, I claim to myself a part of your expense, and,

RELIEF REPRESENTING A SACRIFICE.

like another father, present our young lady with fifty thousand sesterces. The sum should be larger but that I am well persuaded the smallness of the present is the only consideration that can prevail with your modesty not to refuse it.

Fortunate daughter of Quintilian ! Many girls had no such windfalls, and not being marketable, as Plautus's miser would say, were doomed to maidenhood.

When the two families agreed, the young people were betrothed. The occasion of a betrothal was celebrated with much pomp. All the friends received invitations, which etiquette required them to accept. The young man made several presents to his *fiancée*, and among other things he gave her an iron ring as a pledge of his fidelity. But this ceremony led to no change in the relation between the two young people. Their engagement gave them no right to seek to become better acquainted with each other. For what we call "courting" was an unknown thing among the Romans. It was a long time before any one was surprised that two beings, who were to bind themselves to live a common life together, should do so when they were strangers to each other. It was only under the influence of Christianity that this thing was considered strange.

"Courting" unknown.

Before a man buys an ox, a horse, a slave [said Saint Jerome], he tests them; but his future wife he is not even allowed to see, for fear that she may displease him before the marriage.

The spiritual director ·of the Roman ladies of the fourth century, when he said that, failed in courtesy toward the fair sex.

The ceremony of betrothal over, it was time to think of the wedding outfit. Custom made it the father's place to purchase jewels and provide the trousseau for his daughter. He also selected the servants who should follow the young wife into her new dwelling. When all these preparations were over, he had the pleasure of seeing his daughter dedicate her doll and her other toys to the divinities which had protected her childhood. Then came the wedding day.

Preparations for marriage.

Early in the morning the houses of the betrothed were decorated. The throng of friends and relations filled the atrium of the bride's house. This room was brilliantly lighted and trimmed with green branches. The recesses in the wall were thrown open to display the images of the family ancestors. Soon the bride appeared. On her head she wore a flame-colored veil, flowing at the back and at the sides, so that only her

The wedding.

The bride's attire.

face showed. A girdle with a jasper buckle encircled her waist. Precious stones sparkled in her hair, and she wore about her throat a necklace of gold, and pearls in her ears. When the ten required witnesses had placed their signatures below the contract, a matron chosen for the purpose led the bride up to the bridegroom and joined their right hands. The couple then offered a sacrifice upon the family altar, after which, conducted in festal procession, they set out for their new home. They had to pass through a crowd who were mingling cheers with the music of flutes and with gay songs, and who did not disperse until they had seen the bridegroom lift the bride over the threshold of her new dwelling. It was thus that the husband symbolized his right of possession. · Finally, the festivities were ended by a feast given in the husband's house, when husband and wife sat side by side. We have reason to believe that much money was lavished upon this repast, for Augustus sought to limit by law the expenditures upon such occasions. Moreover, when a

Origin of the wedding tour.

couple wished to avoid this showy entertainment, they went to get married in some country house. This was the course that Apuleius adopted when he married Pudentilla.

> We wished [said he] to escape from the eager crowd, who would have claimed our hospitality, . . . and to avoid also those numerous and wearisome feasts which custom imposes almost always upon a newly married couple.

Here we find the origin of the wedding tour, and although this beginning of married life is sometimes condemned on grounds of health, it will never lose its charm until young married people shall cease to wish for solitude—so favorable to intimacy and love.

Roman law at first was very severe for the wife.

Our ancestors [said Livy] required that women, even in their private affairs, should always be under the guardianship of some man—father, brother, or husband.

The condition of the wife.

But custom was less rigorous than law. From the earliest period in Roman history the wife, enthroned near the family hearth, was queen in the atrium. Gide, in his study upon the condition of the wife, says :

The atrium was not, like the gynæceum in a Greek house, a secluded apartment, an upper floor, a hidden and inaccessible retreat. It was the very center of the Roman house, the common hall where the whole family assembled, where friends and

LUCRETIA AND HER MAIDS. From a painting by J. Coomans.

strangers were received. There near the hearth was the altar of the Lares, and around this sanctuary were gathered all the most precious and sacred possessions of the family, the nuptial bed, the images of the ancestors, the web and spindle of the mother, the chest containing the family records and the money. All these treasures were placed under the guard of the wife. She, as head of the family, offered herself the sacrifices to the Lares. She presided over the domestic labors of the slaves. She directed the education of the children, who even after they

The family hearth.

passed out of childhood continued to submit to her authority. In short, she shared with her husband the administration of the property and the rule of the house.

We see that from very early times the wife, who legally was in wardship, was in fact emancipated. She obtained still greater independence under the empire, through important modifications in the laws, which no longer secured to the husband his former power over his wife. It ceased to be true that "the personality of the wife was absorbed by the husband, and that all her property inevitably belonged to him, as if she had become his daughter."

The freedom of wives.

The ancient religious form of marriage, by which the wife with her property came under the absolute dominion of her husband, having fallen into disuse, a form called free marriage prevailed, by which the dowry brought by the wife for her support after marriage was reserved and secured for this use. She retained the independent ownership of all her other property, personal as well as real, and the husband had not legally the right even to use the interest coming from it. Under such provisions the women were not satisfied with being no longer slaves—they wished to be mistresses. And ordinarily they exercised their power with tyranny. The tables were turned, and, if we may trust Juvenal, it is the husband now whom we should pity:

The tyranny of wives.

> Naught must be given, if she opposes ; naught,
> If she opposes, must be sold or bought ;
> She tells him where to love, and where to hate,
> Shuts out the ancient friend, whose beard his gate
> Knew, from its downy to its hoary state ;
> And when pimps, parasites, of all degrees
> Have power to will their fortunes as they please,
> She dictates his, and impudently dares
> To name his very rivals for his heirs !

To maintain the rights of women married under the later law of freedom, and even to suggest to them exorbitant demands, a curious class of men arose— business managers for ladies, stewards, as they were called. When these stewards were young and hand-some bachelors, they easily left their rôle of business counselor and became the professed admirers of their clients. Seneca speaks somewhere of the gallant stew-ard, the steward with curled hair. Husbands, to take revenge, declared such men " absurd and insipid in the society of men," as Cicero described for us Ebutius, business manager of the widow Cesennia. But never-theless, husbands, in more than one way, were the dupes and the victims of these schemers and unscrupu-lous experts in handling the law.

However cautious we may be in drawing conclusions from the exaggerations of the pessimistic moralists and the thrusts of the satirists, we are forced to recognize that the institution of marriage was, in the second century after Christ, singularly undermined. Augustus, alarmed at the disturbance which the civil wars had produced in the morals of society, frightened at the increase of celibacy and at so many illegitimate births, had caused two laws to be passed—the Julian Law and the Papia Poppæan Law—designed to check the evil. According to these laws society was divided into two distinct classes. By the Julian Law these two classes were celibates and those who were married ; by the Poppæan Law, childless persons and parents. Against celibates and those without children severe regulations were enacted, while privileges and immunities were granted to married persons and parents. Let us add that the name of celibate applied to any one who was not married, whether a widower or a man who had been divorced.   Hence, in order to avoid the penalties of the Julian Law, it was necessary, upon the dissolution of one's marriage by death or by law, to remarry at once.   Women alone were allowed a certain interval between two marriages—one year after the death of a husband and six months after a divorce.   These intervals the Poppæan Law increased respectively to two years and to eighteen months.

Divorces.

But, after all, few laws can effect a change in moral tendencies.   At any rate, the laws of Augustus did not succeed in this.   We may even say that they produced a new difficulty.   Divorce was granted very easily, and the necessity resting upon divorced parties of entering into new unions resulted in legalizing a certain looseness of life.   Seneca claims that there were women who reckoned years not by consulships, but by their husbands.   Juvenal, in one of his satires, goes still further :

> Thus the virago triumphs, thus she reigns.
> Anon she sickens of her first domains,
> And seeks for new ; husband on husband takes,
> Till of her bridal veil one rent she makes.
> Again she tires, again for change she burns,
> And to the bed she lately left returns,
> While the fresh garlands, and unfaded boughs,
> Yet deck the portals of her wondering spouse.
> Thus swells the list ; *eight husbands in five years*—
> A rare inscription for their sepulchers !

How far removed from the time when the Romans considered marriage as the union of two lives !

Infidelity to the marriage vows.

In spite of the opportunities which the facility of obtaining divorce gave to those who had a taste for variety, open immorality was very common.   The writers of the time blamed the wives for this state of things.   The husbands, however, must bear their share of the responsibility.   Under the ancient system of slavery they always had the leisure to form seraglios, and they doubtless often formed them. There were also the pretty freed-girls and the elegant courtesans of the voluptuous Subura. Infidelity in the husband was made more frequent by the fact that the enjoyments of

domestic life for men were few, and that the irregularities of men entailed no responsibilities. So that probably it was not uncommon for husbands to break their marriage vows, and at the epoch of which we are writing instances of such misdemeanors must have been very numerous. Formerly, infidelity in the wife alone was punished, but the emperor Antoninus, thinking that this

WOMAN'S HEAD.
Farnesian Palace, Rome.

gave encouragement to fickle husbands, abolished this difference, and immorality was punished in husbands as well as in wives.

From the close of the republic, the type of the matron of old times, "who remained at home and spun wool," had ceased to be the ideal toward which the women of Rome aspired. A taste for elegant corruption had been introduced from Greece. Lawful wives felt that they would lose their influence over their husbands if they clung to the austere and cold virtue of the matron, and did not endeavor to acquire more fascinating attractions. Many criticisms were passed upon the first women who departed from the old traditions and tried to excel in dancing or music. Sallust, stricter in his writings than in his conduct, thought that Sempronia "danced better than became a virtuous woman." But soon such prejudices disappeared. The stanch defenders of old-fashioned education were reduced to silence. And at the time of Trajan the poet Statius, too poor to give his daughter a dowry, depended upon her charms and accomplishments to win her a husband. At this time women began to appear in society, and to play a part there. When husbands were invited out to dinner their wives accompanied them. On such occasions the etiquette was the same for both sexes, except that the ladies sat in chairs, according to the ancient style, while the men adopted the Greek custom of reclining at table. There was no more seclusion for women. They became acquainted with life, tasted its charms, but, unfortunately, found pleasure in its intrigues. And, happy in the liberty that they had acquired, in the homage which they had compelled men to render them, they often abused their privileges.

From the time of Augustus women indulged much in coquetry. This excited the indignation of the rhetorician Porcius Latro, who, not confining himself to his rhetoric, traced for us the following true picture of Roman manners :

When a matron wishes to be secure against the advances of the bold, she ought to dress just well enough not to appear slovenly. She ought to surround herself with servants of a respectable age, whose aspect alone will repel undesirable approaches of gallantry. She should walk always with lowered eyes. When she encounters one of those eagerly attentive men who bow to all the women that they meet, she had better appear impolite than pleasantly responsive. If she cannot avoid returning his greeting, let her return it with confusion and a blush. Let her attitude be such that if one is tempted to make her improper proposals, her face will say no before her voice. These are the measures by which women should protect themselves. But, on the contrary, see them seeking by their expressions of countenance to draw attention to themselves, only half dressed, with language so playful, such a caressing manner, that any one and every one feels free to approach them. And then when they reveal their shameful desires by their dress, their walk, their words, their faces, are you surprised that there are people who cannot escape from these shameless creatures who fall upon them?

Porcius Latro's judgment of women.

With the conquest of the world Roman commerce had become more extended. From distant countries merchants imported rich and beautiful stuffs, precious stones, rare and curious jewels. Women then began to spend a great.

Woman's Head—said to be Julia, Wife of Titus.
Museum of Naples.

deal of time upon their dress. Though they were unacquainted with our extravagances in gloves, hats, and coiffures, they delighted in the delicate textures from the East Indies or from China; though fur was used by them only in moderation, they indulged a

Luxury in dress.

fancy for garments of brilliant color — a rather expensive fancy, when you consider that the double-dyed purple wool which came from Tyre cost more than one thousand *deniers*, or about $167, a pound.   Pompey's triumph over Mithridates had introduced into Rome the oriental luxury of precious stones.   People went wild over them.   The diamond seems to have been little employed for ornament, except to be set in rings.   But people were passionately fond of the emerald, the aquamarine, the opal, the sardonyx, and especially of pearls. They trimmed the lacings and buckles of their shoes with pearls.   They even covered their slippers with them.   Luxury had become for women an absolute necessity.

Juvenal, in his Sixth Satire, speaking of a typical society lady, Bibula, says :

> Briefly, for all her neighbor has she sighs,
> And plagues her doting husband till he buys.
> In winter, when the merchant fears to roam,
> And snow confines the shivering crew at home,
> She ransacks every shop for precious ware,
> Here cheapens myrrh and crystal vases, there
> That far-famed gem which Berenice wore.

And the day when the husband's purse was closed or exhausted, his honor was imperiled.   There were so many women ready to tempt him, and Rome offered so many opportunities to one who wished to betray him.

Ovid laid out, for the use of the man in quest of good fortune, a sort of itinerary through those parts of the capital where flirtations prospered.   Ovid knew his subject.   Let us follow him ; he is a good guide :

> The fowler and the huntsman know by name
> The certain haunts and harbor of their game.
> So must the lover beat the likeliest grounds ;
> The assembly where his quarry most abounds.

The wearing of jewels.

Extravagance of women.

Flirtations.

It is first Pompey's portico.   Also Livia's picture gallery ; the painter's art, which freely represented the love-making of mythological characters, served often to awaken the first desires and to encourage the passions just developing.   Other places are the public promenades, beautifully laid out in gardens and parks, where an admirer has leisure to be gallant, to render a thousand little services, among others, to hold his lady's parasol.   The solemn forum itself is sometimes the scene of a flirtation.

Flirtations at the public resorts.

> The crafty counselors, in formal gown,
> There gain another's cause, but lose their own.
> There eloquence is nonplused in the suit,
> And lawyers, who had words at will, are mute.

But the theater and the circus are the chosen resorts of men inclined to gallantry.   The women attend the theater in their finest attire, to see, but, above all, to be seen.   At the circus they sit among the men.   It is then at the circus that flirtations are most conveniently carried on.   The young woman has taken her place next her admirer.   A grain of sand has fallen upon her dress ; he delicately snaps it off with his finger. Her *pallium* (cloak) falls to the ground ; he hastens to pick it up and brush it.   He arranges the cushion where she sits, he fans her, he does not forget to place the stool for her feet, he hands her a program, and applauds at the right places, that is, when she applauds herself.   If she asks for some information, he must never fail to supply it—he must, if necessary, even tell what he does not know.   Thus it is that a gallant man conducts his business.   After paying so many attentions, he will not fail to be invited to some feast where the one whom he loves will be.   The husband is a great drinker.   The lover takes advantage of this.   The hus-

Flirtations at the circus.

band goes to sleep in the midst of the wine, and then, on the table, without fear of being seen, the lover can write with his finger, dipping it in the spilled wine, the confession thus far withheld.

If we consider the legislation alone, we are astonished to see such eagerness in seeking immoral alliances. The Julian Law, passed under Augustus, punished the crime of unfaithfulness to the marriage vow by exile only. But under the same ruler and his successors the punishment was often made death, by several special provisions ; and finally, by the general constitution of the emperor Theodosius, and afterward of Justinian, unchastity was made a capital offense in all cases. No humiliation was spared to women recognized as guilty of infidelity to their husbands. They were no longer allowed to wear the *stola*, but were obliged to appear in public dressed in the *toga*, a garment of men. Death, when pronounced against them, was accompanied with refinements of cruelty. The victim was placed in the arena before a bull trained to pick up with his horns, and toss into the air, large pieces of wood. Such severity, however, was exercised but rarely. The husbands themselves were unwilling to demand it. Many of them, after a wife had committed a fault, preferred to keep silent.

We are compelled to admit that the writers of the second century after Christ did not always draw upon their imagination for their facts, and that chastity no longer prevailed at Rome, as in the age of Saturn. But, on the other hand, we cannot deny that they often greatly exaggerated the evil. It appears certain that, influenced in their moral judgments by the traditions of literature, they often condemned too severely the women of their time, on account of having as their ideal the type of the ancient matron. Public opinion, in fact, clung to the ancient maxims after they were no longer practiced. At the same time that women were allowed by public opinion to lead a freer life, the epoch when they lived in closer retirement was universally praised. The manners of the current age were judged by the ideas of former times ; the new principles were accepted, but their consequences condemned.

And yet social opportunities, enjoyment of the arts, and intellectual interests, had not made all women either frivolous or guilty. Some women, in trying to be beautiful, witty, or cultured, had no other object than to make the family life more charming, or to please their husbands more. Such, for example, was the wife of Saturninus.

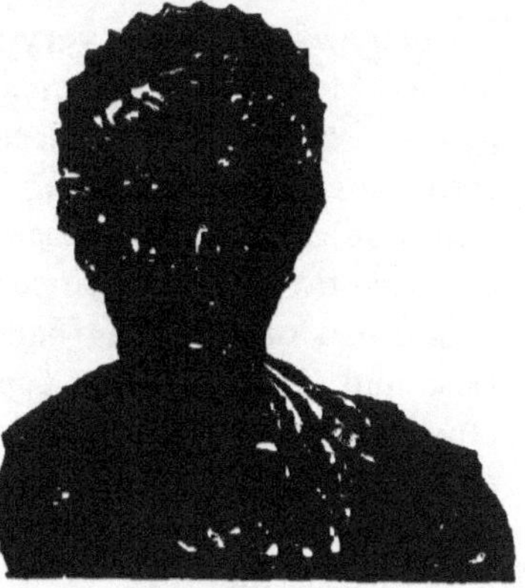

WOMAN'S HEAD.

He read to me, the other day [said Pliny], some letters, which he assured me were written by his wife ; I fancied I was hearing Plautus or Terence in prose. Whether they are that lady's, as he positively affirms, or his own, which he absolutely denies, he deserves equal praise ; either for writing such pieces himself, or for having so highly improved and refined the genius of his wife, whom he married young and uninstructed. .

Such also was the wife of Pliny himself.

She possesses an excellent understanding [he wrote], together with a consummate prudence, and gives the strongest evidence of the purity of her heart by her fondness for her husband. Her affection for me, moreover, has given her a taste for books, and my productions, which she takes pleasure in reading, and even in getting by heart, are continually in her hands. How full of tender anxiety is she when I am going to speak in any case, how rejoiced she feels when it is got through ! . . . When I recite my works at any time, she conceals herself behind some curtain, and drinks in my praises with greedy ears. She sings my verses, too, adapting them to her lyre, with no other master but love, that best of instructors, for her guide. From these happy circumstances I derive my surest hopes that the harmony between us will increase with our days, and be as lasting as our lives.

Such women came very near realizing the dream of all sensible and refined men, who take no pleasure in a learned wife, but who desire a wife cultured, sweetly serious, capable of taking an interest in the pursuits and studies of their husbands, and who now and then can give them a bit of sincere and natural advice.

Women of this time had then gained lovable qualities, and we must not suppose that all had lost the sturdy virtues of the past. Upon a close examination of the matter, we may even say that there are few epochs in which more examples of feminine heroism may be found. It is sufficient to recall the two Arrias, and Fannia, the daughter of Thrasea, who followed their husbands to exile or to death—"valiant women, whose strength was not always without grace, who wished in dying to be associated with the glory of their husbands, whose fidelity and constancy were afterward held up as examples, and whom universal admiration, by a sort of profane canonization, placed among the women Stoics." We must also mention, if only for the fact that the heroine has remained anonymous, an admirable example of conjugal devotion reported by Pliny :

I was sailing lately upon our lake, with an old man of my acquaintance, who desired me to observe a villa situated upon its banks, which had a chamber overhanging the water. " From that room," said he, "a woman of our city threw herself and her husband."   Upon my inquiring into the cause, he informed me that "her husband having been long afflicted with an ulcer, she prevailed with him at last to let her inspect the sore, assuring him at the same time that she would most sincerely give her opinion whether there was a possibility of its being cured.   Accordingly, upon viewing the ulcer, she found the case hopeless, and therefore advised him to put an end to his life ; she herself accompanying him, even leading the way by her example, and being actually the means of his death ; for tying herself to her husband, she plunged with him into the lake."   Though this happened in the very city where I was born, I never heard it mentioned before ; and yet, that this action is taken less notice of than that famous one of Arria's, is not because it was less remarkable, but because the person who performed it was more obscure.

These are, one will say, exceptions, and exceptions provoked by a reaction against the general disorder.   It seems, however, that after the reigns of Nero and of Domitian society had been for a short space purified by suffering.   The virtue of the women was certainly renewed by it.   The Palatine, where Messalina and Poppæa had reigned, was occupied under Trajan by good princesses, modest in their dress, without parade, affable in manner, who practiced all the domestic virtues.   In the great world, also, which imitates its leaders, morals seemed to become purer.   This at least is the impression left by the perusal of Pliny's letters.

But even if the deeds which we have recalled are only heroic exceptions, they prove at least that there is no hour of history where one can cease admiring women, and that expiring antiquity could show to young Christianity heroines not unworthy of being compared with its martyrs.

CHAPTER III.

THE ROMAN HOUSE.

LET us try to replace in their environment these Roman men and women whose education and married life we have attempted to describe.

Let us walk along a street of ancient Rome and observe its aspect.

Even when the city had been rebuilt, after Nero's fire, the streets, with few exceptions, would seem to us scarcely wide enough. But narrow streets, since they serve to secure shade and coolness, are almost a necessity for the peoples of the South, a fact overlooked by the builders of modern Athens. There is, moreover, another explanation of the narrow streets, and that is the natural configuration of the land, with its many hills and ravines. On each side of the long streets rose

houses whose height, while it terrified the ancients, would not excite surprise in our day. Strabo, the Greek geographer, reports that Augustus had forbidden the erection of buildings higher than seventy feet. This restriction applied only to the façade, for a greater height was allowed in that part of the building which did not overlook the public street. Nero reduced still further this limit, and Trajan, if we may trust Aurelius Victor, a Latin historian of the fourth century, finally made the limit sixty feet. However this may be, the citizens of Rome complained very much of this piling up of story upon story. They were always afraid of falling buildings or fire. Listen to the words which Juvenal puts into the mouth of the poor Umbritius :

Who fears the crash of houses in retreat
At simple Gabii, bleak Præneste's seat,
Volsinium's craggy heights, embowered in wood,
Or Tibur, beetling o'er prone Anio's flood?
While half the city here by shores is staid,
And feeble cramps, that lend a treacherous aid :
For thus the stewards patch the riven wall,
Thus prop the mansion, tottering to its fall ;
Then bid the tenant court secure repose,
While the pile nods to every blast that blows.

O! may I live where no such fears molest,
No midnight fires burst on my hour of rest !
For here 'tis terror all ; mid the loud cry
Of "water! water!" the scared neighbors fly,
With all their haste can seize—the flames aspire,
And the third floor is wrapt in smoke and fire,
While you, unconscious, doze. Up, ho ! and know
The impetuous blaze which spreads dismay below,
By swift degrees will reach the aerial cell,
Where, crouching, underneath the tiles, you dwell,
Where your tame doves their golden couplets rear,
And you could no mischance but drowning fear.

Danger of falling buildings and of fire.

One feature of the streets of Rome which would have excited the astonishment of a modern was the aspect of the façades. The Romans of the time of the Antonines, although they had already the taste for symmetry of form, which their descendants in Italy have so well preserved and developed, did not seek for symmetry in the construction of their buildings. Our modern architecture sacrifices much to the front elevation ; the ancients scarcely thought of that. Irregular lines were allowed where we should have straight lines. While we seek symmetry in the openings of our dwellings, an ancient Roman house would have windows isolated, or irregularly arranged, in the upper stories. While we wish to have the light pour freely into our rooms,

The aspect of the façades.

while we multiply large windows, in Roman houses there were no rooms upon the ground floor opening on the street. While the two sides of our streets look like the two sides of a trench which have been carefully kept equal in height, it was not rare to see in Rome an inequality in height between the different parts of even a single building. In short, the Romans

Inequality in height.

REMAINS OF A HOUSE AT POMPEII.

seem to have professed much indifference, if not actual disdain, for symmetry in architecture.

The irregular aspect of their streets was increased by numbers of little sheds, put up against the houses and encroaching upon the street. Here small trades were carried on. Here were taverns and shops. Domitian tried to change all this.

Shops.

The audacious shopkeepers [says Martial] had appropriated to themselves the whole city, and a man's own threshold was not his own. You, Germanicus [Domitian], bade the narrow streets grow wide ; and what but just before was a pathway became a highway. No column is now girt at the bottom with chained wine-flagons ; nor is the prætor compelled to walk in the midst of the mud. Nor, again, is the barber's razor drawn blindly in the middle of a crowd, nor does the smutty cookshop project over every street. The barber, the vintner, the cook, the butcher, keep their own places. The city is now Rome ; recently it was a great shop.

Doubtless at this time were constructed some of those arched over streets—arcades—of which the world's capital was proud.

But nothing is more difficult than to remove a little horde of shopkeepers, to break up their habits of life. Moreover, whatever Martial may say, Domitian did not wholly succeed ; for we find in 386 the prefect of the city, Pretextatus, issuing edicts similar to those of the last emperor of the Flavian dynasty.

Domitian's attempt to improve the streets.

POMPEIIAN HOUSE-FOUNTAIN. Museum of Naples.

The Romans enjoy the merited reputation of having been great builders. They owe this above all to their admirable public works—sewers, roads, causeways, and

The Romans as builders.

aqueducts.   But their private architecture, in spite of its late development, is not less worthy of attention.

Up to the time of Sulla, private houses were of a great simplicity.   Under the empire, those who were enthusiastic defenders of the ancient customs would recall with expressions of praise the little house, so small that it could be torn down in one day, of the consul, Valerius Publicola, or the modest dwellings of

Simplicity of private houses under the republic.

ATRIUM OF THE POMPEIIAN HOUSE AT SARATOGA SPRINGS, N. Y.
Franklin W. Smith, architect.

the Ælian family or of Cato Uticensis.   But from the end of the republic this simplicity began to disappear. In 93 B. C., the censor L. Crassus decorated his atrium with columns of marble from Mount Hymettus ; fifteen years later the consul Lepidus had a sill of Numidian marble placed in his house.   Such magnificence at that time caused much gossip.   All the idlers of Rome, and they were numerous, discussed the

Increasing magnificence of private dwellings under the empire.

matter. But this luxury was soon to cease being a cause for surprise. In the half-century which preceded the birth of Christ, the taste for beautiful buildings became general. ˙ It spread on account of the eastern wars, after the expeditions of Q. Metellus Creticus, of P. Servilius Isauricus, of Pompey, and of Lucullus. The splendor and magnificence of the eastern world dazzled the descendants of Romulus, and the immense wealth brought from this marvelous region by the Roman officers and revenue collectors (a freedman of Pompey, Demetrius, left a fortune of four thousand talents, about \$5,000,000) was put into buildings. Then came Augustus, who wished to make Rome the capital of the universal empire which he had founded. His great public works gave an impulse to private buildings, and, according to a famous saying, from a city of bricks Rome became a city of marble.

Vitruvius, Latin author of a work on architecture, expressed the requirements of the new taste as follows :

When you build for important personages, you must make vestibules high and of a royal aspect, a very large atrium, peristyles, parks, and spacious, imposing driveways. You must add libraries, picture galleries, and basilicas as grand as those of public edifices.

Grandeur was in truth the effect sought in private dwellings, beginning from this time, and Ovid and Sallust were not wholly incorrect, if they did exaggerate somewhat, when they said that certain great mansions of Rome might have been taken for towns.

We ask the reader to follow us into one of these abodes of wealth.

In front of the entrance is quite a large place, usually surrounded by porches, called the vestibule. It was there that the clients remained while waiting for their patron to wake up in the morning. A short corridor, called the *prothyrum*, connects the vestibule with the interior. At the right and at the left are situated rooms for the porter and his assistants, the watch dogs. If a man could not or would not have mastiffs for guardians, he replaced them by a painting which represented them showing their teeth, and above these dogs in effigy was written in large letters, "Beware of the dog" (*Cave canem*, or sometimes the abbreviation *C. C.*).

At the rear of the *prothyrum* is a heavy double door of oak. Let us open it and enter the atrium, to which it gives access. The atrium is the essential room of a Roman house, the room to which all the other parts of the house are subordinate. Its importance requires that we pause to examine it a few moments.

It is a vast court, lighted through an opening in the

STUCCO—WALL OR CEILING DECORATION.

roof. Here the family assembles, here is the hearth, the treasure chest, and formerly you would find here the bed of the father of the family. The smoke escapes through the opening overhead in the roof, through which also the rain falls into the *impluvium*, a basin sunk in the center of the floor, whence it is afterward distributed through the rest of the house. Up to the fourth century before Christ, the *lar*, or tutelar divinity of the house, was placed at the entrance of the atrium. In the houses of the nobles, the images of the family ancestors, often made of wax, occupied the wings or recesses of the atrium. New families adorned the atrium with medallions in bronze or silver.

Description of the atrium.

There were five different kinds of atria, distinguished by their architectural peculiarities. But we shall not make a point of these differences, as we wish to consider only what is essential and not to enter into archæological curiosities. We select then a typical atrium for our description.

Different kinds of atria.

It is worth our while to notice the luxury that is displayed in this room. Its dimensions are very large. An idea of the size of the atrium may be gained from the information which we have that the atrium of Scaurus (58 B. C.) was thirty-eight feet high. Cornices of white marble from Mt. Hymettus rest upon columns of Numidian marble ; ivory gleams on the gilded soffits. Between the columns were sometimes planted trees or shrubs. These are what Horace, with a satiric poet's exaggeration, called forests. The floor is paved with mosaic ; for the mosaic art was well advanced at Rome and was much admired. It is said that Cæsar, even in his military expeditions, carried with him mosaics for his tent. At the sides of the atrium are colonnades, whose gutters feed the central basin, the *impluvium*.

The luxury of the atrium.

Decorations
of the atrium.

This basin was often ornamented by a fountain. The opening in the ceiling of the atrium was sometimes covered with hangings of purple stretched from the entablature of one column to that of another. These hangings shut out the hot sun and cast a reddish light upon the bright, polished floor.

Purple hang-
ings.

Painting was also used to decorate the atrium. M.

ATRIUM OF THE POMPEIIAN HOUSE AT SARATOGA SPRINGS, N. Y.
Franklin W. Smith, architect.

Paintings.

Boissier, in his work entitled "Archæological Rambles," speaks of paintings found in a handsome Roman house, during some excavations on the banks of the Tiber. He describes them as "architectural designs painted with much elegance—figures boldly outlined, columns linked by garlands and arabesques, and between them medallions bearing representations of scenes from every-day life, feasts, concerts, sacrifices."

But it is time to continue our trip through the Roman house.

In the rear of the atrium are three rooms. The first, which is opposite the door opening into the *prothyrum*, is the archive-chamber, called the *tablinum*.   The *tablinum*.
Here the archives are stored. On each side of the atrium, right and left, is a recess called a wing, where the family portraits are kept and the busts of ancestors. These precious souvenirs are supported upon shelves, below which are inscriptions recalling the titles and the honors of the individuals represented.

Along the sides of the atrium are the dining-halls,   The dining-halls.
called *triclinia*, of which a Roman house contained several. There is one dining-hall for large receptions, another for a gathering of friends ; there is one fronting west for winter, one fronting east for spring and fall, and for summer one fronting north. Let us enter one of the dining-halls. At its four corners are lampstands. The center is occupied by the table, along three sides of which are couches, where those who are eating recline. The Romans, in fact, borrowed rather early from the eastern nations the custom of reclining at table. *Finally, on the side of the table not occupied by the couches is the abacus or sideboard, upon which, on grand reception days, were displayed, in honor of the guests, costly vases, dishes of gold and of silver, objects of art or of curiosity, in short whatever might convey some idea of the opulence of the owner of the house.

On each side of the *tablinum* are passages, leading to the truly private part of the house, the rooms which no one was expected to enter without being invited.

The first of these is the peristyle. The peristyle,   The peristyle.
like the atrium, is a court ; but while the atrium is

covered, the peristyle is open to the sky. The difference between the uses of the two rooms explains this difference in construction. Visitors are received in the atrium ; the peristyle is reserved for the family. Moreover, the central part of the peristyle, inside the columns, is occupied by flower beds, the *xystus*, and not by mosaic.

Upon this garden open the women's apartments (the *œci*), and also the library, fronting east. But there were few libraries except in the houses of the rich. Books were for the ancients objects of great luxury, the invention of printing not yet having made them cheap. At Pompeii, which was a town of prosperous tradesmen, books have not yet been discovered. The account books of the banker Cæcilius Jucundus, found recently, cannot be regarded as literary relics. The library was made to face east, because those who used it would do their work there usually in the morning, and besides the books would suffer less from damp.

Looking west is the *exedra*. In this hall, usually rather long, furnished with seats along the sides, the owner of the house would seek recreation from his business cares, in conversing with poets, rhetoricians, and philosophers. If M. Jourdain had been acquainted with Roman antiquities, he would not have failed to arrange' in his house a room of this kind. Then he would have been able to escape from the scolding of Nicole, his servant, and the upbraidings of Madam Jourdain, his wife.

A tennis-court, called the *sphæristerium*, and baths occupied the rest of the ground floor of a Roman house.

The use of artificial baths was introduced from Greece. In the early times of the republic, after their rude exercises on the Campus Martius, the athletes would go and plunge into the Tiber. But we know what rapid progress Greek customs made at Rome. Progress of Greek customs at Rome. Although few baths, according to Pliny, were known up to the time of Pompey, there was scarcely a house of importance in the first century of our era that was not fitted up with apartments for bathing.

The bath was a suite of rooms where one could take a cold, a warm, a vapor, or a hot bath. In the houses of the rich there were separate bathing apartments for the women. The usual time for bathing was just before dinner, from one to three o'clock. Few besides the very voluptuous bathed after this meal.

Let us follow a bather through the process of a very elaborate bath, noticing as we go the arrangements of the rooms.

CANDELABRUM.

He enters first the *lepidarium*, a moderately· heated room, not meant for The lepidarium. bathing. Here he sits for a while before undressing and perspires. He then removes his clothes, leaves them in charge of slaves who put them in cupboards kept for the purpose, and he passes to the *caldarium*, The *caldarium*. or hot room. This room is constructed with much care; it is provided at one end with a warm bath, the *alveus*, and at the other end there is a circular alcove or chamber called the *sudatorium* (sweating-room) or the *laconicum*, which is kept much hotter than the main part of the room. The *caldarium* is directly over the furnace, and has under the pavement a number of flues, through which hot air is supplied to heat the floor; the walls, too, of this room are sometimes hollow, and are heated by a circulation of hot air from the furnace. After a plunge in the *alveus* the bather enters the *sudatorium*. This circular recess has a hemispherically vaulted ceiling, with an opening at the top, which is closed by a movable disk. If the atmosphere becomes too suffocating, the disk is lowered by means of a cord worked from below, and some of the hot air is allowed to escape.

The sudatorium.

Running around this domical chamber are steps rising one above another; on the topmost step are niches, containing each one an arm-chair. In the center on the floor there is some gymnastic apparatus, and also a tub of hot water. The bather, if he desires, starts the perspiration by lifting weights, or by some other exercise, and then he begins to ascend the steps, gradually habituating himself to the temperature, which grows hotter and hotter as he rises. When he reaches the top, he sits in one of the arm-chairs and lets the perspiration flow. Before leaving this chamber he bathes in the tub of hot water. From the *caldarium* the bather returns to the *tepidarium*. Here he is treated by the masseurs, by others whose business it is to pull out hairs and trim nails, by those who, with strigils, bronze instruments, thin and flexible like hoops, scrape his skin all over to remove the impurities. The bather, then, if he wishes to omit nothing, passes to the

Masseurs, etc.

frigidarium, or cool room, where he takes a plunge in the *baptisterium*, a basin sunk in the floor, or, if he prefers, gives himself a cool sponge bath, standing before a bowl of moderate size, supported upon legs. Finally he comes back to the *tepidarium*, and before putting on his clothes he is rubbed by slaves with a liniment, to relieve itching and eruptions, wiped with fine towels of linen or of cotton, anointed with oil, and perfumed. Then he feels comfortable.

Some bathers preferred to begin with the cold bath, and often a bather took only the cold bath or only the warm one. None but the most luxurious went through the whole process frequently.

Besides the baths of private houses, there were the public baths.

The first floor only of a Roman house offers much that is interesting to us. There is little to be said about the upper stories, which contained less important rooms. The staircase giving access to them was usually only a steep and narrow ladder. The Romans would have been unable to understand the importance which we attach to this part of our buildings. Their indifference in this matter has been too faithfully preserved in certain provinces of our modern France, where they build a house first and afterward put in the staircase wherever they can, no matter how.

By the preceding description of a Roman house the reader can see that when the ancients constructed their homes they were not influenced by the same considerations that influence us when we build homes. Public life among the moderns is much less intense, if I may use the expression, than in the republics of antiquity. When we speak of the agitations of the forum, we merely make use of a trite metaphor. Among the

Romans the expression was exactly literal, even under the empire, even when Augustus had *pacified* the public square, according to the expression of Tacitus. The men lived much outside of their homes—in the street, at the baths, in the market-places, at the spectacles, at the lecture halls, at the tribunals. Consequently, when they returned home they experienced a need of isolation all the greater. Those who were obliged to receive visitors always reserved a part of their house where no one should intrude or disturb the family retirement. Did a client, a person seeking a favor, or a bore of any kind, insist upon seeing the master of the house? The emergency had been foreseen, and by a rear door leading into some narrow passage, the master, without difficulty, escaped from this troublesome caller. With us, back stairs are not always provided in our houses, and even where they do exist, they do not afford such a sure and secret means of escape as the Romans enjoyed. The world enters freely into our houses, and when it does not enter, we try at least to view it through our wide-open windows. An ancient house, instead of looking toward the street, looked away from it. In short, the comparison between an ancient and a modern house is sufficient to show us that although family life among us may occupy more hours of a man's life, it is less retired and less intimate than it was among the ancients.

Reduce the dimensions of the costly house that we have described, omit some rooms, those that could be serviceable only in a wealthy man's home, the library, the *exedra*, the tennis-court, and you will have an idea of the sort of houses that the middle class dwelt in. The general plan was the same. In the houses discovered at Pompeii, a town of small tradesmen, the

atrium, peristyle, etc., were always found. Only instead of the artistic magnificence displayed in the city
palaces, we observe in these provincial dwellings proofs
of the bad taste always exhibited by those who have not
long possessed means. In the peristyle, instead of
beautiful green grass and fountains there are sickly
shrubs, and mere threads of water, which the people
ostentatiously called channels (*euripi*), and grottoes of

Poor taste exhibited in provincial dwellings.

PERISTYLE OF THE POMPEIIAN HOUSE AT SARATOGA SPRINGS, N. Y.
Franklin W. Smith, architect.

stones or shells. Stucco or poor imitations of metals
take the place of marble and of bronze. Many of the
citizens of Pompeii must have resembled that Parisian
shopkeeper described by M. Sardou in the "Bons Vil-
lageois"; when he retired to the country he had a villa
built for him adorned with vases of imitation marble
and lighted by imitation windows furnished with imitation curtains.

Imitative decorations.

We wish we were as well informed in regard to the dwellings of the poor. Unfortunately, the poets and romancers paid little attention to the poor. The active interest which is felt to-day in the lower classes, the curiosity with which we read the books which depict their manner of life, the craving even which we feel for these representations of humble society—all this did not exist among the ancients. Except for the little poem

MARS AND VENUS. WALL DECORATION. Pompeii.

"Moretum," ascribed to Virgil, the romance of Petronius, and a few scenes from comedy, we find nothing in ancient literature to give us information about the poorer classes. But, after all, what could we learn that we do not know? It is only palaces that change in appearance. Huts remain the same in all times. It is luxury that assumes new aspects. Poverty has not so much variety.

Withdraw from my cottage, little mouse, hiding in the shadow. The kneading-trough of Leonidas cannot feed mice. Here is an old man, content with little; for whom some salt and two barley cakes are enough, and who lives without complaining, as his fathers have lived. What are you looking for in his house, dainty mouse? You will not find here the crumbs from a dinner. Quickly go to my neighbors. There ample provisions wait you.

A poor man's cottage.

Thus spoke from the inside of his home a poor man who lived two centuries before Christ. One hundred and fifty years earlier, Chremylos, a character in one of the comedies of Aristophanes, gives this description of an Athenian hovel :

> The gnats and fleas that buzz about your head,
> I cannot count, so great their multitude.
> They wake you, and their shrill pipe seems to say,
> "Up, wretch, although you're hungry, up, arise."
> You have besides a tatter for a quilt,
> And for a bed your rushes full of bugs,
> That will not let you drop your drowsy lids,
> And for a pillow underneath your head
> A good sized stone.

It is indeed always the same story ; beggars of Athens, beggars of Rome, beggars of Paris—forlorn always, in all countries, your hovels have no history. The houses where people die of cold are all built in the same fashion and their style is eternal.

Let us return, then, to the fortunate inhabitants of the world. Judging from the luxury displayed in the construction of their dwellings, one is tempted to believe that they were sumptuously furnished. This temptation must be resisted, for it will lead us into error. The Romans of ancient times had no more idea of comfort than their descendants and the peoples of the South in general. The great palaces of modern Rome often contain rooms very beautiful, but gloomy on account of

The furniture of a house.

their bareness. There is nothing but some master-piece, picture or statue, for the eyes to rest upon. It was very much the same in the ancient houses. Nothing, or almost nothing, for convenience, everything for show. While the entire house was scantily furnished, the reception halls often contained a few very handsome articles—tables made from citrus wood with ivory legs, couches veneered with tortoise-shell, or ornamented with gold and silver, and covered with Babylonian tapestry, vases of Corinthian bronze and of murrhine ware, dressers decked with silver, and candelabra, like those of which Lucretius speaks :

> What though about the halls no silent band
>   Of golden boys on many a pedestal
> Dangle their hanging lamps from outstretched hand,
>   To flare along the midnight festival !

Vanity may indeed partly account for this manner of furnishing a house, but doubtless a taste for the plastic arts, so keen from this time among the people of Italy, had something to do with it. There were surely among the Romans some enlightened amateurs who were not actuated merely by the single desire of dazzling their visitors. Read the charming description which Pliny gives us of a Corinthian statue which he had purchased:

Out of a legacy that was left me I have just bought a statue of Corinthian bronze. It is small, but thoroughly clever and done to the life—at least, in my judgment, which, in matters of this sort, and perhaps of every sort, is not worth much. However, I really do see the merits of this statue. It is a nude figure, and its faults, if it has any, are as clearly observable as its beauties. It represents an old man standing up. The bones, the muscles, the veins, and the very wrinkles, all look like life. The hair is thin, the forehead broad, the face shrunken, the throat lank, the arms hang down feebly, the chest is fallen in, and the belly sunk. Looked at from behind, the figure is just as expressive of old age. The bronze, to judge from its color, has the marks of great antiquity. In short, it is in all respects a work which would strike the eye of a connoisseur, and which cannot fail to charm an ordinary observer. This induced me, novice as I am in such matters, to buy it. However, I bought it not to put in my own house (for I never had there a Corinthian bronze), but with the intention of placing it in some conspicuous situation in the place of my birth, perhaps in the Temple of Jupiter, which has the best claim to it. It is a gift well worthy of a temple and of a god. Do you, with that kind attention which you always give to my requests, undertake this matter, and order a pedestal to be made for it out of any marble you please, and let my name, and, if you think fit, my various titles, be engraven upon it.

TABLES.

I will send you the statue by the first person who will not object to the trouble ; or, what I am sure you will like better, I will bring it myself, for I intend, if I can get away from business, to take a run into your parts.

In short, comfort, which is a necessity for people of the North, is not required by southerners. What must they have ? Coolness and shade, also rooms reserved for family life, even if they are very small and receive the air and light only by the door. Of what use to furnish such rooms ? A bed, a chair—was anything more necessary for napping at noon or sleeping at night?

Let us not exaggerate, then, the luxury in the furnishing of a Roman house. Doubtless certain articles of furniture were very costly. Doubtless there were candelabra from Ægina which cost 250,000 sesterces (about $10,625). Doubtless Cicero possessed a table of citrus wood worth 500,000 sesterces (about $21,250). But these were curiosities. The possessors of these objects were artists or maniacs. At a much less cost one could furnish his house suitably, even richly. It seems, according to Martial, that about $40,000 of our money was sufficient to furnish a large house. If we remember that the installation of the Countess Kosel in the Château de Pillnitz cost $150,000 ; if we consider that the expense of furnishing of the Northumberland House is estimated at several hundred thousand pounds sterling, we shall conclude that the moderns have progressed since the time of Martial, and that our nabobs have outdone the patricians of ancient Rome.

CANDELABRUM.

Moreover, we must not forget that the greatest private fortunes of antiquity never equaled those of our modern Crœsuses.   It is true that there were fools and eccentric individuals like the Apiciuses, the Caligulas, and the Neros, those people who gave themselves up to senseless prodigalities, which Lucian wittily calls "the solecisms of indulgence."   But we must admit that the estate of the richest of the patricians was not large.   According to Marquardt, the greatest income known in ancient times scarcely exceeded $1,215,000 of our money.   What is that compared to the fortune of Baron Rothschild, which the papers, when he died in 1868, valued at $400,000,000?

Thus private wealth at Rome never had the proportions which it has reached in our modern society.   Now the Greek artisans and oriental merchants sold very dear the beautiful objects which they made, while the system of slavery brought down the price of manual labor in the work of building.   This explains the splendor of the buildings and the plainness of the furnishings in a Roman house.

CHAPTER IV.

THE SERVANTS.

In our day domestics have been called "household enemies." The epithet unfortunately applies too well, but it applied still better to the slaves of ancient times.

The source of slavery is known. At first the slave, as is indicated by the etymology of the Latin word for slave *servus* (*serere*, to bind), was a prisoner of war. Hence the severity of the legislation to which he is subjected. He is regarded as a thing. His master possesses him absolutely, having the right to use him or to abuse him. The slave has nothing of his own. The savings which he has been able to make from his *peculium*, or allowance, usually by depriving himself of nourishment, do not belong to him. According to law, they belong to his master. The slave cannot marry; the union which he contracts resembles concubinage. He cannot make a will; he cannot witness in a court of justice. Is he ill-treated by his master? He must keep silent, for he has no redress. Insult, dishonor, anything he must bear without protest. Has not his master the right over him of life and death?

The harshness of this legislation explains certain facts which appear to us to-day monstrous. Seneca tells us how a certain Vedius ordered a slave to be thrown into the fish-pond as food for the murænas because he had broken a vase. Nero's father, Domitius Ahenobarbus, killed his freedmen (freedmen were often servants to their former masters and liable to punishment from them) because they refused to drink as much wine as he wished them to.   In the comedies masters never speak to their slaves without threats ; they have at their tongue's end a whole catalogue of instruments of torture, crucifixes, whips, hot irons.   And the mistresses are no more tender.   To illustrate, we quote from Juvenal's Sixth Satire.   A lady is speaking.

> " Go, crucify that slave."   For what offense ?
> Who the accuser ?   Where the evidence ?
> For when the life of man is in debate,
> No time can be too long, no care too great.
> Hear all, weigh all with caution, I advise—
> " Thou sniveler ! is a slave a *man?*" she cries.
> " He's innocent ! be't so ;—'tis my command,
> My will ; let that, sir, for a reason stand."

Slaves were sometimes driven to extremities by these cruelties, and took terrible revenge.

The vengeance of slaves.

The horrid barbarity [writes Pliny] which the slaves of Largius Macedo, a person of prætorian rank, lately exercised upon their master is so extremely tragical that it deserves to be the subject of something more considerable than a private letter ; though at the same time it must be acknowledged there was a haughtiness and severity in his treatment of them which showed him little mindful that his own father was once in the same station.   They surrounded him as he was bathing, at his villa near Formiæ, and some beat him about the face and head, while others trampled upon his breast and his belly ; when they imagined they had thus completed their intentions, they threw him upon the burning pavements of the hot bath, to try if there was any remaining life left in him.

But the vengeance of slaves always cost them their lives.   Further, when a master was assassinated by a slave, and when the culprit could not be fixed upon, all the slaves who dwelt under his roof were executed. Thus perished, under Nero, the four hundred slaves of Pedanius Secundus, prefect of the city.   Tacitus, in the fourteenth book of his " Annals," represents the

Its punishment.

senator C. Cassius urging their execution in a speech which exhibits with striking fidelity the cruelty of the ancient prejudice against slaves and the harshness of the inhuman legislation in regard to them.

But war early ceased to be the only origin of slavery. The citizen who had undergone civil degradation and the insolvent debtor were reduced to servitude. Those who were born of slave parents were slaves themselves.

Under the influence of these facts, the treatment of slaves became milder than the laws, and gradually the laws themselves were modified.

Cato the Old was certainly a faithful representative of the ancient manners. He cannot be reproached with being easily moved to pity,

DOOR KNOCKER.

and the lot of the slave awakened no feeling within him.

It is necessary [he said] to sell old cattle, old wagons, old iron implements, old or diseased slaves—in a word, whatever is useless.

He did not pamper his slaves.

As a relish for them [he said] save as many fallen olives as possible, next, those olives which do not promise to give much oil.

We know what kind of wine he would have them drink.

Pour into a cask six amphoræ [the amphora was a measure of six gallons and seven pints] of sweet wine and two amphoræ of very sharp vinegar. Add to this two amphoræ of boiled must and fifty of fresh water. Stir the whole with a stick three times a day for five consecutive days ; after which mix into it thirty-two gallons of old brine. This wine will last good up to the solstice. If any is left over, it will make excellent vinegar.

He exercised as much economy in dressing them as in feeding them.

Every other year a tunic, three and a half feet long, and a *sagum* [coarse blanket]. When you give them a new *sagum* or tunic, have them return the old one, as it will do to make over into patchwork garments. Every other year a good pair of shoes.

And yet this master, whose heart was of iron, as Livy says, used to eat and drink with his slaves, and had his wife take care of them when they were sick.

These germs of humanity developed fast. In the time of Augustus, Horace condemned the severity of Albucius, who did not pardon a single fault in the slaves who served him at table. Augustus also, when a wicked man, Hostius Quadra, had been killed by his slaves, pretended to be ignorant of the crime, for, although he aimed to observe rigidly the laws, he feared he would offend public sentiment if he prosecuted the criminals. Half a century later, when the slaves of that Pedanius Secundus of whom we have spoken above were punished by death, the military forces had to be called out to prevent the people from snatching the wretches from the executioner.

We read, also, of a Roman mother who having lost a son and a slave of the same age had them buried near each other. Their sepulchers were side by side and just alike. The inscriptions contained nearly the same words. Those who were thus united in death, those to whom she rendered the same religious rites, must have been loved by her during their life.

Philosophy exerted an active influence in ameliorating the condition of slaves. We know that the Romans had very little taste for pure speculation. A doctrine, in their eyes, was of value according to its practical results. They did not enjoy ideas except as they could be translated into facts. So the philosophers sought to improve the public morals by direct means, either by friendly counsel after the manner of Seneca, or by popular preaching, like that of Dion Chrysostom. They had especially at heart the welfare of the slave. From Cicero to Seneca all recommend to masters the exercise of clemency and gentleness. Seneca spoke of slaves as our "humble friends," and Juvenal, who in more than one passage protests against the ferocious caprices of the great nobles, affirms boldly

> that slaves have powers,
> Sense, feeling, all, as exquisite as ours.

. These ideas and these sentiments found a ready welcome in the soul of Pliny, and suggested to him one of his most beautiful letters :

The sickness which has lately run through my family, and carried off several of my domestics, some of them, too, in the prime of their years, has deeply afflicted me. I have two consolations, however, which, though they are not equal to so considerable a grief, still they are consolations. One is, that as I have always very readily manumitted my slaves, their death does not seem altogether immature, if they lived long enough to receive their freedom ; the other that I have allowed them to make a will, which I observe as religiously as if they were legally entitled to that privilege. I receive and obey their last requests as so many authoritative commands, suffering them to dispose of their effects to whom they please ; with this single restriction, that they leave them to some in my family, which to persons in their station is to be esteemed as a sort of commonwealth.

But though I endeavor to acquiesce under these reflections, yet the same tenderness which led me to show them these indulgences still breaks out and overpowers my strongest resolutions. However, I could not wish to be insensible to these soft impressions of humanity; though the generality of the world, I know, look upon losses of this kind in no other view than as a diminution of their property, and fancy that by cherishing such an unfeeling temper they discover a superior fortitude and good sense. Their wisdom and self-control I shall not dispute. But manly, I am sure, they are not; for it is the very criterion of true manhood to feel those impressions of sorrow which it endeavors to resist; and to admit, not to be above, the want of consolation. But perhaps I have detained you too long upon this subject—though not so long as I would. There is a certain pleasure in giving vent to one's grief; especially when we pour out our sorrow in the bosom of a friend, who will approve, or at least pardon, our tears. Farewell.

Such pages prove that philosophic instruction could produce happy results. In fact, beginning from the empire, philosophy, and particularly the Stoic philosophy, inspired the Roman lawmakers. So, from the reign of Tiberius, the Petronian Law forbade delivering without reason slaves to the wild beasts. An old custom permitted the exposure of sick slaves upon an island of the Tiber sacred to Æsculapius. There they died of hunger and cold. Claudius put an end to this barbarity. Under Nero slaves could go to law. "There is a judge," Seneca tells us, "before whom slaves may relate the injuries inflicted upon them by their masters."

Laws for the protection of slaves.

DOOR KNOCKER.

Difficulty of enforcing these laws.

It is true, they might seek redress "with discretion, and only if they had been too cruelly beaten, if they had been compelled to suffer from hunger, or if an attempt had been made upon their honor." It is true, also, that such complaints, at this epoch, could have been but little heeded, since the magistrate whose duty it was to listen to them was the prefect of the city, that very Pedanius Secundus who was assassinated by his slaves. Nevertheless, protective measures for slaves had been started, and the emperors who followed developed them still further. Hadrian exiled a matron who was in the habit of cruelly maltreating her slaves, under the most trivial provocations. Antoninus established the principle that it is no more permissible to kill one's own slave than another's slave, and he made the punishment the same for both crimes. Finally, the progression of public opinion reached the point at which the lawyer Gaius declared that slavery was contrary to natural right.

Slaves protected by the self-interest of masters.

But more than by philosophy or by law the slave was protected against the caprices of cruelty by his master's self-interest. According to M. Boissier, economy was exercised in regard to slaves, as well as in regard to other perishable property :

Varro takes great pains to instruct his farmer to employ, in a dangerous piece of work, work in the marshes for instance, where fatal fevers are likely to be contracted, a hired laborer, rather than one of his slaves. If the hired laborer succumbs, it is his own misfortune. When a slave dies, it is his master's loss.

Does not this remind us of La Rochefoucauld's maxim, "Self-interest, which we accuse of all our misdeeds, deserves often to be praised for our good actions" ?

In short, it seems that the various causes which we

have just indicated had made slavery under the Antonines a supportable condition, although it was always a sad one.   At no epoch did slavery cease to be a plague-spot in the Roman civilization.   Ancient society carried
thus within itself a germ of destruction. But, as we have shown, the evil had its alleviations. And, moreover, the Romans, in struggling against it, were supported by a strong and skilful organization.

Our most important magistrates of to-day do not live in such style as to give us any idea of the large attendance of domestics in an elegant house at Rome.   Pliny the

BRONZE HAMES (HORSE HARNESS).

Elder narrates that Cæcilius Isodorus said in his will that although he had lost much in the civil wars, he left 4,116 slaves.   Petronius certainly did not exaggerate when he said that Trimalchio did not know by sight one tenth of his slaves, and that when the steward of this upstart came to render his account to his master one day, he informed him that during the night, in his estate of Cumæ alone, thirty boys and forty girls had been born.

We naturally wonder why the Romans should be

willing to undertake the burden of these innumerable bodies of slaves.   There is only one explanation—the private estates were of vast extent.   The conquered territory, which was rapidly and incessantly augmented by the Roman armies, became public land.   This public land, when not sold or otherwise disposed of, was allowed to fall into the hands of private individuals on the condition that they should work it, or farm it, giving the state a share of the profits.   Such an arrangement as this, being of necessity loosely administered, gave an opportunity, first to patricians, afterward to men of senatorial rank, and to rich and powerful families, to accumulate vast tracts of land which they held as private property.

Thus were developed those large landed estates

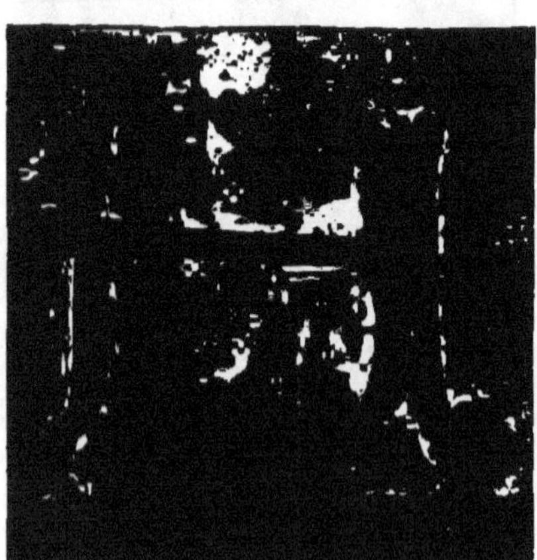

HORSE BIT.

which, according to the writers of the time, were the ruin of Italy.   Thus a rich man's domains became so vast that a kite's wings would have been wearied in flying across them. As private individuals possessed veritable provinces, they needed, to work them, veritable nations.

But many people, who were not forced to do so by circumstances, nevertheless owned many slaves.   They were influenced by vanity to imitate the great nobles, and wished to appear what they could not be.   They played the eternal comedy:

> Every little prince ambassadors must send,
> Every marquis, too, his pages must attend.

Women have more of a taste for display than men, and Juvenal shows how the women of his time were true to their character :

> Whene'er Ogulnia to the circus goes,
> To emulate the rich, she hires her clothes,
> Hires followers, friends, and cushions ; hires a chair,
> A nurse, and a trim girl, with golden hair,
> To slip her billets.

Manias quickly become necessities. Accordingly the middle-class citizens of Rome almost always had a body of domestics out of proportion with their property. Scaurus inherited from his father only 37,000 sesterces (about $1,572.50), yet he was served by ten slaves. It is natural to judge from appearances, for this is the easiest and quickest way. When two people met upon a road, the one who had the fewer attendants would give room to the other. Thus the respect which was a man's due was indicated by the number of servants he had about him. A magistrate who kept only five slaves was pointed at with the finger of scorn. If a lawyer wished to attract clients, he would not succeed if he relied upon eloquence. He must rather appear in public carried in a sedan-chair by eight slaves, and have a troop of very submissive dependents following him.

We see that slaves very often became a heavy burden upon their masters. To support this burden a miracle of economy would have been required, if the treatment of domestics in ancient times had been anything like the treatment which they receive to-day. A character in one of Labiche's comedies sums up the requirements of our servants :

What do I ask? To be well fed ; . . . to be well paid ;
. . . to be allowed to grow fat in peace.

These are modest requirements ; many of our servants are more exacting, and we have to yield to them.
But at Rome domestics were cheaper. The price of
an ordinary slave was about $100, which would be
equivalent to the payment of $5 a year as wages. His
food and clothes also were very inexpensive. Pliny
said that when he received his freedmen at his table, he
let them drink the same wine that he himself drank.
But the Roman to whom he gave this detail appeared
so surprised at it that we must conclude that Pliny was
alone in his generosity. It was much more usual for
masters to keep their slaves upon the diet which Cato
recommended. Seneca seems to say that it was customary to give a slave every month five bushels of
corn and five *denarii* (about 83 cents). Calling the
price of a bushel of corn 4 sesterces (about 17 cents),
that would make the total expense for one slave about
$1.68 a month — a modest outlay, especially in com-
parison with the princely salaries which we allow our
cooks and coachmen. Let us add that the master of a
well-ordered Roman house bought nothing ; his own
estate was supposed to furnish him the commodities
necessary for supporting his family, and his city house
contained artisans of every trade.

But even when a householder was not burdened with
the support of slaves, he had enough to do. In order
not to be overtaken by want, he piled up provisions of
every kind in immense storehouses, whose contents he
could not always remember. It is related that at the
epoch when the theater tried, like the theater of modern
times, to draw crowds by the splendor of its scenery, a
manager, who had to dress a large number of his

figurants and who was unwilling to go to great expense, applied to Lucullus, begging him for the loan of one hundred tunics. "One hundred tunics!" replied the rich Roman. "Where do you expect me to find them? Nevertheless, I will have a search made." The next day he sent the manager five thousand tunics. The administration of these immense fortunes must have been very burdensome.

When a master had provided for the support of a vast number of slaves, he was not rid of his responsibility. He had to organize his force, form it into companies like an army, so that commands might be given to it and obedience enforced, and so that each slave might have an employment suited to his ability and strength.

The discipline of slaves.

The slaves who were born in the house, the *vernæ*, as they were called, were naturally less of a care to the master than the others. Their fathers had had a trade, an office of some kind, and the children had learned to work by watching them at their tasks. If the *vernæ* were destined for some new service, there was plenty of time to educate or to train them. Moreover, they were easily managed ; they inherited habits of servitude. They almost always submitted, they were often contented, and many a slave was proud of his title of *Verna*, and had it inscribed upon his tombstone.

The vernæ.

There was greater difficulty with slaves that had been purchased. These were brought from the market where they had been exposed on a platform, their feet whitened with chalk, if they had just been imported from across the sea, and each one with a label round his neck announcing his good qualities and his faults. But it is not to be supposed that these labels were always truthful. The slave merchants had a well-

Purchased slaves.

merited reputation for bragging and falsifying. Horace has cleverly described one of these shameless rascals, and we may well believe that if they had not all the wit which the poet ascribes to them, they were not lacking in impudence and roguery.

What was to be done with these purchased creatures, whose masters were little, if at all, acquainted with their qualities? After a sorting process, some were sent to the fields, the others were retained for the city house.

Out-door slaves.

The lot of the former was by no means enviable. They were treated about like cattle. At night they were shut up in buildings no better than stables— underground prisons, lighted by narrow windows placed so high above the floor as to be out of reach. During the day they had to work alone. For fear that the open air and free space might suggest flight to them, fetters were put upon their feet. For some this treatment was the cause of great suffering. "No," said one of them, "I have often seen the torments of hell represented in painting, but there is no hell more infernal than my condition."

Their toilsome labor.

The labor, besides, which they were compelled to perform was always extremely toilsome. They had to work quarries, to clear up land which had never been under cultivation, to prepare irrigation works, to construct the causeways or the roads necessary for making a piece of property valuable. And yet many of them were contented with their condition. Horace's valet, who, to speak the truth, had the restless disposition which is becoming a poet's servant, wished to leave the city and to be employed at Tibur. For in the country a slave had the advantage of being far from his master. "When one works in a distant field where the master rarely comes," says a character in an Atellan of Pomponius, "he is no longer servant but master." Besides, slaves enjoyed, without doubt, great liberty during the festivals when they were allowed to gather together. There was in the country a freedom during the Palilia and the Saturnalia which the police of the city would not have allowed. Bonfires were lighted everywhere ; wine flowed in abundance, and if the master happened to be near, full of the tranquillity and the gentle kindness which a peaceful country life fosters, he would retire, without doubt, as did Pliny the Younger, into some secluded room, in order not to check the explosion of joy which these poor creatures exhibited when left to themselves unchained. Festivals.

The slaves reserved for the city house, being nearer their master, had more to suffer from his caprices, but also they had a better opportunity to profit from them. Moreover, being relatively more numerous, their work was less laborious. House slaves.

Slaves were classified, first, according to their nationality and their color. The Asiatics were musicians or cooks ; from Egypt came those beautiful children whose mission it was to enliven their master by their frolicsome humor. The Africans, agile and strong, ran before his sedan-chair to make a way through the crowd. As to the Germans, with their great bodies and towering height, they were saved for the gladiatorial show. Classification of slaves.

But thus far we have only made the first rough classification ; for the division of labor was carried to a degree that is difficult for us to realize. There were slaves to open the door for a visitor, others to show him in, others to hold aside the hangings before him, others to announce him. A man had slaves to whisper in his Division of labor.

ear the names of those whom he ought to recognize upon the street. There were house-porters, stewards, ushers, cup-bearers, bath-keepers, sweepers, etc. The tomb has even been discovered of an unfortunate mortal whose unique duty was to paint the aged Livia. May we not trust that this office was a sinecure?

The Romans had become so accustomed to let their slaves act for them that they came to rely upon their slaves also to think for them. The Roman household was a machine in which the intellectual faculties of the slaves and freedmen belonged to their masters, and in which the master who knew how to govern his forces worked, as it were, with an infinite multiplicity of intellects. Greece furnished in abundance learned and literary slaves, who read, took notes, made researches, prepared material for authors. It has been thought that Pliny the Elder's "Natural History," that encyclopedia of antiquity, was written with such assistance from slaves. Quintilian said that Seneca had often been led into error by the false information of those who had been directed to make researches for him, and he evidently refers to slaves and freedmen. Not only did the Romans have slaves for secretaries, they had slaves for prompters. The story of Calvisius Sabinus is familiar. He was ignorant and had no memory. But he required one of his slaves to learn by heart all Homer, another Hesiod, and others the nine Greek lyric poets included in the Alexandrian canon; and when he gave a dinner, he had them crouch at his feet under the table and furnish him with such quotations as the occasion might suggest to a learned and witty man, and these he repeated, often with absurd mistakes. He did not hesitate to incur expense. Each one of these prompters cost 100,000 sesterces, or about

$4,250. A man who could afford it would let slip no opportunity for getting possession of such valuable assistants, whether he wished to use them himself or to trade them off. They were articles of luxury, and they sold easily, literary vanity being quite in the style. There was, then, in connection with every well-appointed house, a department where a complete course of study was provided for slaves. The ancient inscriptions make frequent mention of these slave-schools. *Slave-schools.*

When each slave had had his special duty assigned to him, the next step was to establish a system of discipline. It is at this point that the Romans displayed their genius for organization. The slaves were divided into groups of ten, and each group was commanded by a decurion. The decurions, again, were under the authority, in the country, of the farmer, and in the city, of the steward. The farmer and the steward had to render each day an account of their administration to the master, or to the one whom he deputed in his place. This organization, which required certain slaves to assist in the government of the house and interested them in its management, this division of the domestic force into little groups, which gave to the decurions authority over their companions, without interfering with the supremacy of the master, this incessant oversight rendered the administration of a vast household possible, if not easy, and afforded an excellent training to those great optimates who were to play one day a public rôle. *The organization of a body of slaves.*

The country slaves had their festivals, and the city slaves, occupied by tasks which were, as we have shown, so narrowly circumscribed, would have been indeed subjects for pity if they had not enjoyed now and then a few hours of pleasure. Their Saturnalia, *Recreations of slaves.*

boisterous without doubt, were nevertheless held more closely within bounds than the same festival in the country. But the city slaves made up for this restriction by many minor pleasures. Horace gives us an idea of the amusements which occupied the leisure moments of those of somewhat low taste. They used to take long strolls through the busy streets of the capital, stand in front of the pictures done in charcoal or red chalk, which adorned the white walls of the buildings, gossip at the public baths, while waiting for their masters, or loiter in the low corner tavern, where some girl played the flute, while the clowns danced to her noisy music. Sometimes, too, huddled together on the highest seat of an amphitheater, they would become so absorbed in the games as not to notice the loud voice of the vender as he went about crying that his cakes were hot from the oven.

The more cultured slaves found pleasure in their master's society, and liked to take part in his life without his suspecting it, to exert a quiet influence among the members of his household, to make himself indispensable—in short, to rule. With a good master this was not difficult. Pliny ingenuously confesses that he did not always wield undisputed authority in his own house, and that he had to call upon his mother-in-law to support him :

The elegant accommodations which are to be found at Narnia, Ocriculum, Carsola, Perusia, and particularly the pretty bath at Narnia, I am extremely well acquainted with. The truth is, I have a property in everything which belongs to you ; and I know of no other difference between your house and my own, than that I am more carefully attended in the former than in the latter. You may, perhaps, have occasion to make the same observation in your turn, whenever you shall give me your company here ; which I wish for, not only that you may partake of *mine* with the same ease and freedom that I do of *yours*, but to awaken the industry of my domestics, who are grown something careless in their attendance upon me. A long course of mild treatment is apt to wear out the impressions of awe in servants ; whereas new faces quicken their diligence, as they are generally more inclined to please their master by attention to his guest than to himself. Farewell.

But the slaves would often succeed in securing their ends, even with masters who had not the indulgent and kind spirit of Pliny, and many a Cæsar, who held the world in terror, was himself governed by one of these obscure persons, whose power was all the greater and more formidable because it was concealed.

Having tried to show the relation of slaves with their masters, it remains

HEATER. Naples.

for us to indicate the feelings that existed among the slaves themselves, and this is not the least interesting part of our task.

If the reader remembers what we have said of the organization of the domestics in a Roman house, of the

system of government which was practiced, he will have
no trouble in seeing that hatred and rivalry among
slaves must have been frequent. Accusations, of course,
were often made, and masters had no need of encour-
aging them. But frequently, also, their community of

suffering drew the slaves into sympathy with each
other, and made them form strong friendships. Upon
the tomb of one of his friends, a freedman once had the
following inscription engraved :

> Between us two, my dear comrade, no difference ever arose ;
> I call upon the gods of Heaven and Hades to witness the
> truth of this statement ! We were made slaves at the same
> time, we served in the same house, we were freed together,
> and this day, which has taken thee away from me, is the first
> which has separated us.

These friendly relations were not limited to a few
individuals. In a rich man's house associations were

formed among the slaves—*collegæ* (colleges), to use the
Roman word—whose members were regularly assessed
to meet the common expenses. Sometimes all the
slaves of a house would assemble, like the people in
the forum, to vote, after solemn deliberation, some
recompense to the one in command over them. If
they were satisfied with him, they would join in erecting
a monument to him to thank him for having exercised
his authority with moderation. Sometimes, on such occasions, they would imitate very successfully the official
style, and express themselves as follows : "The dining-
room slaves, in token of the services and the kindness
of Aurélia Crescentina, have decreed a statue in her
honor." Does it not sound like a decree of the senate?
Liberty is such a beautiful thing that these poor people,
who had lost it, or had never known it, found a sweet
delight even in imitating its forms and its language.

The law refused a slave the privilege of having a family. Marriage, with its resulting civic rights and its moral character, was reserved for the free man. But when the law is in such manifest contradiction to nature it has no effect; it remains a dead letter. That is what happened at Rome. The slaves intermarried, and the lawyers, by pronouncing their unions mere concubinage, could not prevent the slaves themselves from regarding them seriously. The slaves had no scruples against appropriating the titles husband and wife, a privilege which the free man claimed exclusively for himself. Some of them imitated the style of the inscriptions placed upon the tombs of the women of noble family, and in praising a wife did not hesitate to apply to her the adjective "incomparable." They also, and with more sincerity perhaps than their masters, would speak of eternal regret, and refer with sorrowful pride to a union which no storm had ever troubled and which had never brought them any pain except in the death of the loved one. These marriages, freely contracted, in which only mutual liking was consulted, in which questions of birth never had· weight and money considerations very seldom, were likely to be happy marriages. But sometimes, also, slaves would not wait for true affection to come before concluding a marriage, but

Marriage among slaves.

KEY.

would obey a mere caprice. Such caprices were not always regulated according to our notions of propriety. Sometimes, instead of a union of two, a union of three was established. Plautus, in his "Stichus," has described one of these singular combinations, where perfect harmony reigned, as the following song of one of the husbands shows :

> We love the same girl,
>   And we ne'er disagree.
> No envy we know.
>   Funny rivals are we !
> We live in accord,
>   And we drink from one bowl,
> Yet we love the same girl !
>   Oh, is it not droll?

The reader may be tempted to think that we have here the mere wild fancy of a comic poet, which his bold gaiety allowed him. But no ; graveyard inscriptions, which of course are not humorous, show us that there were instances in which two husbands, at the death of their common wife, joined in mourning her—and in erecting her tombstone. Plautus has not imposed upon us. The reality was far more bizarre than the inventions of the poet. A slave whose wife was his sister mentions the fact in an inscription, as if it was the most natural thing in the world.

Fortunately, however, instances of this kind must have been somewhat rare. Marriage, in general, far from depraving the slave, had the effect of improving his morality, and was therefore encouraged by masters. Moreover, it was a means of attaching the slave to the house, of removing the temptation to escape. The children born from slaves were valuable property ; and Cato, who was a practical man, conceived the idea of selling to his slaves the right of marrying. This was making them pay for the privilege of enriching him. Masters, then, willingly presided over the marriages of slaves, and attended their noisy celebrations, perhaps even paying for them. These customs became so well established that, under the empire, marriages among slaves obtained a sort of legal recognition, and the jurist Paulus, who lived under the emperor Alexander Severus, allowed that a slave might legally apply the term "wife" to the mother of his children, a privilege which earlier jurists had refused.

Thus, as the plebeians formerly had acquired, in spite of the law, the power to conclude valid marriages with the patricians, so now slaves succeeded in getting their marriages with each other legalized. They were no longer denied the consolation of remembering those who had given them life, and the joy of anticipating the future of those who had received life from them. Often, it is true, this joy was mingled with much bitterness. Was not the future full of dark uncertainty? Was it not in the power of their master to take away their dear children? Was not the life, and above all the honor, of their children, at the mercy of his caprice? What would become of this little girl, who was growing up full of grace? Might she not please her lord too well? And this young boy, handsome and strong, might he not become the victim of those hideous passions which the morals of the ancients regarded with too little severity? Even the true happiness of the children sometimes cost the tears of the parents. The children might be freed, and that meant separation. A master might marry the daughter of a slave, and in that case he naturally would not allow her to visit her parents. In spite of so many fears, in spite of so many anxieties for the future, the desire for a family is so natural and so profound that slaves were not deterred from marriage by the thought of the possible consequences. This praiseworthy perseverance began to reap its reward when a law of Constantine forbade separating the members of a slave family, even by an act of manumission.

The time has come to speak of the important act which gave to the slave the liberty which he had never known, or restored to him the liberty which had been taken from him. Reinach has given the following brief but complete description of the bestowal of freedom upon a slave:

The manumission of slaves.

Manumission [he says] might be effected without formalities, but in case a regular form was observed, the slave was released in one of the three following ways : 1st. By *vindicta*, the Latin word for staff. This was a ceremony in which a third party, who must be a Roman citizen, touched the slave with a staff in the presence of a magistrate and of the master. The master, who was holding the slave, let him go, and the magistrate pronounced him free. 2d. By census, when the master had the slave's name inscribed by the censor upon the list of citizens. 3d. By will, or even by a wish expressed for the heir to carry out.

Modestus.

It was probably this last method that Sabina used in the case of her slave Modestus, but she had neglected to state formally her desire. Fortunately, she had made Pliny the Younger one of her legatees, and he chose to respect the intentions of her will rather than hold strictly to its letter. We cannot deny ourselves the pleasure of quoting the letter, in which Pliny tells us how he adopts a course upon this occasion which does honor to his character.

Your letter informs me that Sabina, who appointed you and me her heirs, though she has nowhere expressly directed that Modestus shall have his freedom, yet has left him a legacy in the following words: "I give, etc.—to Modestus, whom I have ordered to be made free"; upon which you desire my sentiments. I have consulted upon this occasion with the most learned lawyers, and they all agree Modestus is not entitled to his liberty, since it is not *expressly* given, and consequently that the legacy is void, as being devised to a slave. But it appears plainly to be a mistake in the testatrix; and therefore I think we ought to act in this case as if Sabina had directed in so many words what it is clear she imagined she had. I am persuaded you will join with me in these sentiments, since you so religiously regard the will of the dead; which indeed, where it can be discovered, will always be law to an honest mind. Honor is to you and me as strong an obligation as necessity to others. Let Modestus, then, enjoy his freedom and his legacy in as full a manner as if Sabina had observed all the requisite forms; as indeed they effectually do who choose their heirs with discretion.

Pliny's decision in the case of Modestus.

Emancipation gave to the slave the rights of a citizen, but up to the time of Augustus freed people could not contract marriage with those of free birth. They were also excluded from military service, and were not eligible to office. Moreover, they were under certain obligations toward their liberator. They could not bring an action against him, nor witness to his disadvantage.

The rights of freedmen.

The law Junia Norbana, of uncertain date, perhaps belonging to the time of Tiberius, divided freedmen into two classes, citizens and Latins. The former enjoyed full liberty, the latter a more incomplete liberty and the rights only of Latin colonists. But history shows us that the tendency of Roman legislation was toward unity, and we find under Justinian all freedmen raised to the same rank. This emperor conferred upon them all the rights of freeborn citizens.

By what means could a slave succeed in escaping from servitude? How could he win the privilege of

How freedom might be won.

putting on that Phrygian cap which was the sign of freedom?

.He was obliged first to fulfil certain conditions required by the law. Up to the end of the empire a master could not give freedom to a slave under thirty, nor to one who had suffered during his slavery any ignominious punishment. The law indicated also the cases in which a slave could claim freedom. A slave who had been exposed sick on the island in the Tiber sacred to Æsculapius, and who recovered, also a slave

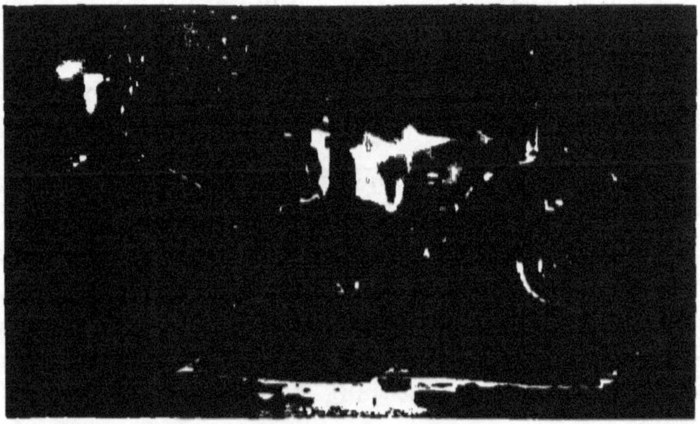

Conditions required by the law.

COOKING UTENSILS.

who had informed against certain criminals, were thenceforth free. Slaves were also allowed to buy their freedom from their masters with their savings.

But most emancipations were the result of a master's willingness to give freedom. When a slave had rendered his master some extraordinary service, or had succeeded in winning his master's favor by his agreeable ways, he might hope to be led before the prætor and to be touched by the liberating staff. Those who belonged to the higher class of slaves, who had literary

The purchase of freedom.

culture, were more likely than others to be presented with their liberty, and often, after becoming freedmen, they lived in intimacy with their masters. It is known that Cicero had a strong friendship with his freedman Tiro, and Pliny the Younger shows in the following letter that he had no less affection for Zosimus :

Friendships between masters and freedmen.

As I know the humanity with which you treat your own servants, I do not scruple to confess to you the indulgence I show to mine. I have ever in my mind Homer's character of Ulysses,

> "Who ruled his people with a father's love."

And the very expression in our language for the head of a family [*pater familiæ*, father of a family] suggests the rule of one's conduct toward it. But were I naturally of a rough and hardened cast of temper, the ill state of health of my freedman Zosimus (who has the stronger claim to a humane treatment at my hands, as he now stands much in need of it) would be sufficient to soften me. He is a person of great worth, diligent in his services, and well skilled in literature; but his chief talent, and indeed his profession, is that of a comedian, wherein he highly excels. He speaks with great emphasis, judgment, propriety, and gracefulness; he has a very good hand, too, upon the lyre, which he understands better than is necessary for one of his profession. To this I must add, he reads history, oratory, and poetry as well as if he had singly applied himself to that art. I am thus particular in enumerating his qualifications that you may see how many agreeable services I receive from him. He is indeed endeared to me by the ties of a long affection, which seems to be heightened by the danger he is now in. For nature has so formed our hearts that nothing contributes more to raise and inflame our inclination for any enjoyment than the apprehension of being deprived of it—a sentiment which Zosimus has given me occasion to experience more than once. Some years ago he strained himself so much by too vehement an exertion of his voice that he spit blood, upon which account I sent him into Egypt; from whence, after a long absence, he lately returned with great benefit to his health. But having again exerted himself for several days together beyond his

The character of Zosimus.

His ill-health.

strength, he was reminded of his former malady by a slight return of his cough and a spitting of blood. For this reason I intend to send him to your farm at Forum-Julii, which I have frequently heard you mention as having an exceeding fine air, and I remember your recommending the milk of that place as very good in disorders of this nature. I beg you would give directions to your people to receive him into your house and to supply him with what he shall have occasion for; which will not be much, for he is so temperate as not only to abstain from delicacies, but even to deny himself the necessaries his ill state of health requires. I shall furnish him toward his journey with what will be sufficient for one of his abstemious turn who is coming under your roof. Farewell.

But the stigmata of slavery were not easily effaced. Public opinion refused to place these newcomers into civic life in the same rank with those who had always been free. We know that the enemies of Horace reproached him with his birth, and when, long after (178) Pertinax, who, like the poet, was a freedman's son, succeeded, by his military achievements, in winning the consulship, people did not fail to circulate scornful remarks about his humble origin. "Look," they would say, "at the results of cursed war."

It is not hard to understand this feeling of contempt for freedmen. The conditions of the slave and of the free man were separated by barriers so wide that it was not easy to cross them, and any one who accomplished this feat was regarded with ill-will.

But we must confess also that freedmen often furnished cause for this prejudice and distrust. They were probably not responsible for the degradation in their characters produced by slavery. Nevertheless, they were degraded, although they were not to blame for it. The touch of the prætor's staff was not the touch of a fairy's wand, and liberty could not change them completely in a single day.

They had usually received mental training ; but honor is not learned without a teacher. So they were almost all of an equivocal morality, if they were not notoriously immoral.

When they entered civic life they were usually without means, and they lived by their wits. They could not afford to be too particular about the choice of a profession. The important thing was to make a living. No pretense of an occupation would do. They became trumpeters, itinerant musicians, assistants in funeral obsequies, barbers, town-criers, scavengers ; their taste was not very delicate, neither was their conscience. They swelled the number of legacy-hunters, false witnesses, and brokers. Active, shrewd, unscrupulous, knights of industry, convinced that business meant other people's money, they often quickly amassed a fortune. And then they exhibited those vices that in all ages come with a sudden elevation of fortune. Might not their vices of to-day afford them some compensation for yesterday's repression ? Might they not even be the punishment of those masters from whom they had been learned—learned almost under compulsion ? Juvenal has drawn several striking portraits of these insolent and vain rich freedmen. Let us reproduce one of them :

The scene is the open space, filled with people, before the door of a palace whose owner is distributing free gifts among the expectant crowd. We see a patron and his clients. A dispute has arisen in the crowd about a question of precedence.

> "Dispatch the Prætor first," the master cries,
> "And next the Tribune." "No, not so," replies
> The Freedman, bustling through, "first come is, still,
> First served ; and I may claim my right, and will !—

Though born a slave ('tis bootless to deny
What these bored ears betray to every eye),
On my own rents, in splendor, now I live,
On five fair freeholds ! Can the purple give
Their Honors more ? when to Laurentum sped,
Noble Corvinus tends a flock for bread !—
Pallas and the Licinii, in estate,
Must yield to me : let, then, the Tribunes wait."
Yes, let them wait ! thine, Riches, be the field !—
It is not meet that he to Honor yield,
To sacred Honor, who, with whitened feet,
Was hawked for sale, so lately, through the street.
O gold ! though Rome beholds no altar's flame,
No temples rise to thy pernicious name,

.   .   .   .

Yet is thy full divinity confest,
Thy shrine established here, in every breast.

Petronius, in his " Satiricon," has depicted the
finished type of those freedmen, who, trying to
imitate their former masters, substitute for magnificence, display ; for elegance, affectation ; for
pride, insolence; and for rudeness, vulgarity. His
Trimalchio, at the same time that he makes a show
of his riches, tries to appear a lord. He even
aspires to literature. He would like to pass for
a Mæcenas, for a patron of arts. He prides himself on a beautiful passion for music. So he has
himself served at table to the sound of musical
instruments, and his valets carve in rhythmic
measure. However, in his sincere moments, he
confesses that, as to artists, he cares only for rope-
dancers and cornet-players; thus M. Jourdain preferred to everything else the sound of the trumpet
marine.

This kind of upstart was only ridiculous. But
the more intelligent ones became often formidable.

KEY.

Pliny once made the following profound observation about the Cæsars : " They are the masters of the citizens, and the slaves of the freedmen."

The power of freedmen.

What motives led the emperors to depend so largely upon the services of freedmen ? They desired to impress the masses, whose temper it was important not to irritate, with the idea that the imperial court was not essentially different from a private family. Furthermore, they were influenced by a political consideration which, although diametrically opposed to this affectation of simplicity, is not inconsistent with it. They tried, by employing freedmen in places of honor, to show plainly how little importance they attached to the differences of social rank ; they wished to make it understood that they had adopted a system of leveling, and thus to break down the resistance of the ancient patrician class, and to teach all that the imperial pleasure was the source of every honor, that it could raise a man from the humblest condition to the highest, and that before it all the subjects of the empire were equal.

Social leveling.

This power of the freedmen, it is true, was checked under the Antonines ; for Pliny says to Trajan : " You advise them to keep themselves within bounds. . . . You know that the presumptuous airs of the freedmen make the prince appear insignificant." But this power could not have been destroyed, for Pliny adds, " Besides, they are all the more worthy of receiving respect when we are not compelled to pay it to them."

The rapid accumulation of wealth by the freedmen, their sudden attainment of political elevation, excited the anger and surprise of the Roman citizens. This explains their exclamations of wrath against freedmen ; this excuses the unjust satires of Juvenal, who, misled

The wealth of freedmen.

by a feeling of hatred, sometimes makes random flings at them, and even goes so far as to reproach them for gaining their livelihood by working. He represents his friend Umbritius, who is on the point of leaving Rome, as saying :

> Here, then, I bid my much-loved home farewell—
> Ah, mine no more !—there let Arturius dwell,
> And Catulus ; knaves, who, in truth's despite,
> Can white to black transform, and black to white.

Now, these freedmen, so severely condemned by the wrathful Umbritius, are nothing but engineers, manufacturers, and merchants ; for he continues his indignant strain by explaining in just what the knavery of these knaves consists.   They

> Build temples, furnish funerals, auctions hold,
> Farm rivers, ports, and scour the drains for gold!

But let us not, in trying to understand the irritation of the ancient Romans at the sight of the rapid ascent of these men who started from so low a position, fail to observe one of the greatest facts in the history of civilization.   Emancipation opened the avenues for true democracy.   We owe to the manumission of slaves the gradual disappearance of pernicious prejudice, of the unjust and aristocratic contempt for work, commerce, and industry.   And as the breaking down of one barrier always drags along another, the prosperity of freedmen resulted at last in the abolition of slavery.

CHAPTER V.

THE TRANSACTION OF BUSINESS.

THE ancients regarded historical composition as belonging to the realm of the artistic imagination. A history was for them a beautiful drama, whose scenes should follow each other in a style of sustained elevation of oratorical grandeur, without any prosaic interruption. They carefully excluded all that could break this unity of tone or destroy this harmony of color. Tacitus illustrates this ancient conception of history when, instead of quoting the official text, which he had at hand, of the speech delivered by the emperor Claudius in favor of extending to Transalpine Gaul the right of admission to the senate, he remodels it, and imbues it with his own personality. The province of history was, then, among the ancients, much more limited than among us. They attempted to describe only the most attractive aspects of the society in which they lived. Consequently they have told us almost nothing about questions of the economic order. Since the historians neglected this subject, can we not go to the dramatic writers or to the romancers? They would doubtless be a valuable source of information, but, unfortunately, the comedies which represent scenes from the lives of tradesmen and workmen—we refer to the mimes and the Atellans—have been lost, and the interesting romance of Petronius, which depicts the lives of the uneducated classes, is too strongly local in color, belonging exclusively to the south of Italy, to be serviceable as a source of general information. To treat the commerce of antiquity is therefore a difficult undertaking. In fact, nearly all our knowledge about it is derived from monumental inscriptions. Let us try to sum up the results arrived at by those who have devoted their time to research in this subject.

Scanty as our information is, we are safe in affirming that commerce, in ancient Rome, never reached the same degree of activity as among modern nations. There was nothing at Rome which resembled even faintly the rush of business affairs which sweeps along in its feverish movement the men of the present time. When we consider how practical the Romans were we are inclined to feel much surprise that commerce among them held so unimportant a place, and we wonder how it could have been so dormant in an atmosphere which, at first thought, seems very favorable to its development.

Some have sought an explanation in the origin of Rome. The first settlers, we know, were farmers. During long years agriculture was the principal means of existence for Italian communities, and especially for the Latins. The beautiful custom of beginning the foundation of a city by tracing a furrow with a plow where the future encircling wall was to stand, proves how profoundly the feeling that the existence of cities depended upon agriculture was impressed upon all minds.

So agriculture was a profession eminently honored by the ancient Romans. Listen to the views of the elder Cato :

When our forefathers pronounced the eulogy of a worthy man, they praised him as a worthy farmer and a worthy landlord; one who was thus commended was thought to have received the highest praise. The merchant I deem energetic and diligent in the pursuit of gain; but his calling is too much exposed to perils and mischances. On the other hand, farmers furnish the bravest men and the ablest soldiers; no calling is so honorable, safe, and inoffensive as theirs, and those who occupy themselves with it are least liable to evil thoughts.

Nothing is better than to praise agriculture. But, unfortunately, the respect in which farming was held was offset by a contempt for commercial activity. We learn from Livy that a Claudian law, passed at the suggestion of Caius Flaminius, forbade senators and the sons of senators to possess ships, except for the transport of the products of their own estates, and probably also forbade them to engage in public business enterprises; in a word, excluded them from all that the Romans understood as speculation or trade. There is an oft-quoted passage in Cicero's writings which has a significant bearing upon this question. In his treatise on "Duties," the orator distinguishes between liberal and servile occupations as follows:

The contempt of commerce.

Liberal and servile occupations.

Those callings are held in disesteem that come into collision with the ill-will of men, as that of tax-gatherers, as that of usurers. The callings of hired laborers, and of all who are paid for their mere work and not for skill, are ungenteel and vulgar; for their wages are given for menial service. Those who buy to sell again as soon as they can are to be accounted as vulgar; for they can make no profit except by a certain amount of falsehood, and nothing is meaner than falsehood. All mechanics are engaged in vulgar business; for a workshop can have nothing respectable about it. Least of all can we speak well of the trades that minister to sensual pleasures—

"Fishmongers, butchers, cooks, poulterers, and fishermen,"

as Terence says. . . . The professions which require greater skill, and are of no small profit to the community, such as medicine, architecture, the instruction of youth in liberal studies, are respectable for those whose rank they suit. Commerce, if on a small scale, is to be regarded as vulgar ; but if large and rich, importing much from all quarters, and making extensive sales without fraud, it is not so very discreditable.　Nay, it may justly claim the highest regard, if the merchant, satiated, or rather contented with his profits, instead of any longer leaving the sea for a port, betakes himself from the port itself to an estate in the country.　But of all means of acquiring gain nothing is better than agriculture, nothing more productive, nothing more pleasant, nothing more worthy of a man of liberal mind.

Agriculture the noblest occupation.

One hundred and fifty years after Cicero, Juvenal expresses the same ideas.　It was considered in his time less unbecoming for a free man to go and beg for the *sportula* (gifts of money doled out by a patron to his clients) than to engage in a lucrative employment. Have we not still retained something of this prejudice? Are we not too fond of the liberal professions, which have been ironically defined as '' those which allow the least liberty and bring in the least money'' ?

This contempt for commerce was probably sincere with some of the great nobles and literary men among the Romans.　But it seems to us that it was more often a pretended contempt, assumed by those who wished to appear stylish and cultured.　At bottom, the Romans, whom Pliny the Elder considered so devoted to utility, were mercantile in spirit.　Cato, who expressed his mind freely, confesses, in the practical instructions which he prepared for his son, that this is so.

Mercantile spirit of the Romans.

A man [he says] ought to increase his fortune.　And the man whose account books prove at his death that he has gained more than he received as an inheritance is worthy of praise, and is filled with a divine spirit.

Let us not, then, look for the cause of the slight

development of commerce at Rome in the disdain which people boasted for the merchant's calling and their respect for agriculture only.   The true explanation is to be found in the social constitution of Rome.   From an early point in its history Rome had no middle class. The small farmers, the small plebeian property-holders, who had constituted the strength of the city in the first era of its existence, soon disappeared.   In fact, how could they sustain the war which capital, in the third and fourth centuries after the founding of the city, had declared against labor?   For war it certainly was when the landowner, who never worked, took away from the farmer, under the pretext that it was the interest upon his debts, the profit coming from the land which he toiled to cultivate.   These ancient citizens, thus driven out of agriculture, which had become a burdensome profession for them, would doubtless not have scorned trade or manufacture.   But how could they succeed in either?   How meet the formidable competition of slave labor?   In almost every branch of traffic business was carried on by slaves.   The historian Mommsen says :

The money-lenders and bankers instituted, throughout the range of their business, additional counting-houses and branch banks under the direction of their slaves and freedmen.   The company which had leased the customs duties from the state appointed chiefly their slaves and freedmen to levy them at each custom-house.   Every one who took contracts for buildings bought architect-slaves ; every one who undertook to provide spectacles or gladiatorial games on behalf of those to whom that duty pertained, purchased or trained a company of slaves skilled in acting, or a band of serfs expert in the trade of fighting.   The merchant imported his wares in vessels of his own under the charge of slaves or freedmen, and disposed of them by the same means in wholesale or retail.   We need hardly add that the working of mines and manufactories was conducted entirely by slaves.

It is plain that to engage in trade without a large capital was, on account of the competition of slave labor, disheartening even for the boldest citizens. Moreover, what deterred the plebeians more than anything else from such an enterprise was that measures had been adopted to render it unnecessary for them to do business. What was the use of working when one could live without it?

The chiefs of the democracy [says M. Boissier, in his "Archæological Rambles"], at length risen to power, paid the people for their kindness by a liberality whose consequences were necessarily fatal to the republic. C. Gracchus caused it to be decided that henceforth the state should undertake partially to feed the poor citizens. Corn tickets were distributed to them, which allowed them to receive corn at half price. It being natural not to stop at half measures, some time after the Gracchi it occurred to another demagogue to give it for nothing. The less people paid, the more the number increased of those who desired to enjoy this favor. When Cæsar took possession of the supreme power their number mounted to 320,000.

If we consider how temperate the people of the South are, and how few their needs, and if we bear in mind that besides these gratuitous distributions which the masses received, these gifts of public assistance, clients were given presents by their patrons, and that the people sold to candidates for office the support of their votes, we shall understand how aptly the familiar phrase, "a commonwealth composed of millionaires and of beggars," applies to Rome during the two centuries before the Christian era. This condition of things was but little bettered under the empire, in spite of the efforts of some of the princes to restrain this mendicity. At the death of Augustus 200,000 citizens were still receiving corn from the state. This enormous disproportion in the distribution of wealth, these premiums awarded to idleness, constitute in our opinion the true cause of the stagnation of commerce at Rome.

However this may be, commerce did exist, and it is time for us to describe it.   In the first place, commerce was purely passive, and consisted in importation.   How could it be otherwise?   Ruined by the capitalization of wealth, by the encroachments of the large estates, and by the civil wars, Italy produced nothing.   Pliny the Elder says that on the peaceful waters of the Tiber could be seen the commodities and the merchandise of the whole world.   This is not an exaggeration.   Rome was the vast emporium for all that the world pro-

Importation.

CUP.

Rome becomes a vast emporium.

duced.   It absorbed everything and returned nothing. Look at the picture which Ælius Aristides traced in the second century after Christ of this immense bazaar:

Into this city are brought, from all countries and from all seas, the fruits of all the seasons and the products of all lands, rivers, and lakes ; and whatever is created by the skill of the Greeks and of the barbarians.   So that the man who wishes to view all these things must either travel over the whole world or visit this city, where there is always an abundance of whatever is grown or manufactured among all nations. In the course of a season so many freighted ships come into its port from all countries that a person there might almost think he was in a universal manufactory. So many cargoes from India and from Araby the Blessed are to be seen there that one might imagine that the trees of those countries are forever stripped of their fruits, and that the people who live in those countries will be forced to come to Rome to ask back again as much of the products of their own soil as their necessities require. The stuffs of Babylonia and the jewels from the barbarous region of interior Asia reach Rome in much larger quantities and far more easily than the products of Naxos and of Cythnus reach Athens. In fact, whatever commerce can lay hold of and ships can carry, whatever agriculture and the mines produce, whatever industry and the arts create, whatever exists in the earth, and whatever grows upon it, all this is gathered together in the market of Rome.

Rome thus had become a truly universal city, a microcosm, a miniature world, according to the expression of a Greek rhetorician. Its appearance was as cosmopolitan as that of our modern Paris. There one might hear a confusion of tongues as various as those which buzz in Paris. The costumes of all the countries, the types of all the races, presented there a mixture even more picturesque than can be seen to-day in that city. For if the Roman civilization had created unity, it had not been able to impose uniformity. Here were fair-haired Germans and woolly negroes. Oriental princes with their pointed caps, such as the Persians of our day wear, ran against tattooed savages from the island of Britain. Rome attracted men as it absorbed things. It was at the same time the museum and the inn of the universe.

Under such conditions, transmarine commerce was naturally more fully and more quickly developed than other commerce. In a comedy of Plautus, a slave who has just found a bag in the bottom of the sea, and who, judging by its weight, thinks he has made a valuable find, builds, as we say, castles in Spain—castles in Asia, as the Romans would have said. After Its extensiveness. he shall have purchased his liberty from his master, he proposes to equip vessels and to engage in commerce on a large scale. He will meet with success, like a certain contemporary of his, who became suddenly rich ; and he will found cities which shall bear his name, and he will be bowed down to as king among kings. A person does not indulge in such dreams unless there is some foundation in reality. In fact, commerce beyond the sea had become very extensive. This is proved by its complicated organization. The historian Mommsen says :

In transmarine transactions more especially and such as were otherwise attended with considerable risk, the system of The system of partnership. partnership was so extensively adopted that it practically took the place of insurances, which were unknown to antiquity. Nothing was more common than the nautical loan, as it was called—the modern "bottomry"—by which the risk and gain of transmarine traffic were proportionately distributed among the owners of the vessel and cargo and all the capitalists who had advanced money for the voyage. It was, however, a general rule of Roman economy that one should rather take small shares in many speculations than speculate independently ; Cato advised the capitalist not to fit out a single ship with his money but to enter into concert with forty-nine other capitalists, so as to send out fifty ships and to take an interest in each, to the extent of a fiftieth share.

The empire, which had made the comfort of the masses a subject of its incessant care, and, as it were, The harbor of Ostia. an instrument of control, did not fail to encourage this commerce, which tended to create activity and was a source of wealth. Great public works were undertaken, harbors were dredged ; and the excavations of Ostia, so prosperously conducted by Signor Visconti and continued by Signor Pietro Rosa, have shown us what intelligence and what large ideas the Romans displayed in constructions of this kind.   Claudius and Trajan had successively worked there.   M. Boissier says :

The port of Claudius.

The port of Claudius was shut in to the right and to the left by two solid jetties, "like two arms," says Juvenal, "stretched out in the middle of the waves."   The one to the right, sheltered by its position from tempests, was formed of arches, which allowed the water of the sea to enter, while that to the left was of solid, stout masonry.   It had to be strong enough to resist the billows, when raised by the south wind.   Between the ends of the two jetties the enor-

OSTIA.

mous vessel on which one of the largest obelisks of Egypt had just been brought over was sunk full of stone.   It became a kind of islet, protecting the harbor, and only leaving on either side two narrow passages, furnished with iron chains.   On this little island a lighthouse was raised—that is to say, a tower of several stories, ornamented with columns and pilasters, like the one that lit the port of Alexandria.

Trajan's harbor.

Soon the harbor of Claudius was inadequate.   Trajan had a new one dug.   It was a hexagonal basin, covering an area of almost one hundred acres, and it was lined on all sides by a quay forty feet broad, with granite posts to moor the ships to.   These are still in their places.   The new harbor formed a continuation of the old one, and was joined to it by a canal fifty-nine feet broad, and another canal put them in communication with the river. This latter canal has become a new arm of the river, and is called to-day the Fiumicino. There are remains in the port of Ostia of vast warehouses—docks, as we should say. They all appear to have been constructed at the same time and upon the same model. Great vats are still in existence there, half buried under the ground, where corn and oil used to be stored. The docks at Ostia.

A whole population of sailors, divers, porters, lightermen, and writing clerks were employed in the unloading and storing of the merchandise. A painting found at Ostia preserves for us a life-like picture of these maritime towns. It represents a vessel, with its name and that of its proprietor inscribed upon its side. It was called the *Isis of Geminius*. M. Boissier thus describes the picture :

On the poop, above a little cabin, the pilot Pharnaces grasps the helm. Toward the middle, the captain Abascantus is overlooking the workmen. On the shore, porters, bending beneath the weight of sacks of corn, proceed toward a small plank, which joins the ship to the shore. One of them has already arrived, and is pouring the contents of his sack into a large measure, while in front of him the controller, charged with the interests of the department, is intent on seeing the measure well filled, and holds the sack by its edges, in order that nothing may be lost. A little further, another porter, whose sack is empty, is sitting down to rest, and his whole face breathes an air of satisfaction, explained by the words written by the painter above his head, "I have finished" (*feci*). A picture of maritime life.

Next to maritime commerce, money-dealing was the most brilliant feature of Roman private economics. It constituted the occupation of a whole class of the citizens—namely, the equestrian order. In early times this branch of commercial industry had been Money-dealing.

much despised.   Cato, in his outspoken way, said :

Lending money at interest has several advantages, but it is not honorable. Our fathers consequently decreed, and inscribed it among their laws, that the thief should be sentenced to restore double, but the lender at interest quadruple. We see by this how much more pernicious a citizen they regarded the usurer than the thief.

The basis of the social economy of the Romans.

But neither the law nor the instinctive hate which the masses felt for the business prevented money-dealing and the leasing of the taxes from becoming the basis of the social economy of the Romans. Through such monetary transactions the knights succeeded in gaining in the state a place which permitted them soon to counterbalance the influence of the senatorial order. For almost none of the business men had the good sense to keep aloof from public life. The example of the wise Atticus was but little followed. The mania for holding office seized upon those who grew rich at this time, as in our nineteenth century.

Banking.

We should like to know something about the system of banking among the Romans. Unfortunately, our only source of information is the tablets of a provincial banker, Cæcilius Jucundus, in business at Pompeii. These tablets, recently discovered, comprise one hundred and thirty-two signed receipts, of which one hundred and twenty-seven have been deciphered. Almost all these receipts have reference to sales by auction. We quote from M. Boissier :

He who presided at the sale—the chief auctioneer, as we should call him—had to know how to keep accounts and draw up a regular report, so a professional banker was often appointed to the office. This is how, at Pompeii, Cæcilius Jucundus came to be charged with it. The presidency of the banker had, besides, another advantage. When the buyer, who was obliged to settle at once, had not the needful sum at his disposal, the banker advanced it. So in transactions of this nature he made two kinds of profit—first, the commission levied on the total proceeds of the sale in payment of his trouble, and then the interest required of the buyer for the money lent to him. Our tablets, which, with a few unimportant differences, are all written the same way, contain the receipt of the seller to the banker who furnishes the funds, and represents the real buyer of whom he is the intermediary. These documents have special interest for lawyers. Others, unfortunately in too small numbers, give us curious information touching the finances of Roman municipalities, and the way in which they administered their properties. They are signed by the town treasurer, and show us that Cæcilius, who was not satisfied with the emolument accruing to him from sales by auction, also undertook to manage the communal estates. He had thus taken farm pastures, a field, and a fuller's shop belonging to the municipality, perhaps either sub-letting or working them himself. Such were the means hit upon by the banker of a small town in order to enrich himself.

A banker's profits.

Below the bankers were those who lent money on the security of personal property deposited. For already this means had been discovered of exploiting the poor and needy. Martial, in one of his epigrams, depicts a man who tried to appear rich making a display of sumptuous elegance at the forum, although the evening before he had presented himself at the counter of the pawnbroker Claudius to pawn his ring in order to get enough money to buy his supper with. In short, whatever the social standing of money-dealers in Rome, it seems to be evident, in spite of the scarcity of information on the subject, that financial activity was divorced from morality. The evil results of the unscrupulous management of money reached a climax at the end of the republic. Then occurred seditions like those of Cinna, of Catiline, and of Clodius, which were merely battles between those who had property and

Pawnbrokers.

Business immorality.

those who had none.   The reforms of the empire perhaps resulted in improving somewhat this situation, but we do not believe that the emperors succeeded in supplying financiers with true principles of business morality.

We do not entertain for commerce on a small scale the aristocratic disdain of Cicero.   Although they are at the bottom of the ladder, the shopkeepers and the artisans interest us as much as the bankers and the ship-owners, if not more than they.   We should like to have in regard to this class of Roman society abundant and exact information.   But, as we have already said, our information at this point is meager.   However, let us try to make the most of it.

In the first place, we are struck by the great variety of trades.   If the theory of the division of labor is recent, its practice is very ancient.   This division of labor was carried very far at Rome, especially in the manufacture of objects of art and of luxury.   Besides the gold and silversmiths we find ring-makers, as well as gold-beaters and gilders.   Plautus has made a humorous enumeration of the different trades ,which supplied the wants of women.   Let the reader imagine pay-day in a wealthy family :

There stands the scourer, the embroiderer, the goldsmith,

SHOP OF AN OIL MERCHANT AT POMPEII.

street, the belt-makers' street, the sandal-makers' street, the wood-dealers' street, the glaziers' street, etc.

We have enumerated the methods, more or less honest, of gaining a livelihood at Rome. There were other means, shamefully dishonest, of making fortunes. Money became a god. Juvenal, in one of his satires, exclaims :

> O gold ! though Rome beholds no altar's flame,
> No temples rise to thy pernicious name,
> Such as to Victory, Virtue, Faith are reared,
> And Concord, where the clamorous stork is heard,
> Yet is thy full divinity confest,
> Thy shrine established here, in every breast.

But, although this god had no formal worship, it had nevertheless faithful worshipers.

One of the favorite expedients for arriving at a fortune was the hunting of legacies. In the epoch which we are studying this had become more than a business—it was an art systematically practiced according to certain rules. Already Horace had tried to expose the theory of this art, in the satire in which he represents to us the shade of the divine Tiresias teaching Ulysses how to repair his fortune, ruined by the prodigalities of Penelope's suitors. But the instruction of Tiresias was rudimentary ; he was a babe in the art. The employment of legacy-hunting rapidly gained in extent. This was due to the enormous increase of celibacy and childlessness among the upper classes, two evils that the laws of Augustus had not succeeded in curing.

Here in Crotona [wrote Petronius, who transfers to this city the characteristics of Rome] learning is in no esteem ; eloquence finds no acceptance ; nor can temperance and morality meet with commendation, much less lead to profit ;

but all the men you see in that city know for certain that they belong to one or other of two classes ; for they either hunt or are hunted for legacies. No one there rears children ; for whoever has natural heirs is not admitted to any public shows or entertainments, is excluded from all social privileges, and herds obscurely with the dregs of the people. On the contrary, those who have never married, and have no near kindred, are advanced to the highest honors ; they are the only brave, the only fit to command, and, in short, the only virtuous. You will see a city like those fields in the time of a pestilence in which there are only torn carcasses, and crows tearing them.

Development of the art of legacy-hunting.

As legacy-hunters became more numerous, their art became more highly developed.

The most servile obsequiousness, flattery, according to the person practiced upon, the most ingenious, or the most fulsome—such were the methods employed. Those Greeks of whom Juvenal wrote

> They batten on the genial soil of Rome,
> Minions, then lords, of every princely dome !
> A flattering, cringing, treacherous, artful race,
> Of torrent tongue, and never blushing face,

were they not in all probability legacy-hunters ? Juvenal thus continues his description of them :

> A Protean tribe, one knows not what to call,
> Which shifts to every form, and shines in all ;
> Grammarian, painter, augur, rhetorician,
> Rope-dancer, conjurer, fiddler, and physician,
> All trades his own, your hungry Greekling counts ;
> And bid him mount the sky—the sky he mounts.

Waiting for a rich man's death.

The legacy-hunter knew how to satisfy and even to forestall all the whims of the rich man whose death he was waiting for. If the rich man fell sick, his legacy-hunters would lavish upon him their most solicitous attentions, they would pray for him in the temples, they would even go so far as to offer to sacrifice, in case of his recovery, elephants and men. If the rich man wrote verses, his legacy-hunters would declare that in comparison with him Homer was a scribbler. If the rich man had a lawsuit on hand, his legacy-hunters would hasten to court to defend him. And it was not enough for them to be obsequious, they had to be skilful enough to make it appear that so many thoughtful acts, so many kind services, had their source in a disinterested friendship. They would express the wish that the rich man whom they were waiting upon might be blessed with children. They would even make wills in his favor, naturally with the hope of reciprocity. Devices of legacy-hunters.

It sometimes happened that the would-be dupers were duped. Many a clever rich man could attract a following, if not devoted, at least active and eager to render services, by setting a bait for legacy-hunters. Junius Vindex, for instance, the general who rebelled against Nero's authority, used to dose himself, in order to lure on his legacy-hunters, with a drug which had the effect of producing an artificial pallor of countenance. So he was humored and fawned upon up to the last day that he practiced his deception. · Domitius Tullus used a similar method. After having allowed himself to be pampered by those who were aiming at his fortune, he made his niece, whom he had adopted, his heiress. He left besides a number of bequests, and large bequests to his grandchildren, and left something even for his great-grandson. So his will was received by those who had counted upon his neglecting his family in their favor with a vexation which they could not conceal. Respectable people, and Pliny the Younger foremost, applauded, and were overjoyed. For Traps set for legacy-hunters Some legacy-hunters disappointed.

> 'Tis a double delight to deceive a deceiver.

But the legacy-hunters did not often allow themselves to be caught in a trap. Had they not studied the lessons of Arruntius and Haterius, who, according to Seneca, were accomplished in the art of hunting legacies? But, above all, had they not before their eyes the examples of the great masters, Cassus and Regulus? Pliny has given a place of honor to the latter, and has shown him to us in the exercise of his trade. Let us quote the passage ; our readers will then become acquainted with a typical example of this class of men who play so important a part in the · history of manners in the second century after Christ.

Are you inclined to hear a story, or if you please two or three ? for one brings to my mind another. 'Tis no matter which I begin with, so take them as follows. Verania, the widow of Piso, who was adopted by Galba, lay extremely ill. Upon this occasion Regulus made her a visit. By the way, mark the assurance of the man, to visit a lady to whom he was so extremely odious, and to whose husband he was a declared enemy ! Even barely to enter her house would have been imprudent enough ; but he had the confidence to go much farther, and very familiarly placed himself by her bedside. He began very gravely with inquiring what day and hour she was born. Being informed of these important particulars, he composes his countenance, fixes his eyes, mutters something to himself, counts his fingers, and all this merely to keep the poor sick lady in suspense. When he had finished this ridiculous mummery, "You are," says he, "in one of your climacterics ; however, you will get over it. But for your greater satisfaction, I will consult with a certain diviner, whose skill I have frequently experienced." Accordingly away he goes, consults the omens, and returns with the strongest assurances that they confirmed what he had promised on the part of the stars. Upon this the credulous good woman calls for her will, and gives Regulus a handsome legacy. Some time afterward her distemper increased ; and in her last moments she exclaimed against this infamous wretch who had thus basely deceived her, though he wished every curse might befall his son if what he promised her was not true. But such sort of imprecations are as common with Regulus as they are impious; and he continually devotes that unhappy youth to the curses of those gods whose vengeance his own frauds every day provoke.

Velleius Blæsus, a person of consular dignity, and remarkable for his immense wealth, in his last sickness had an inclination to make some alteration in his will. Regulus, who had lately endeavored to insinuate himself into his friendship, hoped to receive some advantage by the intended change, and accordingly applies himself to his physicians, and conjures them to exert all their skill to prolong the poor man's life. But the moment the will was signed, his style was changed. "How long," says he to these very physicians, "do you design to keep this man in misery? Since you cannot preserve his life, why will you prolong his death?" Blæsus is since dead; and as if he had overheard every word that Regulus had said, he has not left him one farthing.

The plot of Regulus against Blæsus.

And now have you had enough? or, like a truant schoolboy, are you for listening still to another tale? If so, Regulus will supply you. You must know, then, that Aurelia, a lady of distinguished accomplishments, designing to execute her will, had dressed herself for that purpose in a very splendid manner. Regulus, who was present as a witness, turned about to the lady, and "Pray," says he, "leave me these fine clothes." Aurelia at first thought him in jest; but he insisted upon it very seriously, and obliged her to open her will and insert this legacy; and though he saw her write it, yet he would not be satisfied till he read the clause himself. However, Aurelia is still alive; though Regulus, no doubt, when he solicited this bequest, expected soon to enjoy it.

How Regulus obtained a bequest from Aurelia.

A clever man, like this Regulus, was always able finally to escape from justice, but it was difficult for him to avoid entirely legal complications. Less skilful adventurers were almost sure to become seriously entangled in difficulties with the courts.

Difficulties with the courts.

This brings us to our next subject for consideration—the Roman bar.

CHAPTER VI.

THE BAR.

As we have indicated, the unscrupulous conduct of legacy-hunters and sharpers was a prolific source of lawsuits. If the reader will reflect upon the social disturbance caused by the civil wars that followed the death of Nero, and upon the fact that the political platform had become silent, he will see why judicial eloquence, under the Flavians and the Antonines, developed in a way that merits our attention.

Under the Cæsars the Roman bar was very corrupt. The beautiful relation between patron and clients had disappeared. To be a successful advocate one no longer needed the science of law, nor oratorical power. Still less necessary was it that an advocate should command respect by an honorable life. It was sufficient if he had big lungs and an effrontery difficult to dis-concert. Look at Vatinus ; yesterday he was a baker, to-day he pleads. Look at Attalus ; yesterday he drove mules, to-day he wins cases. And Ciperus ! He has abandoned his baker's oven, and is now a successful barrister. Has he not a voice sonorous as a trumpet? Was he ever known to perspire or spit during a speech ?

Some advocates, on the other hand, are steeped in letters. They come from the schools of the rhetoricians. Do not expect them to study their cases, to try to understand men, to know how to read hearts, to appeal to right or eternal justice ; they have no interest in all that. They are mere acrobats in eloquence ; you could sing and dance, as Tacitus says, to their speeches.

"You are a villain," some one said to Pedius, a jurist. And what did Pedius reply? He met the accusation with antitheses, skilfully balanced, and brand-new metaphors.

Quintilian summed up the faults of the bar at this epoch in two words—ignorance and frivolity. He expressed the truth.

Quintilian had the praiseworthy ambition to change this condition of things, and he had the good fortune to meet with partial success in his attempt. His education prepared him for undertaking this reform. His father, and even his grandfather, had been rhetoricians of some merit. The taste for public speaking had therefore been handed down in his family as an honorable tradition. Quintilian was admitted to the bar at an early age, and made a mark for himself. We know that he pleaded for

AN ORATOR.   Museum of Naples.

Marcus Arpinianus, accused of having thrown his wife out of a window, and for the queen Berenice, who acted as judge in her own cause. Nothing remains to us of his speeches in defense of these clients, but they were much praised by his contemporaries. We have therefore lost the record of Quintilian's law practice. But, fortunately, he has not hesitated in his book on "The Education of the Orator" to quote from himself by way of illustration. Thus he has made it possible for us to obtain a very good idea of his theory, and to know against what evils his efforts at reform were directed.

He held, in the first place, that the advocate should be versed in the law. He was loud in condemnation of flowery talkers and composers of academic phrases, and he insisted that it was necessary for one who wished to win success at the bar to understand the prætor's edicts and the text of the civil law. Protesting against those adventurers, those ignorant tricksters, whose aim was to dispatch their cases with the greatest possible speed, he claims that the advocate should not concern himself only with the written law, but also with natural right, with eternal justice. He affirms that one can be truly eloquent only if he has reflected upon the nature of happiness, on the foundation of morality, on all that pertains to the good and the true. Finally, he advises any one who seeks to attract about himself a circle of clients to renounce the affected and puerile style of the schools of declamation, and to return to the tradition of the most ancient masters, of Cicero especially — to speak, in short, a language straightforward, manly, and elevated.

Why could not Quintilian have completely escaped the evil influence of his time? Why could he not have condemned without qualification the unscrupulous devices of the sophists and the rhetoricians? Why did he conceive the unfortunate idea of formulating into a theory the art of lying? Remarking that there are causes where every effort fails, he advises the orator to use on such occasions what he calls *colors*, that is to say, specious conjectures, false narrations. In this kind of oratorical fiction, he says, it is important, first, to take care that the story which one invents is possible, and that it suits at the same time the person of whom it is told and the time and place involved; and secondly, it is well, as far as possible, to connect what one invents with something true, "for when all is false, the lie betrays itself." Oh, admirable rules, indeed! Quintilian forgot, alas! that virtue should be exercised even by an orator.

But in spite of these errors the influence of Quintilian on the eloquence of the bar was very salutary. Under Trajan real progress was made. Encouraged and sustained by the prince, and by honest people, a few distinguished men restored to the advocate's profession the prestige which it had temporarily lost. These benefactors of the profession were Saturninus, poet as well as orator, Voconius Romanus, a shrewd old man of the forum, Erucius Clarus, a Roman of the ancient type, a great and an honest man, Pomponius Rufus, a remarkable improvisor, Titius Aristo, a skilful lawyer, and besides these, above them perhaps, their rival, their friend, Pliny the Younger.

We have been accustomed to consider Pliny the Younger merely as a letter-writer; and it seems as if the fame which he won by his delightful correspondence ought to be enough for him. But he was not satisfied with that. An orator's reputation is more splendid and more brilliant than a writer's. Pliny loved to shine. This was the weakness of that soul, so sound otherwise and so good. Accordingly he took his place among the advocates.

We need not lament this fact, for he helped to glorify Roman eloquence, which was so soon to disappear.

His high ideal of the advocate's profession.

Pliny had, in the first place, the great merit of cherishing a high ideal of his profession. He would not admit that the art of the advocate was a mercenary art, and that his services should be paid. Already, under the emperor Claudius, the consul Silius had severely censured those men who sold their talent as if it was a commodity, and he had demanded a law forbidding advocates to receive a salary. But his words remained without effect. Under Trajan, Tuscilius Nominatus, elected as advocate by the inhabitants of Vicetia, required them to advance him 10,000 sesterces ($425), and then on the day of the hearing he did not appear. That was money easily made. The tribune Nigrinus denounced the scandalous proceeding to the senate,

Unscrupulous conduct of Nominatus.

and the senate decreed a return to the severity of the ancient laws. Pliny heartily applauded this reform, which, however, did not touch him, as he had never made merchandise of his eloquence.

Another thing no less creditable to Pliny's character is that he did not think it right for him to plead any cause that happened in his way, nor did his natural tastes lead him to violate his conscience at this point. He did not wish to resemble that Greek orator, Theramenes, who had been nicknamed "The Trimmer." He had constantly borne in mind that maxim of Thrasea,

Thrasea's maxim.

"There are three sorts of causes which we ought to undertake : those of our friends, those of the deserted, and those which tend to public example." Neither influence, nor flattery, nor bribes, could induce him to plead a case when he thought that his honor imposed silence upon him. In vain did his friend Octavius Rufus beg him to defend a certain Gallus against the inhabitants of Bætica. In vain did he attempt, by sending him figs, mushrooms, and excellent dates, to forestall a refusal. Nothing succeeded. Pliny remained gently inflexible.

But when he once consented to undertake a case, he put his whole soul into it. He did not think he could devote too much care and study to it. Very different from those improvisors who were always satisfied with themselves, Pliny would spend long hours in his private study preparing his speeches. He did not pride himself on being always ready; on the contrary, the hour for appearing before his audience seemed rather to come too soon.

> I had repaired [he writes] to the Basilica Julia, to hear some advocates to whom I was to reply at the next session. The judges had taken their places, the decemvirs had arrived, the advocates were at their bench, when an order from the prætor arrives which breaks up the sitting. We are sent off, to my great satisfaction, for I am never so well prepared that a delay does not please me.

It would be an exaggeration to claim that Pliny was a courageous orator, like the men of the ancient republic. His good soul, endowed with the ordinary virtues, did not know heroism. But on several occasions at least he exhibited a certain firmness. When Nerva succeeded Domitian, some good men conceived the idea of avenging the public honor by prosecuting the wretches who had been the instigators or the accomplices of the crimes perpetrated in the preceding reign. Pliny attacked the informer Publicius Certus, the murderer of Helvidius Priscus, Thrasea's son-in-law. He was blamed for this audacity. Certus was about to be consul; he had the advantage of a large fortune and powerful friends. The senators before whom his case was to be brought up had almost all personal relations of some kind with him. In spite of everything, in spite of advice, in spite of the anxiety of his friends, Pliny persisted in his purpose. He had some difficulty in overcoming the opposition of his audience sufficiently to begin and continue his speech. He reaped, however, the reward of his noble determination, for he completely won over his hearers. When he had finished speaking, "there was scarce a man in the senate," as he says in one of his letters, "that did not embrace and kiss me, and all strove who should applaud me most, for having with the utmost hazard to myself . . . wiped off that odium which was thrown upon the senate by the other orders in the state 'that the senators mutually favored the members of their own body.'"

The qualities in Pliny's character which such conduct on his part illustrates won for him much respect, and this explains in some degree his success as an advocate. This success was very marked ; he has not failed to tell us so himself, and we have no reason to doubt his testimony. His vanity was great, but it did not prevent him from telling the truth.

Pliny spoke five times before the senate, either as a defender or as a prosecutor, in those solemn debates presided over by the consul, and the consul was often the emperor ; he impeached Bæbius Massa under Domitian, and under Trajan, Marius Priscus and Cæcilius Classicus. He defended Julius Bassus and Varenus. He counted among his clients two provinces, Africa and Bætica. Like another Cicero, he secured the condemnation of another Verres. On each of these occasions he won his case, and, what was more important, the speeches he made added to his reputation.

However, his true sphere of activity was not before the senate, but in the centumviral court. Here he found himself master, and without a rival. The centumvirs were a permanent court, established under the republic, at a date which we cannot fix. The members were originally elected in equal numbers from each tribe, but there were not always exactly one hundred of them as the word centumvirs (the Latin *centumviri* means one hundred men) seems to imply ; for Pliny, in his time, counts one hundred and eighty sitting at once. The centumvirs were divided into four sections, or sub-courts, and we learn from Quintilian and from Pliny that cases were brought sometimes before two sections, sometimes before the four united sections, although each one voted separately. We do not know the reason for this division.

The centumvirs, after the time of Augustus, were presided over by judicial decemvirs. Their jurisdiction was limited to civil suits, especially such as related to inheritance and property. They met, first in the forum, and afterward in the Basilica Julia.

The latter place was the scene of Pliny's eloquence. We must not, in imagination, reduce these Roman basilicas to the narrow dimensions of our modern court-rooms. They were vast quadrangular halls, longer, by one half or two thirds, than they were wide ; and their interiors were divided by rows of pillars into a main nave and two side aisles. Over the side aisles, whose ceiling was not so high as that of the nave, was a gallery for spectators. On the days when Pliny was to speak the gallery of the Basilica Julia was not large enough to contain the audience, which was, moreover, as select as it was numerous ; for, as Pliny tells us, the society ladies and the men of quality were not afraid to come and crowd together there at the risk of having their cloaks and tunics torn.

But Pliny, even in the midst of such favorable surroundings, where he was able to gratify his self-love by winning splendid triumphs, was not wholly satisfied. He did not feel that his causes were always worthy of him, and he was annoyed by the use of the clepsydra.

Certain advocates had abused the patience of their audience and the judges ; as they never wearied themselves, they were convinced that it would be impossible for them to weary anybody else.   So they would enter into interminable digressions on irrelevant subjects. Such was the advocate whose client thus complains in an epigram of Martial's (we use a translation by John Hay, who substitutes for events in Roman history more familiar events in English history):

> My cause concerns nor battery nor treason ;
> I sue my neighbor for this only reason,
> That late three sheep of mine to pound he drove ;
> This is the point the court would have you prove.
> Concerning Magna Charta you run on,
> And all the perjuries of old King John ;
> Then of the Edwards and Black Prince you rant,
> And talk of John o' Stiles and John o' Gaunt ;
> With voice and hand a mighty pother keep.
> Now, pray, dear sir, one word about the sheep.

The object of the clepsydra was to prevent this excessive overflow of · talk.   The clepsydra was a little vase which resembled a funnel.   Through the tapering extremity the water, with which the vase had been filled, flowed away drop by drop, thus affording a method of measuring time.   Under the empire a clepsydra, placed beside the orator, limited the duration of his plea.   According to the importance of the cause, the orator was allowed two, three, or even more clepsy-

Capitoline Hill, Forum and Surrounding Buildings.

dræ. When Pliny impeached Marius Priscus, he was granted as many as ten. That was good measure, and he had no reason to complain. But some poor talkers, no doubt, abused their privileges. Martial has the following epigram (the translation is Elphinston's):

Seven glasses, Cecilian, thou loudly didst crave ;
Seven glasses the judge, full reluctantly, gave.
Still thou bawl'st, and bawl'st on ; and, as ne'er to bawl off,
Tepid water in bumpers supine dost thou quaff.
That thy voice and thy thirst at a time thou may'st slake,
We entreat from the glass of old Chronus thou take.

On account of such abuses it became customary to grant and to ask only one or two clepsydræ for an advocate's plea, sometimes even only half a clepsydra. Pliny lamented such a custom, and blamed those impatient advocates who devoted to a case fewer clepsydræ than their ancestors devoted days.

It was not merely the interest of the litigant that inspired Pliny with such sentiments. He experienced a difficulty in pleading according to the methods which he had adopted, when he felt that his time was measured out to him. In order to carry conviction into the minds of the judges, he was convinced that it was not sufficient to aim right and strike hard ; he believed that it was necessary also to strike often.

I remember [he writes, in one of his letters] when Regulus and I were concerned together in a cause, he said to me, " You seem to think it necessary to insist upon every point ; whereas I always take aim at my adversary's throat, and there I closely press him." ('Tis true, he tenaciously holds whatever part he has once fixed upon ; but the misfortune is, he is extremely apt to mistake the right place.) I answered, it might possibly happen that what he took for what he called the throat was in reality some other part. As for me, said I, who do not pretend to direct my aim with so much certainty, I

attack every part, and push at every opening ; in short, to use
a vulgar proverb, I leave no stone unturned. As in agriculture, it is not my vineyards, or my woods alone, but my
fields also that I cultivate ; and (to pursue the allusion) as I
do not content myself with sowing those fields with only one
kind of grain but employ several different sorts, so in my
pleadings at the bar, I spread at large a variety of matter like
so many different seeds, in order to reap from thence whatever may happen to hit.

Pliny complained also that in this Basilica Julia,
which had been the scene of his triumphs, he did not
always meet adversaries who were worthy of him.
Debutants, beardless young men, scarcely out of the
schoolroom, would unceremoniously obtain admittance
to the bar.   And as they were as vain as they were
presumptuous, they were determined to succeed, no
matter how.   Not being able to depend upon their
intelligence and their talent, they fell back upon hired
applauders.   Pliny refers to this in one of his letters :

The youth of our days are so far from waiting to be introduced, that they rudely rush in uninvited. The audience that
follows them are fit attendants for such orators ; a low rout of
hired mercenaries, assembling themselves in the middle of
the court, where the dole is dealt round to them as openly as
if they were in a dining-room ; and at this noble price they
run from court to court ! The Greeks have a name in their
language for this sort of people, importing that they are
applauders by profession ; and we stigmatize them with the
opprobrious title of table flatterers ; yet the meanness alluded
to in both languages increases every day. It was but yesterday two of my servants, mere striplings, were hired for this
goodly office at the price of three denarii [about 50 cents] ;
such is the easy purchase of eloquence ! Upon these honorable terms we fill our benches and gather a circle ; and thus it
is those unmerciful shouts are raised when a man who stands
in the middle of the ring gives the word. For you must
know, these honest fellows, who understand nothing of what
is said, or if they did could not hear it, would be at a loss,

without a signal, how to time their applause ; for those that do not hear a syllable are as clamorous as any of the rest. If at any time you should happen to .pass by while the court is sitting, and would know the merit of any of our advocates, you have no occasion to give yourself the trouble of listening to them ; take it for a rule, he that has the loudest commendations deserves them the least. Largius Licinius was the first who gave rise to this custom ; but then he went no further than to solicit an audience. I remember to have heard my tutor Quintilian say that Domitius Afer, as he was pleading before the centumvirs, with his usual grave and solemn manner, heard on a sudden a most immoderate and unusual noise ; being a good deal surprised he left off; the clamor ceased and he began again ; he was interrupted a second time, and a third. At last he inquired who it was that was speaking. He was told Licinius. "Alas !" said he, "Eloquence is no more !" The truth is, it then only began to decline, when, in Afer's opinion, it was entirely perished ; whereas now it is almost utterly lost and extinct. I am ashamed to say with what an unmanly elocution the orators deliver themselves and with what a squeaking applause they are received ; nothing seems wanting to complete this sing-song oratory but the claps, or rather the music, of the stage. At present we choose to express our admiration by a kind of howling (for I can call it by no other term) which would be indecent even in the theater. Hitherto the interest of my friends and the consideration of my early time of life has retained me in this court ; for it would be thought, I fear, rather to proceed from indolence than a just indignation at these indecencies were I yet to leave it ; however I come there less frequently than usual, and am thus making a gradual retreat.

Considering the way in which the tribunal of the centumvirs was made up, we presume that Pliny had another grievance against them which he has not expressed. These men, chosen from each tribe, could scarcely have been cultured men. Their taste was doubtless somewhat crude. How could they appreciate all the fine points in the elocution of this accom-

plished man of letters? Pliny, in fact, spent as much
care upon the style of his orations as upon the subject
matter.   He read and reread the great models : Cicero,
whose harmonious periods and large manner of treatment he imitated ; and Demosthenes, the secret of
whose vehemence and figures he tried to catch.   But
he was not satisfied to limit himself to the simplicity of
these men.   He could not deny himself the pleasure of
plucking some flowers from the roadside as he passed
along his way.   It was not without its effect upon
Pliny that Seneca had been his predecessor in Latin
letters.   Pliny could not resist the seduction of Seneca's
attractive faults.   His taste, which was not bad, lacked
severity, and he could not refrain from ambitious
attempts, he could not avoid seeking expressions that
were rare, curious, or bold, and if he was criticised for
this, he would defend himself, formally, after his fashion.
See how he replies to Lupercus, who had probably
passed some criticism upon him :

I said once (and I think not improperly) of a certain orator
of the present age, whose compositions are extremely regular
and correct, but by no means sublime and ornamented, "His
only fault is, that he has none." Whereas he who is possessed
of the true spirit of oratory should be bold and elevated, and
sometimes even flame out and be hurried away with all the
warmth and violence of passion; in short, he should frequently soar to great, and even dangerous heights ; for
precipices are generally near whatever is towering and
exalted. The plain, 'tis true, affords a safer, but for that
reason a more humble and inglorious path ; they that run are
more likely to stumble than they that creep, but the latter
gain no honor by not slipping, while the former even fall with
glory. It is with eloquence as with some other arts ; she is
never more pleasing than when she hazards most. Have you
not observed what acclamations our rope-dancers excite at the
instant of imminent danger? Whatever is most unexpected
and hazardous, or, as the Greeks strongly express it, what-

ever is most daring, has always the greatest share of our admiration. The pilot's skill is by no means equally proved in a calm as in a storm ; in the former case he tamely enters the port, unnoticed and unapplauded; but when the cordage cracks, the mast bends, and the rudder groans, then is it that he shines forth in full luster, and is adored as little inferior to a sea-god. The reason of my making this observation is, because, if I mistake not, you have marked some passages in my writings for being tumid, exorbitant, and overwrought, which in my estimation are full and bold and sublime. But it is material to consider whether your criticism turns upon such points as are real faults, or only striking and remarkable expressions. Whatever is elevated is sure to be observed, but it requires a very nice judgment to distinguish the bounds between true and false grandeur, between a just and enormous height. We select an instance out of Homer, both of the grand and elevated style, in the following lines ; which can scarce, I imagine, have escaped any reader's observation :

(margin: Distinction between true and false grandeur in literary composition.)

> " Heaven in loud thunder bids the trumpet sound ;
> And wide beneath them groans the rending ground."

Again :
> " Reclined on clouds his steed and armor lay."

So in this whole passage :

> " As torrents roll, increased by numerous rills,
> With rage impetuous down their echoing hills,
> Rush to the vales, and poured along the plain,
> Roar through a thousand channels to the main."

It requires, I say, a very delicate hand to poise these metaphors, and determine whether they are too figurative and lofty or truly majestic or sublime.

What could the triumvirs appreciate in this eloquence so labored, or, to express it more fully, so over-refined? How many of the flowers must have wasted their perfume upon them ! How many the shafts whose point they never felt ! It is not difficult to understand the secret of Pliny's disgust with the bar, which led him to retire early. He was to find a public more to his taste in the lecture halls, where we shall not delay in following him.

(margin: Secret of Pliny's disgust with the bar.)

CHAPTER VII.

SOCIETY.

AMONG us moderns family life and public or private affairs do not engage a man's whole activity. Besides the relations of affection or of business we have what we call social relations. They act and react continually upon our sentiments and our ideas, and no one can escape their influence. Whatever we do, however misanthropic we may be, we are compelled to take them into consideration.

In the ancient cities social life held, it is true, a less important place than in our modern communities, but we must not suppose that it occupied no place. We might almost fix the date when society began to crystallize at Rome. We are certainly safe in saying that when Greek manners and literature were introduced into Italy social life also awoke there. Was it not almost a salon that the younger Scipio established in gathering about him so many artists, so many lettered and distinguished men? The women who previously had lived at home in retirement now begin to visit each other, they go out to dinners with their husbands, they take an interest in intellectual matters, they have their own tastes and express· them, and often succeed in making them generally respected. Beginning from the time of the Gracchi, women take their part in social life. No argument is necessary in support of this statement. It is sufficient to recall the name of the mother of the Gracchi; for we may be sure that when women wield such an influence as did Cornelia, society is in existence.

This society, which had sprung up spontaneously as a result of the continued progress in refinement of manners, became more regular and acquired forms more fixed and definite as soon as a court was set up in Rome.

The establishment of the empire being in the beginning nothing but the elevation of a private family, the organization of the imperial court was at first modeled upon the pattern of a wealthy household. But soon, as absolute power existed in fact, its forms began to appear. A few emperors made attempts,

Organization of the imperial court.

A ROMAN MATRON.

more or less sincere, to return to the ancient simplicity, but notwithstanding this, the court came more and more to resemble the courts of the great kings of other ages. And the customs and tastes which reigned in the court were adopted by the high Roman society.

Docile subjects [said Pliny, in his panegyric on Trajan], we are led by our prince wherever he pleases, and we follow him unquestioningly. For we desire to be loved and approved by him, and those who are not like him cannot succeed in this. It is through such eternal compliance that it has come about that nearly all men live after the fashion of one man. . . . The life of the emperor is a censorship, and that, too, a perpetual one. We look toward his life for our model, we copy it. We do not need commands, the example is sufficient.

The emperor imitated by his subjects.

And this was not the result of the personal influence of Trajan ; the worst emperors wielded the same power.

"Sovereigns who love music," said Plutarch, "make musicians." And the poet Claudianus later expressed this same truth in the famous verse :

All men delight to imitate their king.

Such dependence upon a ruler for inspiration and guidance in intellectual matters may not seem to be justified by good reasons. Certainly there are stronger reasons for imitating the etiquette and ceremonial of the court. In the first place, it saves trouble, and then society knows what to count upon. In order to exist at all it must have forms. The more definite these forms are, the easier is social life. And if social life is tending constantly to disappear in the democratic atmosphere of to-day, is it not because these forms were broken down by the French Revolution?

Reasons for copying court etiquette.

Let us seek, then, to show the nature of the hierarchy and the ceremonial of the imperial court. Under the republic, when statesmen had become party chiefs they tried to organize their followers. C. Gracchus and Livius Drusus are the first who divided their partisans into three classes. Those of the first class were received into their chief's circle of intimate friends,

The hierarchy of the court.

and they were invited by him to attend his smallest and most exclusive receptions ; those of the second class were admitted to larger social gatherings ; those of the third class were allowed to be present only at his public functions. The Romans called these three classes, respectively, friends of the first, second, or third admission. The emperors remembered this division and imposed it upon their courtiers. In the first two classes were the principal senators, the consuls, and ex-consuls, those connected with the royal house by blood or by marriage, and a few other very prominent men, or men much in favor with the emperor, like Lucian under Nero. They might be called into the councils of the empire, might exercise a political influence, or acquire by reason of their constant relations with the emperor an occult but very formidable power. So the choice of friends of the first and second admission was an act of the greatest importance. As it was they chiefly who formed the train of the emperor upon his travels and campaigns, they were called his cohort, and were given the title *comites* (companions), from which our word *count* is derived.

As to the friends of the third class, whose rôle was naturally less important, they were drawn from among the artists, scholars, and poets. Professional jesters, also, belonged to this class. Although their position was subordinate, a small number of the friends of the third admission by their attractive personality or by the dignity of their character won a large share of the imperial favor. Among these fortunate few under Augustus was the philosopher Arcius of Alexandria, who obtained for his compatriots the clemency of the emperor after the battle of Actium ; under Trajan Dion Chrysostom, who was seen more than once in the

emperor's carriage ; and Fronto under Marcus Aurelius. Several court jesters received similar favors ;
under Nero Vatinius was all-powerful. His ascendency
had a rather curious origin ; what had called the
emperor's attention to him was the enormous length
of his nose ; in fact, so remarkable was this feature of
his countenance that a certain kind of drinking cup
which had a nozzle bore the name of Vatinius. This
third class was bound by very stringent obligations.
They were required to live in the palace, where special
apartments were reserved for their use. It may easily
be imagined what a sense of dependence such an
arrangement would naturally create.

The ceremonial was not less inflexible than the hierarchy.

Louis XIV. used to hold early morning receptions, a
small one for his most intimate friends; followed by a
larger, more general one. The Roman emperors had
not devised this distinction, but they had their early
reception, which was called the morning salutation.

This ceremony commenced at dawn. Regular attendance upon it constituted for the most intimate friends at
first a privilege, but afterward a duty which could not
be neglected except for a more important engagement.
Upon all occasions when congratulations were in order
and upon all formal celebrations the senate in a
body attended this reception. Sometimes the emperor
opened the doors of his palace to the knights, and even
to persons of no rank, if they were well recommended,
or if they had petitions to present.

Outside the palace, an entire cohort of prætorians, a
thousand men, mounted guard regularly, and there was
almost always a detachment at the entrance. These
soldiers were supposed to keep out suspicious char-

acters, and sometimes even to search those who solicited an audience.   At the time of Claudius, who was very cowardly, no one could be admitted to the presence of the prince without being subjected to this annoying process.   In the interior of the palace there was a body of servants to maintain order and to announce and show in visitors.   These ushers were called *admission-ales.*   The difficulties of gaining admission varied much according to the character of the emperor.   In order

The *admission-ales.*

ATRIUM OF THE POMPEIAN HOUSE AT SARATOGA SPRINGS, N. Y.
Franklin W. Smith, architect.

to approach a Domitian it was necessary to pass all sorts of guards ; for one who wished to see Trajan the doors opened of themselves.

Here [Pliny says, speaking of Trajan's palace] no bolts, no excruciating ordeal to be passed ; when you have once crossed the threshold, you do not find a thousand doors, and

Easy access
to Trajan.

beyond these other doors which remain closed, or at least obstruct your progress. Before, and behind, but especially around you, profound silence. Everything is done without noise and with all possible deference, so that upon returning to your modest little dwelling you have an impression that the imperial palace is a model of calm and of simplicity.

At these receptions the *toga* was the required dress, as well for the emperor as for his visitors. Some emperors tried to introduce a change in the matter of costume. Nero one day dressed himself in a flowered tunic to receive the senate, but his audacity was the occasion of unfavorable comment. "He had even," said Dion Cassius, "such a contempt for tradition that he would appear in public with his tunic flowing loose without a belt." We see that the tyranny of official costume had begun to be felt. An emperor who gave audience without the *toga* shocked the Romans, as much as we should be shocked to learn that an officer of state dressed in slippers and frock coat had formally received ambassadors.

Dress required at receptions.

The friends, those of the first class at least, were greeted by the emperor with a kiss. Such a salutation was customary between equals at Rome from the establishment of the empire. Tiberius, it is true, felt that this form, which had to be observed so often, was a wearisome duty and he tried to escape from its tyranny. At his departure for Rhodes, when he bade farewell to the persons who were seeing him off, he kissed only a few of them. But this reserve was considered a proof of his excessive pride. Some emperors tried to introduce into the ceremonial certain customs from the oriental courts. Caligula had his feet kissed; Elagabalus tried to require the forms of respect which the king of Persia received. But these attempted innovations were not successful, and the kiss exchanged be-

Greetings between emperor and subjects.

tween emperor and subject-friend remained the customary greeting.

If we consider the crowd of visitors and solicitors who eagerly sought the presence of the prince, and his obligation to speak a few words to the persons of distinction, we can realize how prolonged his receptions probably were. They must have been among the most disagreeable duties belonging to the highest rank. They tested the sovereign's patience, and sometimes even imperiled his health. Antoninus Pius, in his old age, could scarcely endure the fatigue which they occasioned, and he used to fortify himself by a light repast before receiving.

We may be sure also that it was no small tedium that the courtiers had to endure while awaiting their turn in the vestibule of the palace where a suffocating crowd was gathered. But this was nothing compared to the anxiety and torment of every kind to which they were often exposed. Epictetus has drawn for us a picture of what they had to suffer, a little too highly colored perhaps, but correct in its main features :

They are not even allowed to sleep in peace ; but they are awakened early by the news that the emperor has arisen, that he is about to appear. At once they become anxious. If they are not invited to the table of the emperor they are mortified. If they are guests at his table, they dine like slaves with their master, constantly on guard against committing some impropriety. And what are they afraid of? Being whipped like slaves ? That would be getting off easily. No ; they are afraid of exposing their heads, of being obliged even to lay them down with the dignity becoming to friends of the emperor. Even when at a distance from the emperor, and engaged in physical exercise, their minds are never tranquil. In short, who can be so obtuse, or who can so deceive himself, as not to perceive that his lot is all the more wretched, the more he is received into the emperor's friendship.

But this misery was so brilliant that everybody had the ambition to experience it, and when a person had once experienced it, no matter how bitter he found it, he could not resolve to give it up. A great person, Epictetus recounts, had the misfortune of falling into disgrace with the prince, and he was exiled. When the time of his banishment had expired, and he had returned to Rome, "It is all over," he said to the philosopher. "May I be shamed if ever again I place myself at his feet." "You will change your mind," Epictetus returned. The other protested very strongly that his resolution was unshakable. The next day a note from the emperor recalled him to his service. The courtiers of all times resemble each other. Epictetus only described in advance one of La Bruyère's characters.

Two thirds of my life have passed; why be so anxious about the remaining portion? The most brilliant fortune is not worth the torment which I inflict upon myself, nor the pettiness to which I stoop, nor the humiliations and shame which I endure. . . . The greatest of all our blessings, if there are any blessings, is repose, retirement, and a place which we can regard as our domain. R—— thought so in his disgrace, but forgot it in his prosperity.

The actors may change ; the comedy remains the same.

The wealthy families which, as we have said, had furnished the pattern for the court ceremonial in their turn copied it when it had been added to and enriched by the emperors.

The receptions in a patrician household, as at the imperial palace, began at dawn. Clients and visitors mingled on these occasions and the mixture must have been very picturesque. Clients were usually poor people. Many of them wore soiled *togas* and patched shoes. While waiting outdoors for admittance, they would stand along the house wall, in winter impatient for the sun to rise and warm them, and in summer grumbling because it made them perspire under their *togas*—all the while disputing their place with the dogs and the slaves. And near them would be a rich knight, a grave senator, who had been brought in his sedan-chair, carried by slaves in red robes. The house-porter, armed with a rod, was stationed at the entrance, and in order to gain admittance it was usually necessary to purchase his good graces. Many poor people were sent rudely away, and if a few entered gratis, it was that the master's vanity might be satisfied by seeing a long procession of his clients. They would pass, bowing low before their lord, who would return them a disdain-ful nod. Then, after being subjected to a minute examination, they would receive from the treasurer the ten sesterces (about 42 cents), upon which daily allow-ance they lived. Meanwhile the great personages paid their court to the patron ; one, perhaps, was aiming at the consulship, another at a military tribuneship, and they would beg their lord to use his influence in their favor. Altogether they were a swarm of beggars, and Plutarch fitly compares them to flies in a kitchen.

It was in the morning also that calls required by politeness were made, and that such duties were per-formed as attendance upon a marriage or a betrothal ceremony, upon the formal assumption of the *toga* by a boy when he became of age, upon the inauguration of a magistrate, etc. Many were the functions at which a person who had social relations somewhat extended was expected to be present. So the streets of Rome early in the morning offered a lively spectacle ; everywhere people hurrying along, afraid of being late where the rules of etiquette required their presence. Many complained of the wearisome waste of time entailed by these obligations. Pliny, who was of this number, writes :

When one considers how the time passes in Rome, one cannot but be surprised that take any single day, and it either is, or at least seems to be, spent reasonably enough ; and yet upon casting up the whole sum the amount will appear quite otherwise. Ask any one how he has been employed to-day; he will tell you perhaps, "I have been at the ceremony of putting on the *toga virilis;* this friend invited me to a wedding; that desired me to attend the hearing of his case ; one begged me to be a witness to his will ; another called me to a consultation." These are things which seem, while you are engaged in them, extremely necessary ; and yet, when in the quiet of some retirement, you realize that every day has been thus employed, you cannot but condemn them as mere trifles. At such a season one is apt to reflect, " How much of my life has been spent in empty routine ! " At least it is a reflection which frequently comes across me at Laurentum, after I have been employing myself in my studies, or even in the necessary care of the animal machine ; for the body must be repaired and supported if we would preserve the mind in all its vigor. In that peaceful retreat I neither hear nor speak anything of which I have occasion to repent. I suffer none to repeat to me the whispers of malice; nor do I censure any man, unless myself, when I am dissatisfied with my compositions. There I live undisturbed by rumor and free from the anxious solicitudes of hope or fear, conversing only with myself and my books. True and genuine life ! pleasing and honorable repose ! More, perhaps, to be desired than the noblest employments ! Thou solemn sea and solitary shore, best and most retired school of art and poetry, with how many noble thoughts have you inspired me ! Snatch then, my friend, as I have, the first occasion of leaving the noisy town, with all its very empty pursuits, and devote your days to study, or even resign them to ease ; for as my friend Attilius happily observed, " It is better to do nothing than to do nothings." Farewell.

But all did not share this opinion. Some enjoyed

The Ardelions.

this busy idleness, and almost made a profession out of it, so that they came to be considered a distinct class, as it were, in society, and received a special name. They were called Ardelions, or busybodies.

Phædrus and Seneca make us acquainted with these singular persons :

There exist at Rome a certain tribe called Ardelions, hurrying about anxiously here and there, always busy with their idleness, getting out of breath over trifles, doing many things yet doing nothing, burdensome to themselves and most offensive to others.

Seneca compares them to ants who pass up and down a tree, from root to top, and from top to root.

THE APPIAN WAY. From a painting by Gustav Boulanger.

Busy idleness.

There are people [he says] who are driven from their houses by the dawning day. They only go out to swell the crowd. If stopping one of them at his door you should ask him, "Where are you going? What are your plans?" he would reply, "By Hercules, I don't know ; but I wish to make a few calls, to be doing something." . . . We cannot help pity them when we see them running as if they had to put out a fire. They dash headlong through the streets, jostling everybody, and knocking against those whom they encounter. And why such haste? To pay a call which never will be returned, to attend the funeral of some stranger, the trial of some litigant's case, or the betrothal ceremony of a woman who marries frequently. When after having traversed the whole city for the most futile motives they finally return to their Penates, they will swear to you that they have no recollection why they went out, nor even where they have been; which does not prevent them from repeating on the next day, even more frantically, their vagabond wanderings.

Old age might come upon them; no matter; it was useless for Martial to declare that nothing was more hideous than an old Ardelion—still they would go hurrying about.

The receptions and visits of which we have been speaking were all of them characterized by parade, by publicity. They did not allow of conversation, which with us constitutes the charm of social life, and is, for the most part, its only excuse for existence. Where, then, among the Romans, were the pleasures of conversation tasted?

The Romans had no such feature of social life as our modern salon—a gathering of men and women whose keenest pleasure is to talk or to listen according to their tastes and their talents, where you may express your opinion on everything if only it does not offend your neighbor, where wit is not forbidden provided you have enough not to have too much, where feeling is not banished if only it is not allowed to become emotion;—a gathering where the people please each other without loving each other, where they praise without judging, where each one is prudent enough to bring only a part of himself, where one cools the

warmth which he has in his soul and veils the brilliancy
of his intellect, where great qualities are not brought
into play, where only amiable qualities are proper.

Table reunions. But if salons had no existence at Rome, table reunions afforded a very natural occasion for the pleasures of conversation. Horace found that good wine
animated the talkers.

> Is there a man whose tongue no skill or power knows?
> He waxes eloquent whene'er the bright wine flows.

The Greeks, who had received the gift of poesy,
improvised songs at their repasts. The master of the
house would give a couplet, holding a branch of
myrtle in his hand. Then, the couplet finished, he
would toss the branch to one of the guests, who upon
catching it was bound to respond in some more verses.
The Romans, who were less gifted, were nevertheless
intellectual. If they could not sing, they could at least
Table talk. talk. There was conversation, then, at those repasts
which Horace gave to his friends and neighbors in his
country house. They would moralize a little, indulge
much in satire, and the rustic Ofellus would tell some
good story of the time when animals used to talk.
There was conversation, we learn from Horace, at the
house of the advocate Philip, who liked the amusement
of listening to the simple chatter of the auctioneer
Vulteius Menas. There was conversation, too, at
Pliny's house, as he tells us in his letter reproaching
his friend Septicius Clarus for not having come to dine
with him :

Pliny's letter
to Clarus.
How happened it, my friend, that you did not keep your
engagement the other night to sup with me? But take notice,
justice is to be had, and I expect you shall fully reimburse me
the expense I was at to treat you ; which, let me tell you, was
no small sum. I had prepared, you must know, a lettuce

apiece, three snails, two eggs, and a barley cake, with some
sweet wine and snow ; the snow most certainly I shall charge
to your account, as a rarity that will not keep. Besides all
these curious dishes, there were olives of Andalusia, gourds,
shalots, and a hundred other dainties equally sumptuous.
You should likewise have been entertained either with an
interlude, the rehearsal of a poem, or a piece of music, as
you liked best; or, such was my liberality, with all three.
But the luxurious delicacies and Spanish dancers of a certain—

A dainty meal.

PERISTYLE OF THE POMPEIIAN HOUSE AT SARATOGA SPRINGS, N. Y.
Franklin W. Smith, architect.

I know not who, were, it seems, more to your taste. However, I shall have my revenge of you, depend upon it—in
what manner shall at present be a secret. In good truth, it
was not kind thus to disappoint your friend, I had almost said
yourself; and, upon second thought, I do say so. For how
agreeably should we have spent the evening, in laughing,
trifling, and deep speculation ! You may sup, I confess, at
many places more splendidly ; but you can be treated
nowhere, believe me, with more unconstrained cheerfulness,
simplicity, and freedom ; only make the experiment, and if

A pleasant
evening.

you do not ever afterward prefer my table to any other, never favor me with your company again.   Farewell.

Great feasts.

But at those great feasts which are so famous, there was no conversation, because they were only exhibitions.   However, as they hold an important place in the social life of the Romans, we must describe them to our readers.

Let us begin by saying that the luxury of the Roman table has been much exaggerated, or, rather, that it has been represented as too general.

Southerners simple in their tastes.

The people of the South are naturally simple in their tastes, and the Romans were no exception to the rule. Horace, who was an Epicurean, has given us the menu of his ordinary dinner: leeks, gray peas, and a few cakes.   Juvenal, who is inviting a friend to share a meal with him, details to him his intended bill of fare:

Juvenal's dinner.

> From Tibur's stock
> A kid shall come, the fattest of the flock,
> The tenderest too, and yet too young to browse
> The thistle's shoots, the willow's watery boughs,
> With more of milk than blood ; and pullets dressed
> With new-laid eggs, yet tepid from the nest,
> And sperage wild, which, from the mountain's side,
> My housemaid left her spindle to provide ;
> And grapes long kept, yet pulpy still, and fair,
> And the rich Signian and the Syrian pear ;
> And apples, that in flavor and in smell
> The boasted Picene equal, or excel.

Hadrian's diet.

If it had not been for the pullets and the kid a vegetarian might have dined with Juvenal that evening. The emperor Hadrian when he was traveling limited his diet to cheese and milk and he never drank anything stronger than vinegar mingled with water.   We know, moreover, through Galen, the physician, that it was considered a mark of great intemperance to drink pure wine. The Romans do not deserve any special praise for their simple appetites, for their climate obliged them to eat lightly. But how shall we explain the invectives hurled by the moralists against the luxury of the table? Why should Seneca have attributed the corruption of morals to gluttony, as he did when he exclaimed, " The palate has destroyed the world " ?

These lamentations of the moralists were due to the rapid progress made at Rome in the science of dainty cooking. The suddenness of the change from frugality to indulgence made the latter seem all the more shocking. In 161 B. C. the fattening of chickens horrified the Romans to such an extent that the censors issued a decree forbidding it, and this decree had retained its place among the sumptuary laws subsequently promulgated. Sixty years later, even at the most splendid repasts, Greek wine was only served once to the guests. But in the cellar of the orator Hortensius, who lived in the first century of our era, a supply of 10,000 jars of foreign wine was found, and soon after the battle of Actium the luxury of the table reached its height. The world then was conquered ; by way of Alexandria Rome was put into commercial relations with Asia ; the natural products and the manufactured articles of the whole world flowed into Rome. This fact, coincident with the increased fortunes of certain great houses, changed completely the table fare from extremely frugal and simple to abundant and elaborate.

It is certain that from Augustus to Vespasian the luxury of the table was carried very far, but it is no less certain that it was not so extravagant nor so monstrous as might be inferred from certain passages of Pliny the Elder or of Seneca. The virtuous indignation of these writers was especially provoked by the eccentricities of a few fools who wanted to be talked about and who were less influenced by gluttony than by a desire for notoriety. Seneca understood the facts, and he should have avoided making his criticisms general.

Notoriety sought after.

> The spendthrifts [says Seneca] aim to have the life which they lead continually the subject of conversation. They think they have lost their pains if they are not talked about. As soon as one of their actions escapes notice they are dissatisfied. Many of them eat up their fortune in giving gay entertainments, many support mistresses at great expense. In order to make yourself a name among them, it is not enough to lead a voluptuous life, you must pose so as to attract attention. Ordinary dissipation does not create gossip in so busy a city.

It is not difficult to see why a certain P. Octavius paid 5,000 sesterces (about $212.50) for one fish of extraordinary size ; such a glorious purchase could not fail to be a subject for gossip throughout the city.

An expensive trout.

But the Romans had no monopoly on foolish prodigalities. Do we not know that under the First Empire in France, the exchequer reckoned at 6,000 francs ($1,170) the total expense of purchasing, preparing, and transporting an enormous trout with its sauce, sent by the town of Geneva to the archchancellor Cambacérès? Octavius compared to Cambacérès was a miser ; it is true, however, that Cambacérès did not pay for this beautiful dish out of his own pocket ; it was France that footed the bill.

A sumptuous feast.

Examples of still more gluttony there certainly were at Rome. It would be useless to deny it. At a feast which was given half a century before Christ the first course was : sea-urchins, raw oysters, each guest as many as he desired, giant mussels, a thrush on a bed of asparagus, a fattened pullet, a soup of oysters and mussels, black shell fish and white shell fish ; some more shell fish, sea-nettles, and some variety of salt water fish with fig peckers, fillets of wild boar and of wild kid, a poultry pie, and purple fish with fig peckers. The principal course was composed of sows' udders, a boar's jowl, fricassee of fish and of sows' udders, wild duck, teal, which was boiled, hares, roasted fowl, a flour pudding, and loaves of Picentian bread. The menu of the dessert, if there was any, is not preserved. Certainly a copious bill of fare ! Enough to finish off the partakers ! But the feast, we may rest assured, was among the most sumptuous, for otherwise Macrobius, who lived four or five centuries after it occurred, would not have furnished us with our account of it as he has done. Moreover—and this explains everything —the repast was gotten up for some priests.

The principal course.

After all, gormandizing was rarer at Rome than is generally believed. But a Roman loved to cut a dash, and when he received guests at his table he had an opportunity for doing so which he did not like to lose.

Let us try, by gathering together and arranging the scraps of information that Petronius and Martial have left us, to present to our readers a vivid picture of one of these state dinners.

The Romans had three regular meals a day : breakfast, at about nine o'clock ; luncheon, in the middle of the day ; and dinner, at three or four o'clock in the afternoon. The latter was the meal to which friends and acquaintances were, invited. The Romans had a supper sometimes late in the evening, but this was not a regular meal.

Order of meals.

According to Varro, a host who regarded his own comfort, and who wished to make it as pleasant as possible for his friends, would not receive at his table

Number of guests invited.

less than three persons, nor more than nine—"not less than the Graces, nor more than the Muses" seems to have been for a long time at Rome an axiom in the code of etiquette. But under the empire this axiom became obsolete ; for custom authorized those invited to bring with them friends who had not been asked ; the latter were called "shadows," because they were fancifully regarded as the shadows cast by those who brought them. Owing to this custom, the number of guests was often very large. Moreover, at the public

WINTER DINING-ROOM OF THE POMPEIIAN HOUSE AT SARATOGA SPRINGS, N. Y. Franklin W. Smith, architect.

dinners given by the emperors a vast number of covers were laid—as many as six hundred on one occasion. The example set by the court in this, as in many other particulars, was followed by private individuals.

Dress for the table.

Those Romans who were well versed in the rules of etiquette never dined in the *toga*. They wore at table special garments, which they never wore anywhere else ; and when they were going to dine out they would send these garments to their host's house, unless he was to furnish them some for the occasion. When the guests were assembled in the dining-hall, the host assigned to each one his place. In early times, it was the style to have a square table, with a couch or divan on each of three of its sides ; the fourth side was left free for the attendants to put down and remove dishes. Each couch was calculated to hold three occupants. The couch of honor was the center one ; the couch to the left of this was second in point of honor, and the one to the right was the least honorable. The last would be occupied by the host, his wife, and perhaps their child, while the two first would be reserved for guests. At the end of the republic round tables were introduced, and then a single semi-circular couch was used, called, on account of its form, a *sigma*, the name of the Greek letter ϛ (English s), whose ancient form was C.

Precedence at table.

These tables were almost always very costly. The favorite material for them was citrus wood. We have already spoken of the fact that Cicero owned a table of citrus wood worth 500,000 sesterces (about \$21,250), and other tables are mentioned by the ancient authors which cost as much as 1,400,000 sesterces (about \$59,500); they were ornamented with mosaic, mother of pearl, pearls, and ebony. Before table-cloths were used it is easy to comprehend why the ancients should have indulged their taste for elegant tables, but in the time of the Antonines table-cloths began to be fashionable, and still the rich would buy tables as costly as ever.

Costly tables

The Romans had the art of setting a table to produce a most sumptuous effect. A handsome center-piece would occupy the middle. The centerpiece on the table of Trimalchio, a character in the romance of Petronius, was in the form of a globe "upon which were represented the twelve signs of the zodiac. Below each sign the host had caused to be placed dishes which on account of their appearance or their nature had some connection with the constellation represented. Under the Ram were chick-peas, under the Bull, a roast of beef, etc. . . . In the center of this beautiful globe a tuft of grass, artistically carved, supported a honey-comb." But Trimalchio was only an eccentric gentleman of poor taste ; a man of culture as well as of means would adopt a more simple method of decoration. Nonnius Vindex had for a centerpiece a statuette of Hercules, done by the sculptor Lysippus. Although it occupied less room than Trimalchio's globe, it was no less costly.

Other table ornaments were beautiful candelabra from Ægina, murrhine vases, dishes of rock crystal, silver-ware marked with the owner's initials. The father-in-law of Seneca, Pompeius Paulinus, when starting off to command the Roman army in Germany, carried with him between eight and nine thousand pounds of table silver. Such extravagance astonishes us ; but it would surprise us no less, if we were able to take our place at one of those overloaded tables, to find no napkins and no knives. The guests brought their own napkins with them, and as to knives and forks, the custom of serving the food cut up into small bits rendered them unnecessary. At each person's place two spoons were laid, a large one and a small one, and sometimes a few toothpicks. A silver toothpick was a mark of luxury, ordinary ones being of wood or quill.

An elaborate dinner was served in several courses—
the number rose to eight or nine under the empire.
But there were three indispensable courses—the antepast or relish, the dinner proper, and the dessert. The
antepast consisted of shell fish ; but oysters, which
served to awaken the appetite of the diners, seem to
have been eaten in the middle of the repast to revive it.
At the dinner proper the *pièces de résistance* appeared ;
then the waiters brought in the sauces—poppy sauce,
made from the juice of poppy seeds roasted and crushed ;
garum sauce, made of the entrails of fish preserved in
wine or vinegar and seasoned with pepper, salt, etc.
Next fowls, fattened pullets, pheasants, sows' udders,
and, finally, larger animals, which in the most elegant
mansions were brought on the table whole. The dessert
was composed of pastry and fruit. Since Priapus was the
god of the gardens, it was natural that he should preside
over this part of the meal ; so the pastry cooks used to
make out of their dough figures of Priapus gathering up
his robe in front so that a deep pocket was formed in
its folds ; when these figures appeared as dessert the
pockets would be filled with all kinds of fruit, which the
god would seem to be offering to the guests. The final
course, moreover, was the time for surprises. Sometimes the ceiling of the dining-room would open and
flowers would rain down ; sometimes a fountain of perfumed water would rise from a hidden pipe ; sometimes
even—and this was a less charming surprise—a skeleton
would be brought into the dining-room. Petronius, in
his romance, records such an occurrence as follows :

While we were drinking and admiring in detail the magnificence of the feast, a slave placed upon the table a silver
skeleton, so well contrived that the vertebræ and the joints
moved easily in all directions.

This was not an extravagant invention of Trimalchio's, but a custom which the Greeks had learned from the Egyptians and transmitted to the Romans.

Wines.

In what order were the wines served? It is difficult to say. But we know that first came the mead or honey-wine. Martial has left us an enumeration of the famous wines of his day. Just for the sake of curiosity let us run over them. They were the Albanum, the Surrentinum, the Setinum, the Fundanum, the Trifoli-

THE VINTAGE FESTIVAL.   From a painting by L. Alma-Tadema.

num, which was not considered very good, the Signinum, which was rather sour, the Pelignum, very muddy, the Massilian, very fragrant, the Tarentine, the Cæretanum, the Nomentanum, and finally the delicious Cæcubum, and the generous Falernum, whose praises the verses of Horace have immortalized.

But a host's chief duty was, not to furnish food and drink—this was the business of the steward and the cook—but to devise with ingenious taste the amusements, for some kind of entertainment always accompanied a feast.

Entertainment at table.

The question in a host's mind always was, "What new diversion can I provide for my guests? Shall I have an artist in the dining-room to mold under their eyes plastic figures from soft clay? Shall I have readings from epic poetry? Shall I have some beautiful Andalusian girls exhibit their famous dancing, accompanied by the flute and castanets, and a choir of singers? Shall I have a concert of zither players? Or shall I entertain my guests with a farce or a mime?''

There was plenty to choose from. The difficulty always was to make a choice. For custom had rendered some program indispensable.· But many complaints were made in regard to these entertainments —in the first place that they were too costly, and furthermore that they were carried to excess. Pliny, with his usual prudence and tolerance, expresses his views on the subject as follows :

I have received your letter, in which you complain of having been highly disgusted lately at a very splendid enter- Pliny's views tainment, by a set of buffoons, mummers, and wanton prostitutes, who were dancing about round the tables. But let me advise you to smooth your knitted brow somewhat. I confess, indeed, I admit nothing of this kind at my own house ; however, I bear with it in others. "And why, then," you will be ready to ask, "not have them yourself?" The truth is, because the gestures of the wanton, the pleasantries of the buffoon, or the extravagances of the mummer, give me no pleasure, as they give me no surprise. It is my particular taste, you see, not my judgment that I plead against them. And, indeed, what numbers are there who think the entertainments with which you and I are most delighted are wholly without interest ! How many are there who, as soon as a reader, a lyrist, or a comedian is introduced, either take their leave of the company, or, if they remain, show as much dislike to this sort of thing as you did to those *monsters*, as you call them ! Let us bear, therefore, my friend, with others in their amusements, that they in return may show indulgence to ours. Farewell.

But Martial is less tolerant ; one of his epigrams reads as follows :

The eloquent page of Priscus considers "what is the best kind of feast?" and offers many suggestions with grace, many with force, and all with learning. Do you ask me, what is the best kind of feast? That at which no flute-player is present.

Martial certainly was not fond of music. But we should remember that the best things may be rendered unendurable by abuse, and that many hosts, in their excess of zeal, made amusements a bore.

These interludes at a meal must, in any case, have seriously interfered with talking among the guests. We shall not expect to find, then, at dinner-parties any examples of conversation in Rome.

Private conversation, as formerly public speaking, developed in the open air. Let us enter an *exedra* at Rome and watch those who are enjoying an hour's recreation there. We find a group of men discussing some topic which seems to be of the most absorbing interest, for their voices are loud, their gestures violent, and their faces expressive of the greatest animation. But soon the conversation becomes less general ; now two or three only sustain it ; the others, one by one, quietly drop away. Those who remain and continue talking with unabated zeal are philosophers, scholars, or grammarians, who could not resist the temptation to enter into a discussion upon some difficult or abstract question. They have driven away the rest of the company, who could not follow them through the intricacies of their argument.

Outside the temples, near the libraries, in the bookshops, literary people would gather together and discuss the latest publications.

"Pliny," some one would say, "has just sent some new hendecasyllables to Titius Aristo."

"Have you heard," some one else would ask, "about the stupid mistake of Javolenus Priscus? Why, a poet was reading aloud one of his poems, and the first line commenced 'You, Priscus, command'—and what did Javolenus do but burst right in, 'I! why, I don't command anything.' The blockhead didn't know it was part of the poem."

The stupid mistake of Priscus.

"Statius," some one else would contribute, "is

PERISTYLE OF THE POMPEIIAN HOUSE AT SARATOGA SPRINGS, N. Y.
Franklin W. Smith, architect.

going to give a reading from his 'Thebaïs.' The whole city is overjoyed at the prospect."

And then struggling authors would complain of their lot. One of them, who had been unsuccessful in securing an audience when he gave readings from his manuscript poems, would exclaim :

Complaints of unsuccessful authors.

"Alas ! how unfortunate it is to have a mania for

writing! I might as well put my verses in the cupboard and let the bugs and spiders eat them up, for the day is past of such men as Mæcenas; our rich misers don't know enough to bestow upon talent anything but praise and empty admiration."

No more Mæcenases.

"But," a sympathetic friend would reply, "Maculonus lent you a hall in his house in which to give a reading from your poems; he even had his freedmen help swell the audience, and he distributed here and there applauders possessed of vigorous lungs."

"Yes," the other would reply, "but he did not meet the expense of the banquet, nor did he pay for the platform and the chairs for the orchestra which had to be supplied. Just think! I shall have to pawn my cloak."

Compliments exchanged.

And the self-satisfied poets would overwhelm each other with compliments.

"You are an Alcæus," one of them would say.

"And you a Callimachus," would be the reply.

"Your poems have power from all others to wean us."
"In yours hold sway all the Graces and Venus."
"You marshall your words as if 'twere by magic."
"And you are supreme in the realm of the tragic."

This complaisant dialogue between Vadius and Trissotin in Molière's comedy, "Les Femmes Savantes," strikingly resembles the conversation of their Roman ancestors.

Lively criticism.

But praise becomes insipid. There is more spice in criticism; and we may be sure that it had a large place in the every-day talk among literary men.

"Piccus," some one would say, "writes his epigrams on the back side of his pages, and then complains that they are opposite to good sense."

"You make a great mystery, Cinna," some one else

would continue, "out of your poems that no one has seen.

> "Just publish them, friend,
> And the talk will soon end."

We must suppose, also, that general theories were often discussed. Fruitful topics of conversation were furnished by the never-settled differences between the partisans of native literature and the lovers of Alexandrianism. Juvenal probably often indulged his keen wit at the expense of the latter, and it is not likely, whatever he may say about it, that he waited until he wrote his first satire to express his disgust at Codrus, the poet who made himself hoarse by reciting his own verses, and who had compelled him so many times to be an unwilling listener to the reading of his "Theseid." *Literary discussions.*

The ladies and gentlemen of fashionable society used to enjoy meeting each other in the porticoes, richly adorned with statues, and in the public promenades and walks, under the shade of the laurel and plane trees. Here they would chat together, praise the latest exhibition of ballet-dancing, discuss the merits of this or that gladiator, wax enthusiastic over the triumph of the horse that had won in the last races of the Circus Maximus, or take sides for the blues or the reds, colors worn to distinguish the contestants in the games of the circus. There was much talk, too, about love affairs, especially among the ladies. *Chat.*

In short, gossip flourished in Rome as much as in any little country village. A girl could not be pretty in Rome with impunity. Slander, Propertius tells us, was the punishment for beauty. This eager delight in gossip led to frequent intrusion into people's private affairs, and sometimes even to espionage. *Gossip.*

Hence arises [said Seneca] the most frightful of all forms of baseness—spying into the secrets of individuals, besides attempting to find out many things that one can neither listen to nor communicate without danger.

Espionage.

It was of no use to try to escape from eyes always on the watch, from ears always strained to hear. You could not conceal your life; you lived in an open house.

Juvenal, in one of his satires, writes :

> And dost thou seriously believe, fond swain,
> .The actions of the great unknown remain?
> Poor Corydon! even beasts would silence break,
> And stocks and stones, if servants did not, speak.
> Bolt every door, stop every cranny tight,
> Close every window, put out every light;
> Let not a whisper reach the listening ear,
> No noise, no motion; let no soul be near;
> Yet all that passed at the cock's second crow,
> The neighboring vintner shall, ere daybreak, know,
> With what besides the cook and carver's brain,
> Subtly malicious, can in vengeance feign!

Martial, in his portrait of the coxcomb, has taken off marvelously well the commonplaces of conversation often exchanged among the idle, society people of his day. The following is his epigram (we use Elton's translation):

Portrait of a
coxcomb.

> They tell me, Cotilus, that you're a beau;
> What this is, Cotilus, I wish to know.
> "A beau is one who, with the nicest care,
> In parted locks divides his curling hair;
> One who with balm and cinnamon smells sweet,
> Whose humming lips some Spanish air repeat;
> Whose naked arms are smoothed with pumice-stone,
> And tossed about with graces all his own;
> A beau is one who takes his constant seat,
> From morn to evening, where the ladies meet;
> And ever, on some sofa hovering near,
> Whispers some nothing in some fair one's ear;

Who scribbles thousand billets-doux a day ;
Still reads and scribbles, reads, and sends away ;
A beau is one who shrinks, if nearly pressed
By the coarse garment of a neighbor guest ;
Who knows who flirts with whom, and still is found
At each good table in successive round ;
A beau is one—none better knows than he
A race horse, and his noble pedigree "—
Indeed ? Why, Cotilus, if this be so,
What teasing, trifling thing is called a beau !

Slander and frivolity—such was the substance of the fashionable conversation at Rome. We must admit, however, that the Romans had an excuse, which happily we of to-day have not, for idle and mischievous conver-sation. They slandered private individuals because they could not criticise public men ; they discussed petty subjects because great ones were forbidden.

Why the Romans gossiped.

To-day we are not afraid to talk about politics and to express ourselves very freely ; there is scarcely a social gathering where they are not touched upon. Every one thinks he has a right to his own opinion on this subject, and even the ladies must have their say. At certain epochs of the empire politics were a forbidden topic of conversation. There were, indeed, even at such epochs, those moving in social circles who liked to make a show of knowledge in matters of state ; but what was their information worth ?

Politics a forbidden topic of conversation.

The following epigram of Martial's throws some light upon this question :

These are the contrivances, Philomusus, by which you are constantly trying to secure a dinner : inventing numbers of fictions, and retailing them as true. You are informed of the counsels of Pacorus at the court of

WOMAN'S HEAD.
Vatican Museum, Rome.

Parthia ; you can tell the exact numbers of the German and Sarmatian armies. You reveal the unopened dispatches of the Dacian general ; you see a laureled letter, announcing a victory, before its arrival. You know how often dusky Syene has been watered by Egyptian floods ; you know how many ships have sailed from the shores of Africa ; you know for whose head the Julian olives grow, and for whom the Father of Heaven destines his triumphal crowns. A truce to your arts ; you shall dine with me to-day, but only on this condition, Philomusus, that you tell me no news.

But as soon as a person began to talk about the plans of the emperor, about his friends or his victims, he was in danger. There were spies everywhere and it was no safer to listen than to talk.

We should have lost [said Tacitus] with our free speech, our memories, if it had been as easy to forget as to keep still.

The informers were always on the alert, and hovered about armed with the formidable law of *majestas*, which made it treason to utter a syllable reflecting criticism upon the government, and they spread terror everywhere. The ancient writers have left us startling testimony upon the subject of this universal dread that rested upon Roman society.

Never [said Tacitus, speaking of the reign of Tiberius] did greater consternation and alarm prevail in Rome. People trembled in the presence of their nearest relatives. They scarcely dared approach each other or speak to each other. Every ear was suspected, whether known or unknown. Even mute and inanimate things inspired dread. People glanced anxiously at the walls and the ceiling.

There had been so many examples of the terrible power of the informers. It was an informer who had caused the death of Valerius Asiaticus ; it was due to an information that Rusticus Arulenus, Helvidius Priscus, and so many other worthy men had been sent into exile. There were so many instances that could be cited of the perfidy and wickedness of these odious men. No one had forgotten the story of Sabinus. A traitor by long and skilful maneuvering had won his friendship; then he invited him to his house, and while Sabinus, in perfect trust, gave vent to his indignation against the tyranny of Tiberius, three senators were listening, crouched in the roof of the informer's house, so that they might report what they heard to the emperor.

These despicable rascals often became important personages. Domitius Afer and Regulus, both informers, had speedily attained wealth. The latter, according to Pliny, possessed 40,000,000 sesterces (about $1,700,-000). They were powerful, and enjoyed their power with insolence. One day some one spoke before the informer Metius Carus of one of his victims, furiously attacking his character. "What business have you," exclaimed Carus, "with my dead?"

The wealth of informers.

Their insolence.

It was not only under the bad emperors that informers exercised their detestable influence. Pliny, at the succession of Trajan, uttered a cry of joy upon seeing the punishment which a few of them suffered.

Memorable spectacle! [he wrote]. A flotilla loaded with informers is abandoned to the winds. It is compelled to spread its sails to the tempests and to follow the angry waves wherever they may carry it. One loves to watch these ships as they scatter after leaving the harbor. And it is not for one day only, it is forever that you [Trajan] have repressed the audacity of these informers by overwhelming them with fearful punishment. They try to seize wealth which does not belong to them—let them lose what they have of their own. They burn to drive others out of their homes—let them be snatched away from their own hearths, . . . let their hopes cease to be greater than their fears, and let them feel as much dread as they inspire.

Informers punished.

But is not this the exaggeration of the panegyric style? Was such complete safety as Pliny claims secured under Trajan? It seems doubtful. Under Nerva, who was neither a bad emperor nor a wicked man, Martial, inviting six friends to dinner, warns them to avoid dangerous subjects of conversation.

Let my guests [he said] talk about the blues and the greens of the circus [colors worn by contestants], for I do not want my hospitality to be the cause of any one's being accused of crime.

Veiento, who made his fortune by informing, used to dine at this same Nerva's table. One day the conversation turned upon a certain Messalinus, an informer under Nero, who had caused many victims to perish. His crimes were recounted, and, as he was no longer to be feared, they were not smoothed over nor excused.

"What do you think," asked the emperor, "would have been his fate had he lived now?"

And one of the guests, who was not afraid to speak out, said, casting a sly glance at Veiento, "He would have dined with you." It is Pliny himself who tells us this anecdote.

The fact is that under the empire informers carried on a systematic business. From the beginning of the empire a secret police existed in Rome. According to Dion Cassius, Mæcenas had declared to Augustus that it was absolutely necessary to employ spies throughout the empire. The celebrated informers, Regulus and Domitius Afer, were, so to speak, volunteers ; but there was a whole class of men who were regularly enlisted in the service and organized after the fashion, perhaps, of the police of the Persian kings. Slavery, from the time that Augustus found means to evade the ancient law making a slave's information worthless in a court of justice, furnished precious auxiliaries to the body of informers; for as soon as a master gave a slave cause for complaint, the slave could take his revenge by informing against his master.

Even the army was employed in this wretched business. We know that Hadrian formed a special corps of soldiers, called "foragers," who were nothing less than spies.

"Foragers."

It is by allowing your confidence to be too quickly won [said Epictetus] that you fall into the traps set by the soldiers. A military man in citizen's clothes sits down beside you and begins to criticise the emperor. You, following his lead, and taking his boldness as a pledge of his sincerity, you, I say, in your turn, express your opinion; and the result is that you are put in chains and cast into prison.

Let us remember that at Rome there was no free public press, for the official journal contained on the burning questions of the day only what the government saw fit to publish, besides items of court news and announcements of events in families of rank and in high life. Let us not forget that the public rostrum had been torn down. And if we reflect also upon the tyranny which oppressed all the emperor's subjects, which was relaxed only at rare moments, without being ever completely abolished, we shall be more indulgent toward the gossips of Rome, and we shall be able to excuse them for having preferred to say nothings than to say nothing.

No freedom of speech.

CHAPTER VIII.

AMUSEMENTS.

THIS Roman society, whose activity was so limited, whose members were not allowed to express noble thoughts or to engage in the discussion of great questions, felt the necessity for some diversion of absorbing interest. The emperors saw this and provided the spectacles.

The spectacles comprise chariot races and other athletic contests, gladiatorial shows, beast-fighting, exhibitions of trained animals, and dramatic representations. Those of the spectacles which had the character of contests are also called games.

After the close of the republic the games were no longer religious in character ; in the hands of the party chiefs they became simply an instrument for acquiring popularity. The young Cælius, for instance, when tired of pleasure and ambitious for power, begged of Cicero, then prætor in Cilicia, to send him some panthers, convinced that they would be a great attraction in the spectacles which he intended to give for the purpose of winning for himself the popular favor before running for office. Cælius had not the slightest idea of adding to the splendor of the fêtes celebrated in honor of the gods.

The emperors, too, were influenced solely by motives of self-interest when they spent money on the spectacular shows. Juvenal has made familiar the phrase "Bread and games," and this was indeed the cry of the masses, idle, or at least busy, with trifles. If a prince

heeded this cry he was sure to win for himself warm
partisans. Thirty years after the death of Nero there
were still those who refused to believe that he had
perished, who were waiting, and wishing for his return,
and who cherished a tender memory of him. People
had forgotten that he had burned Rome ; they remembered only the magnificence of his spectacles. The

AMPHITHEATER IN POMPEII.

games had become an instrument of power, and this
fact was perfectly understood by that pantomimist
Pylades, who said to Augustus, "Your interest depends
upon our occupying the attention of the people."

These games, which had taken the place of the speeches
given in the public square by the orators and statesmen
of the past, owed their success in part to the fact that
they contained some elements of the passion and storm
that had belonged to the ancient forum. They furnished to the people their only occasions for gathering
together, for manifesting their sympathies or their antip-

athies, for expressing their wishes to the sovereign. The people would ask for the representation of a certain piece, for the emancipation of a certain gladiator, for

the pardon of a criminal condemned to fight with the wild beasts. These southerners, noisy and violent, had a craving for collecting in crowds, for mingling their voices in the shouts that arose from a great amphitheater, for feeling within them that tempestuous breath which Horace compares to the roaring of the Tuscan sea. The rulers did not hesitate to satisfy this craving, for rarely did the popular demonstrations relate to anything but the games themselves. If sometimes they assumed a political character, as when the knights asked of Augustus the abolition of a severe marriage law, or when the people, under Caligula, protested against the burdensome taxes, the emperor had the resource of leaving the entertainment or of suppressing the demonstration, according to his temperament.

So the rulers did not stint their expenditures for these shows, which were free from danger and advantageous in so many ways. In 51 A. D. large sums had been drawn from the public treasury to defray the cost of the games —760,000 sesterces (about \$32,370) for the so-called Roman games, 600,000 sesterces (about \$25,500) for the plebeian games, 380,000 sesterces (about \$16,150) for the games in honor of Apollo, 10,000 sesterces (about \$425) for the Augustan games. And be it understood that these figures represent only the outlay of the state. The individuals who gave the entertainments contributed largely to them from their own resources. Herod

of Judæa spent upon a fête which he instituted in honor of Augustus nearly 500 talents (about \$589,600). And this is only one example among a hundred. We must add also that many who undertook such enormous expenditures did not do so voluntarily, but were driven to it by motives of self-defense; and the senators felt obliged by their position to contribute toward the support of the games. These heavy financial burdens were a sort of tax levied upon the aristocracy in the interests of the masses, and they caused the ruin of many a noble family.

During the early history of the empire the splendor of the shows steadily increased, and the time which they occupied became longer and longer. Under the republic there were seven annual spectacles which lasted sixty-six days in all. Augustus does not seem to have modified this number of holidays, but under Tiberius it was raised to eighty-seven. Celebrations of victories, consecrations of temples, anniversaries of emperors brought the number up to one hundred and thirty-five days in the time of Marcus Aurelius, and under Nero there was a senator, the juris-consult Caius Cassius, who, alarmed at the increasing number of holidays, demanded a law to limit them.

Number of holidays increased.

For the ancients, in fact, the theater was not, as with us, a diversion and recreation after a day's work. The games took place in the morning, that is to say at the only time when it was possible to engage in business, and it was not unusual for them to be prolonged until a late hour of the afternoon, and sometimes even into the night.

This encouragement of idleness justifies the condemnation pronounced upon the spectacles by the moralists of the time. In fact, the games were making of the Roman people a population of beggars. And we shall see, as we study the games in detail, that their demoralizing influence did not stop here.

Idleness encouraged.

The games most in favor with the people and with

society in general were the games of the circus. The horse races, introduced into Rome from Greece, became, according to Tacitus, very popular. At first the spectators sat upon wooden steps—temporary constructions, removed as soon as the races were over. But following the example of Pompey, who had been the first to build a theater of stone, Julius Cæsar gave to the Romans a permanent circus, or race course—the Circus Maximus.

The Circus
Maximus.

The Circus Maximus was among the most magnificent buildings of the world's capital. It was situated in the oblong valley comprised between the almost parallel

CIRCUS MAXIMUS. From a painting by Gerome.

sides of the Palatine and Aventine Hills. It was three and a half stadia (2,121 feet) long, and four plethra (404 feet) broad. An exterior wall, circular at one end and straight at the other, inclosed the entire space. Inside this wall and against it were tiers of seats, the straight end only being left free. These seats were of stone, except those near the top, which were made of wood ; and this seems to have been the case even after

Nero, Domitian, and Trajan had enlarged and embellished the circus. But several terrible accidents must have shown the danger of wooden seats. They frequently gave way, as they did once under Augustus when 1,100 lives were lost. But such catastrophes did not discourage the public. In the time of Cæsar the circus could seat 150,000 spectators; this figure under Titus rose to 250,000, according to Pliny the Elder; and we may well believe that no seats were left empty, for we learn from Seneca that the shouts which arose from the assembly were heard even in the suburbs of Rome. It was, however, only the lower classes who suffered from these accidents; the places nearest the race-course were set apart for the senators, and just above the senators sat the knights. The common people were crowded together on the wooden seats which rose to the top of the exterior wall. Distinguished people, therefore, could attend the circus without danger; the plebeians alone enjoyed this pleasure at the risk of their lives.

Frequent accidents.

A canal ten feet broad and ten feet deep separated the lowest tier of seats from the course, and served as the boundary of the hippodrome.

The vast oblong space which formed the central area, and on which was usually sprinkled a fine brilliant sand, was divided lengthwise into two parts by a wall, called the spine, because its position on the shining surface of the sand was similar to that of the backbone in the human frame. Its top was decorated with statues or columns, and in the middle stood a monolithic obelisk of oriental granite. In addition to these ornaments, at each end of the spine was a set of seven marble eggs mounted upon a shrine. One egg from each shrine was removed by a slave after each round or lap of a

The central area.

The spine.

race was run—there being usually seven laps to each race. The spectators were thus aided in keeping in mind the progress of the race.

The spine occupied less than two thirds of the length of the arena, leaving at either end a passage. At each extremity of the spine, at a little distance from it, was placed a goal, consisting of three tall conical objects, made after the time of Claudius of gilt bronze, and decorated with bands in relief. These goals formed the turning-points for the chariots.

From the straight end of the circus opened thirteen arcades. The central arcade, higher and wider than the others, was an entrance for spectators, and also for the formal procession with which the games began. The other twelve arcades were chambers where the horses and chariots stood before the commencement of a race. They were called *carceres*, or prisons.

Finally, to close this description, let us say that a balcony placed over the principal entrance was reserved for the president of the games. When it was time for a race to begin, he gave the signal for starting by throwing down a purple napkin.

The games, which had at first a religious motive, kept up the tradition of their early character by always opening with a solemn procession, called the Circensian parade.

Let us imagine ourselves among the spectators at one of the Roman chariot races. The procession forms on the Capitoline Hill, passes down its sacred side, crosses the forum, the Vicus Tuscus, the Velabrum, the cattle market, and finally enters the circus, led by the presiding magistrate, standing in a chariot and wearing the dress of a triumphant general. His chariot is followed by musicians playing loudly upon their instruments and by a crowd of clients dressed in white *togas.* Then come statues of the gods, borne upon litters or carried in richly ornamented chariots and accompanied by the priests grouped in their religious corporations. This magnificent parade is welcomed by the cheers and acclamations of the crowd ; but under the empire this demonstration lacks all enthusiasm. It has become an empty form like the procession itself ; for the parade, splendid as it is, has grown monotonous, the religious sentiment connected with it has disappeared, and it no longer arouses curiosity. From the time of Tiberius the words "tiresome as the Circensian parade" were a proverb. The spectators are in a hurry for the formality to end, they are impatient for the races to begin.

An empty form.

At last the signal is given ; the gates of the prisons are flung open and the contestants appear. They are standing in their two-wheeled chariots, which are usually very-light and almost always drawn by four horses abreast. These charioteers are slaves or hirelings who drive for the owners of the horses. They are dressed in short, sleeveless tunics, with close-fitting caps upon their heads ; the reins are wound about their waists, and each one has in his girdle a knife for cutting himself free from the reins in case of accident, and he carries in his hand a whip with a double lash. Their places in the prisons were designated in advance by lot under the supervision of the president of the games.

The
charioteers.

Leaning over the necks of their horses, excited by the cries and the tumult of the crowd, who either hoot them or cheer them, they fling themselves into the contest. They must make the course seven times, seven times they must turn around the goals. As the contestants are usually numerous, as each round is eagerly

The race.

disputed, they often come together in the narrow passage at the end of the spine—often they run into each other, and then there is, according to the expression of Sophocles, a shipwreck of men, horses, and chariots. The one who has been able to avoid this danger, the one who, after the seven eggs have been removed, arrives first at the chalk-line in front of the balcony occupied by the presiding officer, is proclaimed victor by the herald. Descending out of his chariot, he receives from the ædile a branch of Idumæan palm, or a wreath of gold and silver, wrought in imitation of laurel, or the more substantial but less brilliant prize of a sum of money.

The races between four-horse chariots were the most ordinary. But as the games of the circus were very lengthy (under Trajan there would be as many as forty-eight races in one day) it became necessary to introduce some variety into them.

CHARIOTEER. Vatican.

Accordingly, you might see sometimes chariots harnessed to two horses only; some drivers would have a third horse in front of the two; others, but they were veritable virtuosos, would have themselves drawn by six, seven, or eight horses. Of course such daring originality was much admired by the spectators. The way once open for eccentricities, they were carried very far. Did not Elagabalus conceive the idea of having himself drawn by four camels? And is he not also the individual who had two, three, or four beautiful women harnessed to the chariot in which he rode? Yes, he indulged in these whims in his own private circus. But in the time of Nero the Circus Maximus itself was the scene of a peculiar exhibition. The prætor Aulus Fabricius appeared there in a chariot drawn by trained dogs. The regular horse-drivers had refused to drive his horses for him in a race, although he offered them a reasonable price, and this was his original way of showing that he was not beaten.

But the circus offered a more interesting sight than the spectacle, and that was the spectators. One must have been present at a bull-fight in Spain, he must have seen a whole population, as if out of their senses, now stamp with enthusiasm, now howl in anger, now applaud with all their might the bull-fighter, now fling at him a marvelous variety of insults ; he must have seen the women throw their bouquets and even their jewels at the daring or skilful champion, cheer him and waft kisses to him, or hurl upon the coward or the clown the most unexpected weapons—he must have been a witness of this delirium, which is so contagious, if he would form any idea of the conduct of the Romans at these games of the hippodrome. The spectators would take the part of this horse, or this driver, they would encourage their favorite with gesture and voice, hooting his adversaries. If your neighbor did not sympathize with you in your preferences, then followed quarrels, and often even blows.

Moreover, there were no actors in these games more fêted than certain celebrated horses. It was not unusual to gild their hoofs, and it even became customary for them to receive money and presents. Volucris, the favorite horse of Lucius Verus, obtained one day a bushel of gold pieces. Hadrian constructed for his horse, Borysthenes, a tomb bearing an inscription which is still preserved; and this is not an isolated fact; it would be easy to cite many other similar examples. Can we be surprised after this at the stories about Caligula and his horse Incitatus? He gave him a complete house, with slaves and furniture, and insisted upon his friends going to dine with him, and invited him to his table. He did not have time to raise his horse to the consulship, but, having had himself made pontifex, he took Incitatus for his colleague in the priestly office. Such follies astonish our most rabid sportsmen; but perhaps they only caused a smile to curl the lips of the Romans, who were conscious that they all had a taint of this mania in their blood.

The charioteers were second to their beasts in the favor of the people, and yet they were treated in a manner to satisfy the most exacting. They were lionized; if they appeared in public a numerous retinue of faithful admirers surrounded them. They could with impunity indulge in excesses the most intolerable. From the beginning of the empire the shameful custom was established of allowing them, on certain days, to wander through the city, committing, as if in fun, tricks of cheating and theft. Under Nero a law was passed to check this singular license, but it could not put an end to the insolence and effrontery of these drivers. Had they not succeeded in winning all that heart could desire—fortune and honors? Did not Caligula make to Eutyches a present of 2,000,000 sesterces (about $85,000)? Did he not employ the prætorians to con-

struct stables for the horses of this favored driver?
Did not Elagabalus raise the mother of the charioteer
Hierocles from the condition of slavery to consular rank?

The people were partly responsible for the extravagance of the emperors ; at the circus they would take
the side of a certain faction, and applaud the charioteers
who represented it. Their enthusiasm for the greens or
the blues was among the liveliest passions which they
were capable of feeling. What, then, were these factions which are mentioned so frequently by the historians of the Roman Empire?

The factions.

As the magnificence of the games constantly increased, it became impossible for the donors to meet
the expense which was involved. Companies were
then formed of capitalists and owners of studs who
undertook the running of the games. As there were
usually four chariots which entered the lists at a time to
contend for the prize, so there were four great companies who were distinguished by the color of their
chariots and the tunics of their drivers. Hence we
have the four factions represented by the colors white,
red, blue, and green. Domitian established two new
factions—the purple and the gold. It seems that later
the blues and the greens absorbed the other factions.
This must have been an important event, for these
were the colors which especially excited the passions of
the people, more even than the betting or the skill of
the drivers. Pliny, in the following letter, laments this
symptom of intellectual and moral decadence :

*The power of
the colors to
excite the
people.*

I have spent these several days past in reading and writing,
with the most pleasing tranquillity imaginable. You will ask,
"How can that possibly be in the midst of Rome?" It was
the time of celebrating the Circensian games, an entertainment
for which I have not the least taste. They have no novelty,

no variety to recommend them, nothing, in short, one would wish to see twice. It does the more surprise me, therefore, that so many thousand people should be possessed with the childish passion of desiring so often to see a parcel of horses gallop, and men standing upright in their chariots. If, indeed, it were the swiftness of the horses or the skill of the men that attracted them, there might be some pretense of reason for it. But it is the dress they like ; it is the dress that takes their fancy. And if, in the midst of the course and contest, the different parties were to change colors, their different partisans would change sides, and instantly desert the very same men and horses whom just before they were eagerly following with their eyes, as far as they could see, and shouting out their names with all their might. Such mighty charms, such wondrous power reside in the color of a paltry tunic ! And this not only with the common crowd (more contemptible than the dress they espouse), but even with serious-thinking people. When I observe such men thus insatiably fond of so silly, so low, so uninteresting, so common an entertainment, I congratulate myself on my indifference to these pleasures ; and am glad to employ upon my books the leisure of this season, which others throw away upon the most idle occupations. Farewell.

But what could avail against this general frenzy the words of a few literary men ?

Next to the chariot races, the gladiatorial contests attracted the population of Rome.

The amphitheaters, where these contests took place, were at first, like the circus, constructed of wood. Their architecture was a modification of that of the Greek theaters. In the year 53 B. C. Caius Scribonius Curio built, according to Pliny the Elder, a double theater, composed of two semi-circular wooden theaters set on pivots, so that they could be whirled around, spectators and all. When turned back to back they formed two separate theaters, and when turned face to face they formed an amphitheater of the usual shape in

which all the spectators faced the center. In the
morning dramatic exhibitions could be given in the two
theaters separately, and in the afternoon the two
assemblies of spectators, without having been disturbed,
could be thrown into one, and could witness together a
gladiatorial show.

But soon buildings were erected on purpose for these
shows. Wood alone was used in the construction of
Construction of amphitheaters.

THE COLOSSEUM AT ROME.

the amphitheaters of Julius Cæsar and of Nero. But
during the ten last years of the first century of the
Christian era, under the Flavian emperors, that colossal
structure of stone was built which well deserves its
name, the Colosseum, and which we still admire as the
The Colosseum.
most imposing relic of a crumbled world.

At first the gladiatorial shows were closely associated
with religion. They constituted a part of funeral ceremonies. Instead of sacrificing defenseless men on the
tomb of the dead, it seemed less cruel to make them

fight and kill each other ; it was, to use Tertullian's expression, a more humane atrocity. The first contest of this sort was witnessed by the Romans in 264 B. C., when Marcus and Decimus Brutus, at the obsequies of their father, had three pairs of gladiators fight in the cattle market.

This kind of spectacle was rapidly developed. Its original object was soon forgotten ; gladiatorial contests were not long limited to funerals, but were given a place in almost all public solemnities and entertainments. They became so popular that the magistrates felt obliged upon their entrance into office to amuse the people with them, and candidates would give them as a means of winning votes. It even became necessary to pass a law limiting the number of gladiators that might be brought forward upon a single occasion. But this law did not prevent Julius Cæsar, in 65 B. C., from giving a spectacle in which three hundred pairs of combatants fought at once. Certainly progress had been made in the two centuries since Marcus and Decimus Brutus. But the limit had not been reached. In the games given by Augustus ten thousand men descended into the arena, and Trajan, when he celebrated his victory over the peoples of the Danube, exhibited the same number.

The Romans were not satisfied with the tragic emotions which these vast slaughters must have excited in them ; they brought to the amphitheater their taste for sumptuous elegance and their refined curiosity. The victims in these bloody sports had to array themselves for death in brilliant apparel. At the games which Julius Cæsar gave as ædile, the equipment of the gladiators was silver ; at games given by Nero it was of amber, or at least of amber mosaic work. The people

required also that there should be variety in the spectacle ; and therefore it was necessary that the combatants should be of different races, and should exhibit
their skill in the use of their national weapons. So the
Samnites, the Thracians, and the Gauls, who had succeeded in amusing the people under the republic, gave
place, under the empire, to tattooed savages from the
island of Britain, to blond Germans from the banks of
the Danube, to Suebi and Dacians, to dusky Moors,
brought from the villages of Atlas, to negroes from the
interior of Africa, and to the nomads from some steppe
of the region now known as Russia.

How was the army of gladiators recruited?

When a man committed a capital crime, such as
highway robbery, sacrilege, or incendiarism, he was
sent to one of the gladiatorial schools, of which we
shall presently speak. But Roman citizens were not
liable to this punishment. Another source of supply
was furnished by prisoners of war. Slaves also were
often trained as gladiators, their masters having during
the first century of the empire the unrestricted right to
sell them for the arena. Hadrian, however, tried to
put a stop to this by law. But the slaves themselves
were not unwilling to enter the schools of gladiators.
For was not this a means, perilous without doubt, but
quick, of escaping from servitude? At the end of
three years they might receive an honorable discharge
from the arena, in token of which a foil would be
presented to them, and at the end of five years they
might even win their freedom and have the right to
wear the *pileus*, or liberty-cap. The ranks of the
gladiators were also recruited by freedmen and Roman
citizens, who having squandered their estates vol-
unteered to bind themselves to a trainer of gladiators

for a certain time. Even men of birth and fortune sometimes entered the lists to gratify their pure love of fighting.

When we consider the perils of such a profession, when we remember the infamy with which it was branded by the Roman law, we are tempted to suppose that the number of these volunteers must have been very limited. But such was not the fact. The gladiators enjoyed a popularity almost equal to that of the charioteers of the circus. Although under the ban of society, they were often the favorites of fashion. Their portraits were displayed in shop windows ; they were multiplied upon vases, glass lamps, and gems, and, what was not less flattering, they were sketched as decorations upon walls. Like our legendary bandits, they made fair ladies sigh, and society women thought it

The popularity of gladiators.

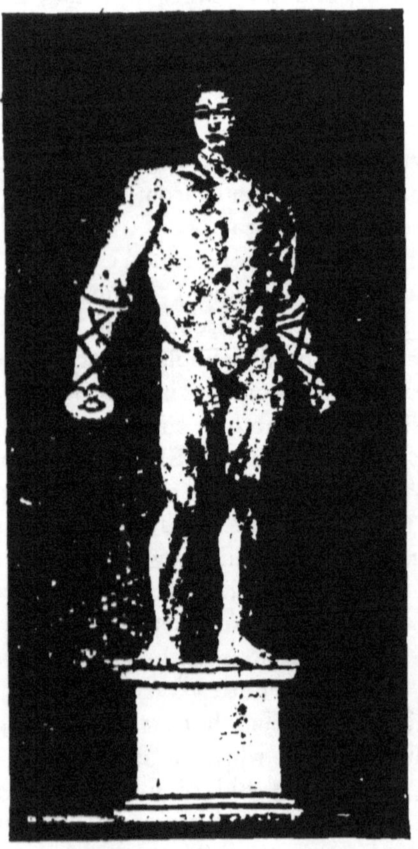

GLADIATOR IN MOSAIC. National Museum, Naples.

quite the thing to have a gladiator for a lover.   Juvenal,
in one of his satires, expresses his disgust at this condition of public morals :

> Hippia, who shared a rich patrician's bed,
> To Egypt with a gladiator fled.
>
> .   .   .   .   .   .
>
> Without one pang the profligate resigned
> Her husband, sister, sire ; gave to the wind
> Her children's tears ; yea, tore herself away
> (To strike you more)—from Paris and the Play !
> And though, in affluence born, her infant head
> Had pressed the down of an embroidered bed,
> She braved the deep (she long had braved her fame ;
> But this is little—to the courtly dame)
> And, with undaunted breast, the changes bore,
> Of many a sea, the swelling and the roar.

To win such glorious triumphs, to make such brilliant
conquests, it was not necessary for the combatants of
the circus to have the beauty of an Adonis.   It was
their profession that the ladies loved.   For Juvenal
continues :

> But by what youthful charms, what shape, what air,
> Was Hippia won ? The wanton well might dote !
> For the sweet Sergius long had scraped his throat,
> Long looked for leave to quit the public stage,
> Maimed in his limbs, and verging now to age.
> Add, that his face was battered and decayed ;
> The helmet on his brow huge galls had made,
> A wen deformed his nose, of monstrous size,
> And sharp rheum trickled from his bloodshot eyes ;
> But then he was a swordsman ! that alone.
> Made every charm and every grace his own ;
> That made him dearer than her nuptial vows,
> Dearer than country, sister, children, spouse—
> 'Tis blood they love ; let Sergius quit the sword,
> And he'll appear, at once—so like her lord !

Did not the women, by their attitude of adoration

toward prize-fighters, supply young men in quest of fortune with a very strong motive for scorning danger and public opinion ? And for many youths was it not a pleasure merely to shock staid and proper people? The Roman patrician, who found himself in the first years of the empire no longer important, sought for means to make himself talked about ; many a young noble, who bore a name honored in the ancient re-public, experienced a strange delight in herding with the rabble, and tried to win celebrity by the excess of his degradation. So it was not unusual for repre-sentatives of the aristocracy to descend into the arena. Such a one was Gracchus, whom Juvenal in one of his satires describes :

The aristocracy in the arena.

Gracchus.

Gracchus steps forth : No sword his thigh invests—
No helmet, shield—such armor he detests,
Detests and spurns ; and impudently stands,
With the poised net and trident in his hands.
The foe advances—lo ! a cast he tries,
But misses, and in frantic terror flies
Round the thronged Cirque ; and, anxious to be known,
Lifts his bare face, with many a piteous moan.
" 'Tis he ! 'tis he !—I know the Salian vest,
With golden fringes, pendant from the breast ;
The Salian bonnet, from whose pointed crown
The glittering ribbons float redundant down.
O spare him, spare ! "—The brave pursuer heard
And, blushing, stopped the chase ; for he preferred
Wounds, death itself, to the contemptuous smile,
Of conquering one so noble, and—so vile !

For those who sought neither the love of women nor the notoriety of degradation, the desire of gain was a sufficient motive to recommend to them the gladiator's profession. Through it they could speedily make their fortunes ; and although some discharged gladiators, probably lawless by nature, tramped the highways as

Fortunes made by gladiators.

beggars, many others who preferred a regular life retired after having made their fortunes into some beautiful country house.

In spite of all precautions, the games of the arena
became so wonderfully popular, the destruction of men
was on so large a scale, that sometimes combatants
were lacking. Then the laws which regulated their
recruital were unscrupulously disregarded. Conscrip-
tions and arbitrary imperial acts were resorted to. The
number of criminals figuring in the arenas of the time is
so great in fact that it excites our suspicion as to the
justice of the decisions by which they had been condemned. Agrippa, king of the Jews, produced in the
amphitheater of Beirut 1,400 wretches, all accused of
capital crimes, and Hadrian, upon one occasion, made
300 fight. The judges of the time would have had
their hands full if they had been obliged to observe all
the legal forms in passing sentence upon such multitudes. The judicial proceedings must then have been
very summary ; and often sentences were executed
before being pronounced to avoid loss of time.

For the training of those who chose the profession
of gladiator, schools were early established. Under
Domitian four such schools were founded—the Great
School, the Gallic School, the Dacian School, and the
School for Beast-fighters. These schools were carefully supervised and conducted on scientific principles.
Besides the sleeping apartments for the pupils (and
what pupils !) they contained each one an arsenal, a
workshop for manufacturing arms, and, what was very
essential, a chamber in which to lay out the dead. A
large faculty of instructors and officers of administration
was connected with each institution. These strange
schools were all under the control of the emperor, who

usually appointed for superintendents men of equestrian rank, and often retired military officers.

A school at Pompeii.

Some of these gladiatorial schools were located outside of Rome. There was one at Capua, one at Præneste, and one at Alexandria. One has been excavated at Pompeii. It is a vast quadrangular area, 973 feet long by 139 feet wide, surrounded by chambers about ten feet square, without windows, opening upon the court within. These cells, seventy in number, belonged to the gladiators. There is no trace of comfort about them.

The discipline of the schools.

The discipline of these schools was very severe. The men who devoted themselves to the business of prize fighting were likely to be dangerous. So when not performing upon the arena they were disarmed and kept in strict confinement. Soldiers were employed to maintain order ; every infraction of the rules was severely punished, often by the application of the whip or of hot irons ; and we cannot suppose that the wretches who were subjected to this treatment found adequate compensation for so much suffering in the careful provisions that were made to keep them in good physical condition.

Grading system in the schools.

It was probably as a precaution against revolt among the pupils of these schools that they were compelled constantly to practise gymnastic exercises. They were frequently subjected to physical tests, and they were graded according to their skill and their endurance. Thus there was established among them a sort of hierarchy. In the lowest rank were the novices, the recruits, who could only lunge at the wall ; with heavy, blunt swords they had to thrust against a manikin. Later, when they had been tried in a real combat, if they acquitted themselves honorably they were rewarded with a rectangular plate bearing the date of their advancement, and henceforth they were veterans. Through later achievements they rose in rank step by step.

In the equipment of gladiators and in their manner of fighting there was great variety. To enumerate and describe the fifteen kinds of gladiators who ordinarily appeared in the arena belongs rather to a treatise on archæology than to a history of manners. Without trying, then, to give the complete catalogue, we shall be satisfied with indicating the principal kinds. There were the *Andabatæ*, who wore helmets without any aperture for the eyes, so that they afforded mirth to the spectators by fighting blindfold ; the *Dimachæri*, who used two swords ; the *Equestres*, mail-clad horsemen, like the medieval knights, who rushed against each other across the arena ; the *Essedarii*, who, mounted in chariots, hurled missiles at each other, or alighted to engage in hand-to-hand sword combat ; the *Hoplomachi*, whose entire bodies, with the exception of the breast, were protected by heavy armor. Foreign gladiators used their national weapons, and fought in the fashion of their own country. Surely the sovereign people had the opportunity of becoming familiar with the various ways in which people killed each other.

As the day approached when a gladiatorial spectacle was to take place, the donors of the entertainment neglected no means of advertising it. Handbills gave to the people all the details which might interest or attract them. The following announcement, for instance, has been discovered at Pompeii : "The gladiators of the ædile A. Suettius Curius will fight May 31st at Pompeii. There will be beast-fighting, and the spectators will be well sheltered by an awning." This

Methods of fighting.

Handbills.

last assurance was very important, for sometimes it happened that the pleasure of the occasion would be interfered with by the rain or the hot sun.   So when a

"Ave, Cæsar, Imperator."   From a painting by Gerome.

donor could not take the precaution that A. Suettius Curius took, he inserted in his handbill the clause, "if the weather permits."

Before the
combat.

The day before the combat the gladiators sat down to a public feast.   This was the prelude to the spectacle, more interesting for the observer than the spectacle itself.   What a sight they were !   Those who had not yet lost all human feelings would bid farewell to their beloved ones, while the others, who had been brutalized by their occupation, would gorge themselves with the meats and wines, careless of the morrow.   At the appointed hour they all descended into the arena.   In full dress they passed in procession before the donor of the entertainment, at Rome before the emperor, whom they saluted in the famous words, "Cæsar, those who are about to die salute thee."   Then an

officer examined their swords to see if they were sufficiently sharp, and this formality concluded the spectacle began.

First there was sham fighting, exhibitions of skilful
fencing. Soon the trumpets gave the awful signal for
the slaughter to begin, and the conflict was taken up in
earnest to the sound of horns, fifes, and flutes ; such
music, well worthy of accompanying such a spectacle,
must have produced discords which would have grated
upon sensitive ears. By turns appeared the different
kinds of combatants which we have enumerated, and
also others whose equipment and methods of fighting
were amusing by reason of their oddity ; for instance,
there were the *Retiarii*, or net-fighters, who were provided with a net to cast about their antagonists, so as to
entangle them in its meshes before attempting to stab
them.

When a combatant is seriously wounded and unable
to defend himself longer, his life or death depends upon
the pleasure of the president, who usually allows the
people to decide the fate of the miserable man.
Stretched upon the ground, the wounded gladiator
raises his finger as a token of submission ; the crowd
shout, clap their hands, wave handkerchiefs—he is
saved ; they depress their thumbs in silence—the conqueror plunges his sword into the helpless body of the
victim.

In the intervals between these horrible dramas,
attendants rush in, drag off the corpse by a hook to an
apartment for the slain, turn over the bloody earth of
the arena with spades, and sprinkle fresh sand.

The public were not always satisfied with single combats ; and the emperors sometimes gave them the
pleasure of witnessing wholesale slaughters. For such

an exhibition the amphitheater was too small, and larger places were sought. Julius Cæsar gave, in the Circus Maximus, the representation of a battle in which five hundred foot soldiers and three hundred cavalry-men took part, besides twenty elephants, carrying upon their backs towers filled with armed men. Claudius, after the conquest of the island of Britain in 44 A. D., gave a representation on the Campus Martius of the taking and the sack of a village of that country. He himself presided over this . exhibition, dressed in a

"POLLICE VERSO."   From a painting by Gerome.

military cloak. Claudius understood well how to obtain good scenic effects, for, according to Suetonius, he succeeded in producing an illusion of reality.

The historians of the empire frequently mention mock sea-fights. The people insisted upon witnessing all forms of death. Julius Cæsar, Augustus, Caligula, and Nero gave spectacles of this kind. But, according to Martial, nothing surpassed the magnificence of the mock sea-fights of Domitian and of Titus, as the following epigram of his bears witness :

Thetis and Galatea have beheld in the waves wild animals previously unknown to them. Triton has seen chariots glowing along the foaming ocean course, and thought the steeds of his master were passing before him ; and Nereus, while he was preparing fierce contests with bold vessels, shrunk from going on foot through the liquid ways. Whatever is seen in the circus and the amphitheater, the rich lake of Cæsar has shown to thee. Let Fucinus and the ponds of the dire Nero be vaunted no more ; and let ages to come remember but this one sea-fight.

In enumerating the different kinds of gladiators, we purposely omitted to mention the beast-fighters. Their profession deserves a separate study.

Early in the history of Rome we find isolated instances of criminals who were punished by being torn to pieces by wild animals. In 186 B. C., M. Fulvius Nobilior, who had collected a large number of lions and panthers, was the first to give as a show a combat in which beasts took part. Such exhibitions soon became very common and exceedingly popular, and they were classed among the regular spectacles, like the games of the arena, to which they served often as a prelude.

Origin of beast-fighting.

The conquest of Asia and of Africa must have been an important factor in the development of this form of amusement. In these recently subdued countries vast expeditions were organized to procure for the amphitheater curious or ferocious animals. A new profession, even, sprang into existence—that of hunting, and the emperor Macrinus, before his elevation to the throne, is supposed to have engaged in the importation of animals. Certain it is that a very general interest was aroused in the catching of wild beasts, as many treatises

Hunting becomes a profession.

on the subject, which are still extant, bear witness.

Nemesianus describes the method of catching bears, stags, wolves, and foxes in nets whose meshes are concealed with feathers; Ælianus tells how to take panthers in Mauritania, by means of traps in which spoiled meat is used for bait; Appianus describes another method for capturing the same animal; Achilles Tatius, the Alexandrine, shows how the hippopotamus may be allured into a pit; and Diodorus informs his readers how the same animal may be harpooned, and also how the crocodile may be caught in a net; Pausanias describes the hunting of the bison, and Arrianus the lassoing of the wild ass in Numidia by horsemen.

Absence of the scientific spirit among the Romans. Hunting we see had become an art at this time, and it seems surprising that natural history under such favorable circumstances did not make more progress. There is scarcely any fact which proves in a more conclusive manner than this the absence of the scientific spirit among the Romans. What excellent opportunities for observation a naturalist would have had in the imperial parks and menageries! The collection of the emperor Phillipus, 248 A. D., contained thirty-two elephants, ten elks, ten tigers, sixty lions, thirty leopards, ten hyenas, one rhinoceros, one hippopotamus, ten giraffes, twenty wild asses, and forty wild horses, besides other varieties of animals. The Romans of this time saw many specimens of rare animals, which have not been seen since in Europe until recently. While the Zoological Gardens of London and the Jardin des Plantes of Paris have experienced much difficulty in obtaining one hippopotamus, the emperor Commodus, as a mere pastime, killed four in one day. In the year 80 A. D., at the dedication of the great Flavian amphitheater, Titus exhibited 9,000 wild animals of

various kinds, and Trajan, at his second Dacian celebration, 106 A. D., produced in the arena 11,000
beasts.

Combats in which animals took part occurred in the
morning, beginning at dawn. Lions were matched Beast-fights.
against tigers, elephants against bulls ; a rhinoceros
sometimes was made to contend with a bear, cranes
fought each other, and wild boars did likewise. But
the interest of the spectators did not rise to its height
until men entered the lists against wild beasts.

The beast-fighters were divided into two classes : the
beast-fighters proper and the hunters. They were The beast-
drawn from the same sources as were the gladiators— fighters.
from among prisoners of war, criminals, slaves, and a
few of them were volunteers. They also had schools in
which they received their training.

The beast-fighters proper appeared in the arena
dressed in a simple tunic, without helmet, buckler, or
cuirass. Sometimes even their right arm was bound ;
the only weapon allowed them was a lance, or rarely a
sword. The hunters, who seem to have occupied a
superior rank in the hierarchy, were better armed. The hunters.
The Parthians, who were very skilful archers, were
probably classed among the hunters, as well as specialists like the bull-fighters.

Sometimes it happened that the spectators had to
wait too long for the sight of death and their interest Undisguised
flagged. There was a very simple remedy for this. brutality.
A criminal was bound to a stake, and the people feasted
their eyes on the victim's agonies as he was torn by the
wild beasts. Sometimes also (for cruelty is ingenious)
the Romans indulged their brutal taste for reality by
making some bloody spectacle represent a mythological
tale. The pantomime of Orpheus is an illustration of

The pantomime of Orpheus.

this form of spectacle. The part of the Thracian poet was taken by a condemned criminal. He appeared coming out of a hole in the ground which was supposed to be Hades. All nature seemed enchanted by his music ; the trees and the rocks moved from their places and followed him ; the wild animals, as if tamed, surrounded him. But soon, when this idyllic scene had lasted long enough, a bear was let loose, which fell upon the victim and tore him to pieces.

Exhibitions of trained animals.

Between these tragic spectacles interludes were often given of a different character. Sometimes they consisted in the exhibition of trained animals. Animal trainers were numerous at Rome from the time of Augustus and even before. Was not Mark Antony seen riding with the courtesan Citheris in a chariot drawn by lions? We may say, and we say it without much regret, that the art of training animals has progressed but little since this time. What prodigies of patience must have been required to teach lions to catch hares in the arena, and then to play with them as a cat does with a mouse, and finally to let them go !

GREAVE.

Stags were taught to obey the rein and panthers to bear the yoke. Peaceful antelopes were taught to be fierce, and a pair of these animals, so mild by nature, would fight together until one or both fell dead. With the elephants especially wonders were

Feats performed by elephants.

accomplished. They could exhibit feats of dancing and

of rope-walking. Four elephants were once trained to carry a fifth. And Pliny the Elder narrates that out of a company of elephants that were being trained together, one of the pupils, who was slower to learn than the others, was discovered one night repeating his lesson.

However strange it may seem, we cannot deny the fact that the Romans were passionately fond of bloody games. Juvenal, who cherishes so many noble sentiments, waxes very indignant when a certain patrician enters a gladiatorial combat. Is it because the satirist has a horror of bloodshed? By no means ; he thinks that this patrician dishonors his noble name, not his humanity. Pliny the Younger, whose soul was so full of sweet and tender feelings, knows of no better way for a husband afflicted by the death of his wife to honor her dear memory than for him to give a gladiatorial show.

Fondness of the Romans for bloody games.

You did perfectly right [he says in one of his letters] in promising a gladiatorial combat to our good friends, the citizens of Verona, who have long loved, looked up to, and honored you ; while it was from that city too you received that amiable object of your most tender affection, your late excellent wife. And since you owed some monument or public representation to her memory, what other spectacle could you have exhibited more appropriate to the occasion? Besides, you were so unanimously pressed to do so that to have refused would have looked more like hardness than resolution. The readiness, too, with which you granted their petition and the magnificent manner in which you performed it is very much to your honor ; for a greatness of soul is seen in these smaller instances, as well as in matters of higher moment. I wish the African panthers, which you had largely provided for this purpose, had arrived on the day appointed, but though they were delayed by the stormy weather, the obligation to you is equally the same, since it was not your fault that they were not exhibited. Farewell.

Pliny's approval of a gladiatorial show.

Pliny, in his panegyric addressed to Trajan, praises the emperor for having revived the taste of the people for these frightful spectacles :

Spectacles have been given, not those characterized by effeminacy and corruption which tend to enervate and degrade the mind, but those which teach men to bear wounds with courage and to scorn death, by showing, even in slaves and criminals, the love of glory and the desire for victory. And what magnificence the emperor has displayed in these games ! With what justice he has presided, entirely free from prejudice ! He has refused nothing that the people asked ; he has offered what they did not ask ; and more than this, he has invited us to express our desires, and then he has anticipated them by pleasant surprises. .

Seneca, perhaps, is the only one at this time who protested against this barbarity ; and, inspired by a feeling of respect for human life, he wrote one of his most eloquent pages.

It happened [he says] that I went to an afternoon entertainment. I was expecting pleasant games, clever jokes, some kind of recreation to rest my eyes, weary with the sight of human blood. What a mistake was mine ! Former contests were child's play. All trifling is put aside and there is nothing but unrelieved assassination. The combatants have no defensive armor ; their naked breasts are exposed. Not a stroke which does not do its work. . . . What is the use of shields? or of skill? Such things only postpone death. In the morning men are thrown as food to the lions and bears, and in the afternoon to the spectators. . . . The issue of every combat is death. . . .

" But," my neighbor says to me, " that man whom you pity was a highway robber."

" Very well, let him hang."

" But he killed a man."

" Let him be condemned to death, in his turn. He deserves it. But you, what have you done, wretch, that you should be condemned to behold such a spectacle ? "

Then the people cry out,

"Kill him! strike him! burn him! Why does he meet the sword so timidly? Why strike back with so little courage? Why die so reluctantly?"

They inflict upon each other wound after wound.

"Bravo! Aim at the breast. Give it to him!"

At last there is an intermission in the spectacle.

"While we are waiting, let's have the men killed, that no time be lost."

Ah! Romans, do you not understand that evil deeds return upon those who commit them?

These noble sentiments, clothed in such strong and emotional language, will be expressed later by Christian preachers and writers. But not a man of them will make a more stirring appeal than the last philosopher of antiquity, not one will proclaim with more eloquence the great principle "man is sacred to man."

The loss of liberty, this taste for coarse or bloody representations of reality, scarcely allowed the true theater to exist under the empire.

The decadence of the drama had already begun toward the close of the republic. As the small farm-ers disappeared the division grew more and more marked between the two classes who listened to the tragedies of Ennius and of Pacuvius, and the comedies of Plautus and of Terence; the knights became more refined and more rare, and the common people coarser and more numerous. The "Clytemnestra" of Attius was tolerated only because the action called for an interminable procession of mules; the attraction in "The Trojan Horse" of Nævius was the exhibition of three thousand craters (mixing bowls for wine). A certain actor would be applauded before he opened his mouth, because he wore a violet robe, dyed at Tarentum. The costume and the scenery were what drew people to the theater. The pleasure to the ears was nothing, the pleasure to the eyes was everything.

The theaters of Rome.

And yet Rome had three magnificent theaters : that of Pompey, which seated as many as 40,000 spectators, that of Balbus, which seated 30,000, and that of Marcellus, which seated 20,000. Dramatic representations were frequently given ; on festival days probably all the theaters were in use at once. But these entertainments were much less popular than those of the circus or the arena ; the actors were not such favorites as the charioteers and the gladiators.

But the donors of the dramatic representations did not scruple to make concessions to the taste of their audiences. There were no plays which made a study of character or a profound and delicate analysis of the passions. An attempt to introduce such plays would have been useless.

The two varieties of the drama which prevailed under the empire, the only ones which the public seem to have tolerated, were the Atellan and the mime.

The Atellan was already popular at Rome about the

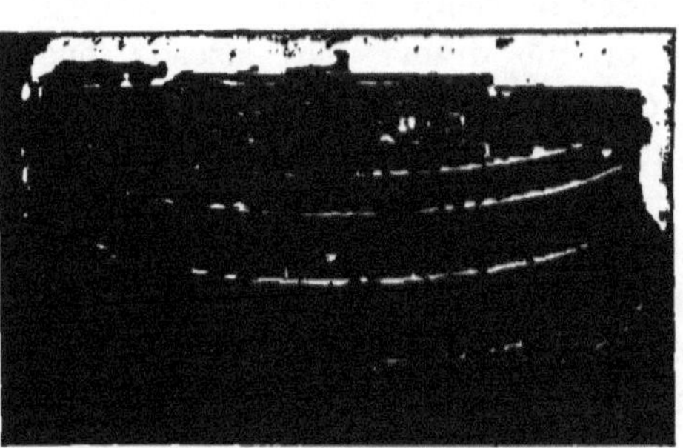

THEATER AT HERCULANEUM. Restoration.

The Atellan.

second century before Christ. It was of Etruscan origin, and it was easier to represent on the stage than the farces and comedies of Greek origin. The Atellan, briefly, was a comic play in which the dialogue was largely extemporaneous. The actors were supplied with a certain theme and then improvised their parts.

The Atellan is the prototype of what is called in Italy to-day the *Commedia dell' arte*. Furthermore, the characters in the Atellan were all masked. The Roman youths therefore could appear in it as actors without losing caste.

About the time of Sulla two men of talent, Pomponius and Novius, wrote Atellans in a truly literary style; after this the fortune of the Atellan was secure. It had won the favor of the people, and it kept it until the end of the empire.

Pomponius and Novius.

It is not difficult to comprehend the popularity of the Atellans if we consider the subjects which they treated. They represented scenes from country life and from the lives of workmen and shopkeepers, and this could not fail to please the low tastes of the public which henceforth laid down the law to the theater. Some of the titles of these dramas have been preserved : "The Cowherd," "The Vintagers," "The Baker," "The Sick Pig," "The Fishermen," "The Fullers," "The Slave Merchant," etc. There was a great deal of caricature in these plays and the wit was broad and vulgar.

The subjects of the Atellans.

However, the freedom of the Atellans was reserve and good taste, charming elegance, as Donatus, the teacher of Saint Jerome, says, compared to the obscenity of the mimes.

The mimes, like the Atellans, became popular about the time of Sulla. In the time of Julius Cæsar and of Augustus flourished the celebrated mimographers Decimus Laberius, Publius Syrus, and C. Mattius. These writers, by their talent, elevated the farce to the dignity of literature, but they could not overcome the power of tradition, and obscenity seemed to be the law of this species of composition. Ovid, who certainly does not

The indecency of the mimes.

err by excess of prudery, expresses indignation upon seeing women at these representations :

It is not simply that the language defiles their ears ; their eyes become accustomed to the most indecent scenes. If a faithless wife has invented a new trick to deceive her husband they applaud, and the palm is awarded to her.

Absence of plot. The mimes can scarcely be said to have had plots. They were burlesque scenes, abounding in coarse humor and practical jokes. A lover, perhaps, would be represented caught hiding in a closet ; he would be dragged out, and blows and kicks would bring the scene to a termination.

Actresses. Besides the brutality of the public, which would be a sufficient explanation of the popularity of this kind of amusement, the presence of women among the actors contributed largely to its success. This feature was a unique exception to the rule of the ancient theater. In all the other exhibitions men only took part. Actresses have always and everywhere exercised a strange fascination ; and the actresses in the mimes, being less numerous than those in our modern comedies, must have been all the more an attraction. Of course they had their adventures. Cicero once pleaded for a young man who had eloped with one of them. And, as is usually the case, their adventures prepared the way for their theatrical success, and their theatrical success for their adventures.

The cast of characters. The list of characters to be taken by the actors and actresses of the mimes presented very much the same variety that we find in connection with modern theatrical companies. There was the eldest son, the father of noble rank, the rich man, the scoffer, and the simpleton.

While these new kinds of dramatic representation

flourished, the ancient tragedy declined. One reason for this was that it received no encouragement or support from the government. For had it not, in the hands of Pacuvius and of Attius, stirred up republican sentiment? Moreover, the people had lost their taste for tragedy. They had no longer any interest in the sublime, the poetical, or the ideal. From the reign of Augustus tragic poetry was only a pretext for the display of stage scenery. Horace has remarked upon this decadence. A little later tragedy became nothing but an exercise in declamation. An actor would select from the work of an ancient poet some brilliant, lyric monologue, and deliver it, isolated from its connection, just as with us a singer will give, at a concert, a selection from an opera. So slight was the interest in the subject matter of the drama that the actors often declaimed in Greek ; a few of their audience, doubtless, knew enough Greek to misunderstand it, but they would loudly applaud.

The decline of the ancient tragedy.

Declamation.

The classic comedy was as much neglected as the tragedy. No new comedies were written, but the plays of Plautus, of Terence, and of Afranius were given now and then. They, however, were only enjoyed by literary people, or people of refinement with a taste for the archaic. Whatever pleasure the general public took in them depended, not upon the poet, but upon the acting.

Ancient comedy neglected.

The mimes attained a marvelous popularity under the empire ; they even came to constitute a distinct form of spectacle by themselves. The art of the pantomimist won the admiration of its most vehement critics and triumphed over the opposition of the partisans of the ancient theater. Under Nero, the philosopher Demetrius expressed the greatest disapproval of panto-

The popularity of the mimes.

The pantomim-
ist Paris.

mimists, and declared them incapable of producing any effect without the accompaniment of choirs and music. But after having seen Paris, the celebrated panto-mimist, he was obliged to confess that he had been mistaken, and he made honorable amends to the artist for his previous hostility.

Schools of
pantomimists.

There were regular schools of pantomimists. Bathyl-lus, the Alexandrine, and the Cilician Pylades were each the founder of a school. Even the great poets did not disdain writing ballet songs for them. Lucan is supposed to have written fourteen such songs.

The success
of actors.

Although not so much raved over as the charioteers of the circus and the gladiators of the arena, the actors of the theater knew something of the intoxication of fame and the triumphs of popularity. Their success often brought them wealth. Vespasian gave 4,000 sesterces (about $170) to each of the actors who took part in the festival celebrating the restoration of the Theater of Marcellus; and yet Vespasian had not a reputation for generosity. But the Roman actors preferred the satisfaction of self-love to the enjoyment of riches. They de-sired success at any price ; and if they could not win it by their talent, they resorted to means which are still employed. Nero, who aspired to be an actor, had skilfully organized the claque. According to his plan there would be distributed over the theater 5,000 vigorous men, divided into squads, each one of

GLADIATOR'S HELMET.

which had as captain a Roman

knight under a salary of 4,000 sesterces (about $170). He had devised a method by which these hired applauders might distinguish between the various degrees of their mercenary enthusiasm. Moderate approval was expressed by ordinary hand-clapping ; when a livelier enjoyment seemed called for, a sharp, almost metallic sound was produced by a peculiar method of striking the flats of the hands together ; the highest admiration was signified by clapping with the hands formed into hollows, creating thus a full, explosive sound. The actors imitated the imperial example, and according to their means made sure of a cordial reception. As far as possible they would enlist voluntary partisans and then hire professional applauders. Factions were sometimes the cause of disturbances and even of violence in the theaters.

Romans is to-day a slang term among the French for hired clappers. Their profession sprang into existence in the Eternal City and there also it became an art.

In the various spectacles which we have mentioned there was not much to please the taste of literary people. To supply this lack public readings were made a regular form of entertainment.

When an optimate, for instance, who has indulged a mania for writing, desires a public for his works, he dismantles some room in his house, puts up a platform, and arranges seats for an audience.. Then all his friends are invited to listen to a reading from his works. His freedmen, clients, and slaves, seated on the rear benches, are responsible for keeping the enthusiasm of the audience at a proper pitch.

Let us illustrate once more how such entertainments were arranged. Rubrenus Lappa, a needy poet, desires to make his verses known. Maculonus, his patron, puts at his disposal a room of his elegant mansion. Posters are scattered over the city announcing the place and the hour of the recitation. When the time comes, Rubrenus Lappa, who for the occasion has donned his best clothes, ascends the platform, unrolls his manuscript, and begins to read it, after having swallowed a glass of warm water to clear his voice. Rubrenus is loudly applauded. The result will be that lovers of literature will go and buy his book, when it appears for sale in the bookstores of the Vicus Tuscus. If he had been hissed, the poor man would have had to pawn his mantle and such articles of furniture as a needy poet might possess.

Others read their works in public in order to have an opportunity, before publishing, to correct and modify them in accordance with criticisms which may be offered. Pliny belongs to this class.

Every author [he writes] has his particular reasons for reciting his works ; mine, I have often said, are, in order, if any error should have escaped my own observation (as no doubt they do escape it sometimes), to have it pointed out to me. I cannot therefore but be surprised to find (what your letter assures me) that there are some who blame me for reciting my speeches ; unless, perhaps, they are of opinion that this is the single species of composition that ought to be held exempt from any correction. If so, I would willingly ask them why they allow (if indeed they do allow) that history may be recited, since it is a work which ought to be devoted to truth, not ostentation? or why tragedy, as it is composed for action and the stage, not for being read to a private audience? or lyric poetry, as it is not a reader, but a chorus of voices and instruments that it requires? They will reply, perhaps, that in the instances referred to custom has made the practice in question usual ; I should be glad to know, then, if they think the person who first introduced this practice is to be condemned? Besides, the rehearsal of speeches is no unprecedented thing either with us or the Grecians.

Still, perhaps, they will insist that it can answer no purpose to recite a speech which has already been delivered. True; if one were immediately to repeat the very same speech word for word, and to the very same audience; but if you make several additions and alterations, if your audience is composed partly of the same and partly of different persons, and the recital is at some distance of time, why is there less propriety in rehearsing your speech than in publishing it? "But it is difficult," the objectors urge, "to give satisfaction to an audience by the mere recital of a speech"; *that* is a consideration which concerns the particular skill and pains of the person who rehearses, but by no means holds good against recitation in general.

Pliny is sincere without doubt when he speaks thus; but it seems probable that in general criticism was less desired than praise, and readers, no doubt, found those listeners most agreeable who understood this truth. If you wish to make your society pleasant to an author, do not be afraid of embarrassing him with your praise.

Poetry, history, oratory, comedy, and tragedy—all these departments of literature furnished matter for these recitations. Pliny read in public his panegyric addressed to Trajan, and some of his pleas; Statius read his "Silvæ" and extracts from his "Thebaïs." The tragedies attributed to Seneca were probably delivered as recitations, for certainly they were never written to be acted upon the stage; we purposely.

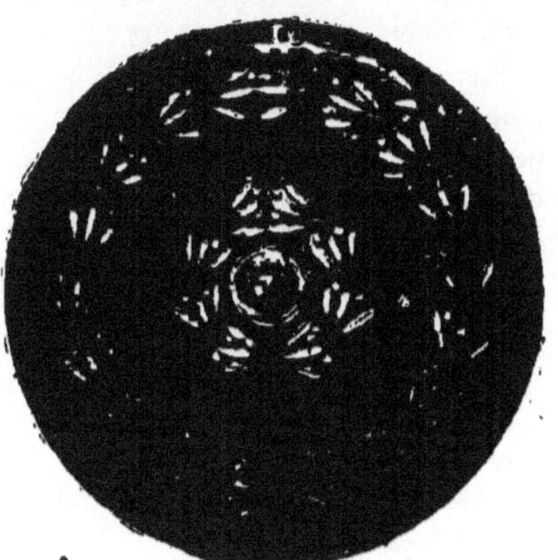

SHIELD.

omitted mentioning them when we were discussing the condition of tragedy under the empire. With their brilliant declamations, their witty aphorisms, and their laborious and cold lyrical strains, they give us a very clear idea of what must have been the taste of those who frequented the recitation halls. These listeners, surfeited by an over culture which prevented them from being surprised into a natural admiration for simple beauties, required to be astonished at the peculiarities of the style and the novelty of the paradoxes. Subtlety, affectation, oddity were not faults in their eyes ; on the contrary, they were merits.

But the time came when both readers and listeners were tired of their amusement and the recitation halls stood empty. Pliny complains of the growing indifference for the public readings, which even in his day was observable.

This year [he writes] has produced a plentiful crop of poets ; during the whole month of April scarcely a day has passed on which we have not been entertained with the recital of some poem. It is a pleasure to me to find that a taste for polite literature still exists, and that men of genius do come forward and make themselves known, notwithstanding the lazy attendance they get for their pains. The greater part of the audience sit in the lounging places, gossip away their time there, and are perpetually sending to inquire whether the author has made his entrance yet, whether he has got through the preface, or whether he has almost finished the piece. Then at length they saunter in with an air of the greatest indifference, nor do they condescend to stay through the recital, but go out before it is over, some slyly and stealthily, others again with perfect freedom and unconcern. And yet our fathers can remember how Claudius Cæsar, walking one day in the palace and hearing a great shouting, inquired the cause ; and being informed that Nonianus was reciting a composition of his, went immediately to the place, and agreeably surprised the author with his presence. But now, were one to bespeak the attendance of the idlest man living, and remind him of the appointment ever so often, or ever so long beforehand, either he would not come at all, or, if he did, would grumble about having "lost a day"! for no other reason but because he had not lost it. So much the more do those authors deserve our encouragement and applause who have resolution to persevere in their studies, and to read out their compositions in spite of this apathy or arrogance.

This indifference was destined to go on increasing. The literary activity of the Romans gradually declined, until the day when their language and literature perished, and in their place sprang up the languages and literatures of modern Western Europe.

Decline in literary activity.

CHAPTER IX.

TRAVELING.

THE splendor of the Eternal City, the magnificence of its buildings, the gaiety of its festivals, the renown of its professors and of its artists attracted strangers to it in crowds. But while the world flowed into Rome, Rome itself spread out over the world.

In our day traveling has become common and very popular. The safety of the roads, the rapidity of the means of transportation, the constant progress toward unity in manners and customs, all this tempts us to leave home, and again enables us to feel at home wherever we go.

The condition of things was the same for the Romans about the second century of the Christian era. To the period of war had succeeded the period of organization. After having conquered the world, Rome "pacified" it.

All parts of the empire were united by a magnificent system of roads.

You have [said the rhetorician Aristides] measured the earth from end to end, you have spanned the rivers with bridges, penetrated the mountains with carriage roads, peopled the deserts, and established everywhere order and discipline. There is no need now for a descriptive catalogue of the earth with an account of the customs and laws of all the nations; for you have become guides for the whole world; you have opened all its doors and given to each man the opportunity to see everything with his own eyes.

Hyperbole is a figure dear to the rhetorician Aristides; but there is no exaggeration in the above passage.

The network of Roman ways covered in truth the entire empire. Everywhere have been found traces of these marvelous constructions. Furthermore, in order to facilitate traveling, road-books were published con- _{Guide-books.} taining maps and information as to stations, distances, and places where one could stay over night. On the site of Vicarello in Etruria were found, among other objects, three silver traveling-cups, shaped like mile-stones, and having engraved upon them a list of stations and distances from Gades to Rome.

The science of geography was dawning. Strabo, whose life extended into the reign of Tiberius, had written his great geographical work, which is a vast and useful repertory. The expression of Aristides did not exceed the truth; the Romans had in fact become guides for the entire world.

The Romans were not satisfied with comfort, they desired rapidity in travel. State post-houses, estab-lished upon the model of the posts of the ancient Persian monarchy, furnished to functionaries of the gov-ernment and to those who bore authorizations from the emperor, horses and carriages which made nearly five miles an hour. Private individuals relied for their accommodations upon private enterprise. Convey-ances were stationed at the gates of towns and at inns. Rich companies kept, for the use of the public, beasts, vehicles, and postilions. You could hire a four-wheeled carriage, or, if you were not very particular about your comfort, a two-wheeled cabriolet. These hired equi-pages were, as might be expected, slower than the post, for the horses were not so good and the postilions, not being accountable to the state, delayed without scruple at the relay stations. It was, however, in a hired carriage that Cæsar traveled the distance of eight hundred miles, which separates Rome from the Rhone —one hundred miles a day. This rapidity astonished his contemporaries, and moderns who have had experience with diligences will share their surprise.

Although traveling by sea was far less common among the ancients than among us, voyages were made with a considerable degree of speed. Spring was the time for setting sail. At this season boats which had been upon the shore all winter were launched by the aid of machines.

According to Pliny the Elder, the prefect Galerus, setting out from the strait of Sicily, reached Alexandria after a seven days' sail. Balbillus made the same trip in six days. In brief, from the items of information that have been left to us upon this subject, we are able to infer that with a favorable wind a ship could make 138 miles a day.

FORTUNE.   Museum of Naples.

We must admit that sea trips were not always free from danger. There were no more pirates, it is true,

Traveling by sea.

Dangers of sea trips.

to interfere with them. The time was past when the corsairs defied the power of Rome, when they carried off the treasure from the Temple of Lacinian Juno at Crotona, and foundered in the very harbor of Ostia a fleet commanded by a consul. Pompey had rid the sea of these bold bandits. Since his day one could sail upon the Mediterranean, even at night, without fear of a dangerous encounter. But the pillagers of wrecked vessels were not so easily disposed of. In spite of severe laws, they multiplied along the coasts and made a living out of their horrible business. Not content with profiting from ships already lost, these rogues often caused wrecks. By false signals they lured vessels upon the rocks and robbed their victims, while pretending to be eager in rescuing them..

Wreckers.

Nor was land-traveling without its dangers. Italy from this time is the classic land of highway robbery, which had begun to flourish immediately after the civil wars. Bands which were recruited from deserting soldiers, fugitive slaves, and refractory gladiators held entire provinces in terror. Augustus and Tiberius took energetic measures to secure safety ; troops were sent to destroy the brigands. But it does not appear that such efforts were ever crowned with success. In the time of Septimius Severus, Felix Bulla, a famous robber, at the head of a band of six hundred men, ravaged all Italy ; he was in the eyes of the people a romantic character ; they talked everywhere of his daring deeds and his generosity upon occasion. It is a singular fact, to which many similar examples may be found in modern times, that people took his part against the police. Was not Fra Diavolo dearer to the Italian peasants than the militia? Finally, to establish his legendary character, Bulla perished a victim of a

Highway robbery.

The popularity of bandits.

woman's treason. Betrayed by his mistress, he ended his life in the arena. Other bandits, more obscure, could never be dislodged from their retreats in the Pontine marshes, in Sardinia, and in the Gallinarian forest near Cumæ. These were the general headquarters of the bandits, as Calabria was at the commencement of our century.

The vicinity of the capital offered naturally more security. Still it was considered somewhat imprudent to venture at night, if one carried money or valuable objects, upon the highways even in the suburbs of Rome. Juvenal, in one of his satires, says :

Vicinity of the capital unsafe at night.

> The traveler freighted with a little wealth,
> Sets forth at night, and wins his way by stealth ;
> Even then, he fears the bludgeon and the blade,
> And starts and trembles at a rush's shade.

We must not, then, accept without reserve the enthusiastic words of the rhetorician Aristides :

> To-day is not each one able to go wherever he pleases ? Are not all the harbors full of movement ? Do not the mountains afford to travelers the same security that towns do to their inhabitants ? Are not all the country regions full of charm ? Is not fear banished everywhere ?

But we should guard against forming an exaggerated impression of the fear felt for the bandits. When travelers set out, the possibility of being robbed on their way was scarcely more in their minds than in ours the possibility of a railroad accident when we take the steam-cars.

Nothing, however, would have been able to check this impulse which had taken possession of the Roman population to go outside of Italy and wander over the world. Cosmopolitism had become almost a favorite doctrine ; the minds of men were full of the idea that

Cosmopolitism.

Rome had established the unity of the world. Poets enthusiastically sang this in their verses. Lucan praises the man "who does not believe that he is born for himself but for the human race and who is inspired by the sacred love of the world." *Lucan.*

Another poet, Prudentius, exclaims : *Prudentius.*

If Rome has bound us, it is with the cord which makes us brothers.

And Claudianus says : *Claudianus.*

Under her pacific government we should all find everywhere our country, we should be willing to move our homes from place to place, we should be able to make a pleasure trip to Thule and to penetrate into retreats formerly bristling with terrors, to drink at our pleasure the waters of the Rhone or those of the Orontes ; in short, we should all form a single nation.

We meet with this idea on every page of Seneca's treatises. The nations are our brothers ; let the boundaries be effaced, let the barriers be removed. *Seneca.*

How ridiculous is man with his frontiers ! The Dacian must not cross the Ister, the Strymon serves as a boundary for Thrace, the Euphrates is a barrier against the Parthians, the Danube separates Sarmatia from the Roman Empire, the Germans must not cross the Rhine, the Pyrenees lift their summits between Spain and the Gauls, vast deserts extend between Egypt and Ethiopia. If ants should be endowed with the intelligence of man, would not they also divide up a garden plot into a hundred provinces ? We must abandon these petty divisions ; we must enlarge our horizon ; we must extend our affections to the entire world. Man should regard the earth as the common habitation of the human race. All that you see constitutes a unit ; we are the members of a great body. . . . I was not born for a corner of the earth ; but my country is the world, and Rome is our common fatherland. *Boundaries between nations to be effaced.*

These are not the hyperboles of a poet or the

humanitarian reveries of a philosopher ; the words which we have just quoted express so well the general sentiment that we find an echo of them in the body of Roman law. "Rome," we read in the Digest, "is the universal country."

Let us add that material prosperity reigns everywhere, that the earth is, as it were, adorned and embellished. Even the enemies of this pagan civilization are compelled to bear witness to its benefits.

Certainly [wrote Tertullian] the world becomes each day more beautiful and more magnificent. No corner has remained inaccessible ; every spot is known and frequented, and is the scene or the object of business transactions. Explore the deserts lately famous, verdure covers them. The tilled field has conquered the forest ; wild beasts retreat before the flocks of domestic animals. The sands are cultivated, rock is broken up, swamps are transformed into dry land. There are more towns now than there were houses formerly. Who now fears an island? Who shudders at a shoal? You are sure to find everywhere a dwelling, everywhere a nation, a state, everywhere life. . . .

How resist the desire to enjoy the sight of so many wonders? How deny one's self the pleasure and the pride of taking a tour through this world which Rome has made after her own image? How could a Roman bear to remain shut up in his small native locality instead of enjoying that universal country which the genius of his people had made his own? Traveling during the two first centuries of the empire and subsequently was therefore as common as in our time. If one was compelled to change his place of abode he did so without reluctance. Many people also traveled merely for their own pleasure.

To-day a functionary obliged to take up his residence in a new place always grumbles, even though the change is accompanied with an advance in his salary. It does not appear, however, that officers of state in the time of the Roman Empire were much incommoded by the necessity of moving. And, moreover, we know that these functionaries were somewhat nomadic.

Men in high stations [says Epictetus], senators for instance, cannot root themselves into the ground like plants, but are obliged to travel in order either to issue or to execute commands, and to fulfil official missions concerning military service or the administration of justice.

The nomadic life of Roman functionaries.

Often they had to make considerable journeys ; they were sent from the swamps of Caledonia to the foot of

BRIDGE OVER THE ANIO, A FEW MILES FROM TIBUR.

the Atlas ; from the towns of Syria to the fortified camps of the German provinces. We know of no example of a functionary's refusing to set out. Not a single ancient author has told us that the Roman officials found these journeys too frequent or too wearisome.

The merchants also led a wandering life. We have shown elsewhere that maritime commerce was well developed at Rome. In order to succeed in it, a never-wearied activity was required and an audacity which nothing could disconcert. Probably our modern business men do not possess these qualities in a higher degree than did these ancient merchants. We learn from an inscription that Flavius Zeuxis of Hierapolis boasts of having crossed to Italy seventy-two times. And did not many a merchant push far beyond the limits of the Roman Empire which pretended to embrace the world? Roman merchants were the first to penetrate into India, which was considered in the time of Horace to be the end of the world.

Like the functionaries and like the merchants, invalids obeyed necessity by going abroad. Some went to Egypt to seek health, others to Anticyra, celebrated for the perfection of its hellebore. Still others journeyed toward the famous sanctuaries of Æsculapius, of Isis, or of Serapis.

There they met religious devotees. Pilgrimages are not an invention of Christianity. Ancient piety delighted in them. Crowds from all parts of the known world flocked to Eleusis at the celebration there of the mysteries ; again, in the time of Aulus Gellius, the Pythian games attracted great multitudes ; and there were always many superstitious people who, like Apuleius, traveled from temple to temple, having themselves initiated into all sorts of religious ceremonies " for love of the truth and for duty toward the gods."

Students and professors, pupils and learned men, also traveled much. For from this time people seem to have been convinced that whoever has seen many things retains in mind many things.

Diodorus, Strabo, Pausanias, Dioscorides, and Galien prepared for their great literary works by traveling. When Apuleius had finished his studies at Carthage, the death of his father having made him the possessor of a fortune of about $40,000, he began to travel through Greece, Italy, and the East, by way of completing his education.

But travelers were not always influenced by motives of curiosity alone. As there are in our time ambulant artists, there were under the Roman Empire rhetoricians and philosophers who went from town to town to give instruction in dialectics and in rhetoric for the money that they might make. They considered that people always like whatever is new ; and before their success in one place began to wane as the novelty of their presence there wore off, they moved on to the next place.

Eunapius and Philostratus, in their biographies of the sophists and the philosophers, have left us curious pictures of the strange lives of these itinerant teachers.

Charlatans of eloquence, these rhetoricians had recourse to singular means in order to make sure of success. When one of them arrived in a town, slaves scoured the streets to collect an audience, proclaiming that marvelous things were soon to be uttered by their master. There was sure to be some wealthy amateur of letters who was willing to lend a hall furnished with benches. There at the appointed hour the rhetorician appeared in full dress, followed by a long retinue of supposed admirers. This train was indispensable to him. Good-natured idlers there were in abundance, who thought they would acquire an air of culture by being associated with a literary man and were very willing to form this escort. Sometimes, however, it was composed in a most unexpected manner. A sophist, for instance, landing at Rhodes, enlisted the oarsmen and sailors whom he found at the port, bought them costumes, and after having arrayed them as lovers of noble eloquence should be arrayed, made a magnificent *entrée* into the assembly at the head of this naval army.

After having taken his place on the platform, the orator would pay a studied compliment to his audience, pronounce a panegyric upon the town, and then proceed to treat his chosen subject with a learnedly affected utterance, assuming regulation attitudes like the poses of a dancer.　If his *toga* was elegant, if the gems upon his fingers were brilliant, if his voice was pleasant, his success was won ; every one thought he had handled his subject well ; whether he pronounced a eulogy upon flies, smoke, or baldness mattered little.　The audience, transported, arose, shouting "crowns! crowns!" and rich presents proved afterward to the orator that the enthusiasm was not sterile.

Disciples desirous of learning the secrets of this fine art which was rewarded with such fame and financial profit followed the caravans of these rhetoricians. Imagine the animation and the gaiety of these youths as they traveled along the highways! What discussions! What bursts of laughter! In these bands no doubt there was many a Gil Blas who could enliven an adventure or create one at need. And then what joyous friendships formed in haste (for brief was the sojourn in each place), when they reached one of those literary centers where studiously inclined young men were wont to gather—Milan in Italy, Autun in Gaul; Appollonia in Epirus, Tarsus in Cilicia, Carthage, Antioch, Alexandria, and Athens.

In his "Sentimental Journey," among the various kinds of travelers which he mentions Sterne distinguishes the idle travelers ; these were, in antiquity, the most numerous kind. People who left their country

The idle travelers.

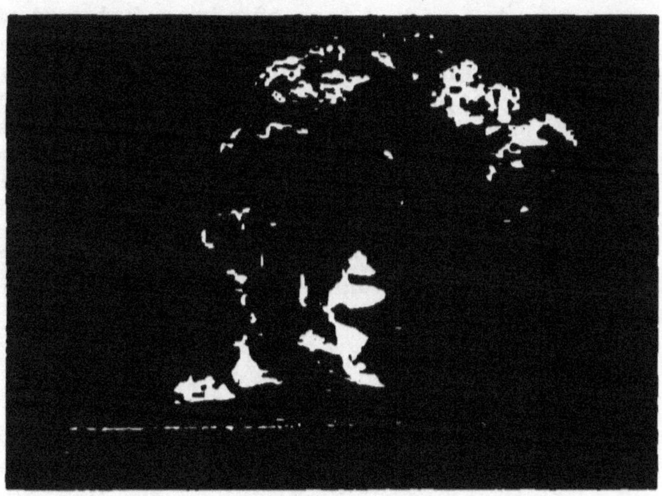

VESUVIUS IN ERUPTION.

with no other end than to have a change, who traveled only to seek pleasure, or rather to escape from ennui; were not rarer then than now.

Nothing in fact was more common, in this refined society of which we have tried to give some idea, than for a man to be oppressed by a feeling of sadness and gloom without his being able to account for it. That languor and discontent for which the English have found the name *spleen* was very prevalent at Rome. How many Romans, exclaiming with Lucretius "always the same thing!" traveled over the world in quest of new pleasures, which, while they sought them continually, they never found ! How many, like those

Prevalent discontent and languor.

sick people who imagine that they obtain some relief by tossing from side to side, exerted themselves to attain a repose which forever fled from them ! As Lucretius says :

A restless man described by Lucretius.

The man who is sick of home often issues forth from his large mansion, and as suddenly comes back to it, finding as he does that he is no better off abroad. He races to his country house, driving his jennets in headlong haste, as if hurrying to bring help to a house on fire ; he yawns the moment he has reached the door of his house, or sinks heavily into sleep and seeks forgetfulness, or even in haste goes back again to town. In this way each man flies from himself.

But such efforts were never crowned by success. Philosophers proclaim aloud the uselessness of setting off on a tour, for

Ennui, a black knight, gallops fast at your side.

Travel as a remedy for melancholy.

But no one listened to the philosophers ; travel, with its excitement and noise, seemed the best remedy for this wretched melancholy, and so when a man became low-spirited he would order his slaves to pack up the luggage quickly.

In summer, at the approach of autumn, when Rome was malarial, the roads leading out of the city were full of pedestrians, horsemen, and carriages. Some directed their way toward the coast of Latium, having in view Antium, Formiæ, Ostia, or Astura. Formiæ, according to Martial, in the following epigram, was a delightful resort :

Formiæ.

At Formiæ the surface of the ocean is but gently crisped by the breeze, and, though tranquil, is ever in motion, and bears along the painted skiff under the influence of a gale as gentle as that wafted by a maiden's fan when she is distressed by heat. Nor has the fishing-line to seek its victim far out at sea ; but the fish may be seen beneath the pellucid waters, seizing the line as it drops from the chamber or the couch. Were

Æolus ever to send a storm, the table, still sure of its provision, might laugh at his railings ; for the native fish-pool protects the turbot and the pike; delicate lampreys swim up to their master ; delicious mullet obey the call of the keeper, and the old carp come forth at the sound of his voice.

The reputation of Ostia was as great. But the most luxurious watering-place of the ancient world was Baiæ, on the shore of the beautiful Gulf of Naples, with the green mountains for a background. Palaces built by the different emperors and sumptuous villas formed, as it were, another city by the side of the real city which was itself richly provided with magnificent establishments for the treatment of invalids or the amusement of those who enjoyed good health. For among all the watering-places, Baiæ was eminently the city of pleasure. Here a perpetual festival reigns, whose gaiety is enhanced by the charm of the sea and the sky. The gulf is covered with barks full of musicians who make the air sweet with melody ; gay companions drink merrily together upon the shore and talk of love ; beautiful ladies and famous courtesans are here, trying to find again the lover of yesterday or seeking the lover of to-morrow. You come here, as Ovid says, to be cured, and you go away with a wound in your heart. Can you be surprised after this that Seneca advises Lucilius to avoid this resort, which he calls a hot-bed of vice?

There is nothing new under the sun. The Romans, who like us had their summer watering-places, had also their winter resorts. The physicians of this time had already conceived the idea of getting rid of their troublesome patients by advising them to seek a milder climate. Thus Antonius Musa directed Horace to pass the winter at Velia or at Salernum. Perhaps these two towns had not yet won the reputation which they afterward enjoyed; for we find Horace inquiring whether the social life there is pleasant and gay, and whether you can find there the good wine which, he says, "can make the blood flow in my veins and awaken rich hope in my heart, loosen my tongue, and restore to me my youth."

Tarentum.

But Tarentum from the time of Augustus had a wide reputation and invited strangers to take up their winter quarters in its delightful vicinity. Horace wished to live and die there.

I will seek [he says] the river Galæsus, delightful for sheep covered with skins, and the countries reigned over by Lacedæmonian Phalantus. That corner of the world smiles in my eye beyond all others; where the honey yields not to the Hymettian, and the olive rivals the verdant Venafrian; where the temperature of the air produces a long spring and mild winters, and Aulon, friendly to the fruitful vine, envies not the Falernian grapes. That place and those blest heights solicit you and me; there you shall bedew the glowing ashes of your poet friend with a tear due to his memory.

Mountains.

The mountains do not appear to have been so popular as they are in our day. People enjoyed, however, the resorts upon the Alban and Sabine Mountains, especially Tibur, Præneste, the Algidus, Aricia, Tusculum, and Alba.

The middle classes limited their trips to Italy, or at most they went as far as Sicily, that they might be able to relate upon their return that they had seen Ætna sung by the poets, the Valley of Enna, and its prairie of violets, the Gulf of Charybdis and the fountain Arethusa.

But the curiosity of the patricians was not so easily satisfied. They wished to go outside of their own country and even of their own age; they sought other skies than the sky of Italy and countries where the past was more vivid than the present. Thus it happened that during the first centuries of the empire there was no Roman somewhat distinguished who had not taken his trip into Greece.

This country always exercised, in fact, over those who had conquered it, a great fascination. However much the Greeks who came to Rome were inclined to disparage their own nationality, Greece inspired in the Romans a sentiment of admiration and respect which Pliny has very well expressed in the following letter to his friend Maximus, governor of Achaia : *Greece.*

My friendship for you constrains me, I will not say to give you directions (for you do not require them), but to remind you of what you already know, so that you may put it in practice, and even know it more thoroughly. Consider that you are sent to the province of Achaia, that true and genuine Greece, whence civilization, literature, even agriculture, are believed to have taken their origin—sent to regulate the condition of free cities, whose inhabitants are men in the best sense of the word—free men of the noblest kind, inasmuch as they have maintained the freedom which nature gives as a right, by their virtues, by their good actions, and by the securities of alliance and solemn obligation. Revere the gods who founded their state ; revere the glory of their ancient days, even that old age itself, which, as in men it claims respect, is in cities altogether sacred. Honor their old traditions, their great deeds, even their legends. Grant to every one his full dignity, freedom—yes, and the indulgence of his vanity. Keep ever before you the fact that it was this land which gave us our own laws—gave them to us, not as a conquered people, but at our own request. It is Athens, remember, to which you go—it is Lacedæmon you will have to govern ; and to take from such states the shadow and the surviving name of liberty would be a cruel and barbarous act ! You see that physicians treat the free with more tenderness than slaves, though their disorder may be the same. Remember what each of these states has been, but so remember *Pliny's letter to Maximus.* *Greece the land of literature and of freedom.*

as not to despise them for being no longer what they were.

Immediately after the conquest of Greece, in the year 169 B. C., Æmilius Paulus went to visit the cities and most celebrated places of that country, and at Olympia he lingered before the Jupiter of Phidias, overcome by an emotion so strong that it seemed as if he was in the presence of the god himself. From this day trips to Greece became fashionable, and the charm of the land for tourists was not diminished by the fact that it was hastening to ruin, that its cities were becoming deserted and its country regions depopulated. Dion Chrysostom describes one of these ancient cities, Chalcis perhaps, where the sheep graze in front of the city hall, where the site of the gymnasium is occupied by a corn-field, among whose waving stalks the heads of ancient marble statues may be seen. There is a fascination about this ruin. Out of these solitudes the image of the past is easily called forth.

But the desolation was not universal. Under the government of the Antonines Athens was restored ; Herod Atticus adorned it with magnificent buildings, and Hadrian tried to make it once more the city of culture.

While Athens served as a studious retreat, Corinth, more animated and more luxurious, attracted pleasure-seekers, and merited its name, "the City of Aphrodite." So Greece remained until the last days of the empire a haunt for tourists, and a poet of the Latin Anthology proclaims that its very ashes are sacred.

Travelers who had plenty of money and leisure did not omit visiting the isles. Bullatius, Horace's friend, took a trip to see Chios, Lesbos, and Samos, those lands of sunny skies scattered upon the waters of the Ægean Sea. From the Archipelago a few strokes of the oar took him to the Ionian coast, where he visited Smyrna. But in spite of their splendors, these rich and beautiful countries could not divert the mind of Bullatius; morose and *blasé* traveler that he was, he did not care to go as far as Ilium.

And yet this wretched village, inhabited then by Æolian Greeks, was frequently visited by Roman tour- *Ilium.* ists. It did not occur to them to wonder whether it was really the ancient Troy, the sacred city of Priam. The descendants of Æneas recognized it without discussion as the cradle of their race, and the least superstitious of them contemplated with emotion the temple where the image of Pallas was formerly kept, a relic since transported to Rome, if we may believe Ovid. Full of the legends of Homer, upon which they had fed their youth, imbued with that patriotic pride which had remained a tradition of the race, after having been a part of its religion and one of its virtues, the Romans allowed themselves to be guided by the people of Ilium, and did not put themselves on guard against the fabrications of these Greek tricksters and liers, who pointed out to them the graves of the Greek heroes, *The fabrications of the guides at Ilium.* the grotto where Paris pronounced his famous judgment, and showed them the trees upon the tomb of Protesilaus, telling them how their foliage withered away when their tops first reached the height whence Ilium could be seen, and then how they leafed out again more beautiful than before. Lucan, in the following passage from his "Pharsalia," represents Cæsar wandering across these famous plains:

Unthinkingly he was placing his step in the thick grass; a Phrygian native forbade him to tread upon the ghost of Hector. Torn asunder lay the stones, and showing no appearance of aught that was sacred.

"Dost thou not behold," said the guide, "the Hercæan altars?"

. . . .

When venerable antiquity had satisfied the view of the

THE JUDGMENT OF PARIS. POMPEIIAN FRESCO.

chieftain, he erected momentary altars with piles of turf heaped up, and poured forth these prayers over flames that burned frankincense, to no purpose :

"Ye gods who guard these ashes, whoever haunt the Phrygian ruins ; and ye Lares of my Æneas, whom now the Lavinian abodes and Alba preserve, and upon whose altars still does the Phrygian fire glow, and Pallas, by no male beheld, the memorable pledge of empire in the hidden shrine, the most illustrious descendant of the Julian race offers on your altars the pious frankincense, and solemnly invokes you in your former abodes : grant me for the future a fortunate career. I will restore the people ; in grateful return the Ausonians shall return to the Phrygians their walls, and a Roman Pergamus shall rise.''

Egypt rivaled Asia in offering attractions to rich and cultivated travelers. Between Puteoli and Alexandria a line of boats had been established. The trip required twelve days and there was nothing unpleasant about it. There were no sailors or shipbuilders of antiquity more skilful than the Alexandrines. Their presence in Puteoli made this port an object of curiosity. Every one admired their neat little boats, that could sail so fast, and their huge transports, which looked like veritable monsters. The *Acâlus*, which under the reign of Augustus had transported the obelisk of the Circus Maximus, could besides this load carry as many as twelve hundred passengers. It was the *Great Eastern* of the ancients.   Egypt. Puteoli.

Those who visited Egypt were usually people interested in curiosities. Everything in this old country seemed strange to the Romans. The antiquity of its civilization did not allow the manners of the people to undergo any transformation. There habits and customs remained what they had been in the time of the Pharaohs. The wonder of the Nile, the peculiarity of the flora and fauna of the country, excited the continual astonishment of strangers. Moreover, there was no city more cosmopolitan than Alexandria ; its population, which amounted to nearly one million inhabitants, presented a most picturesque mixture of all races. City, at the same time, of commerce, of pleasure, and   Alexandria.

of study, its perpetual movement, its feverish activity offered a spectacle which could entertain the most exacting. The emperor Hadrian even, great traveler that he was, wondered at the sight:

Here no one is idle. Every one has his work and practices a calling. Even the blind, the gouty, and the halt find something to do.

Canopus.

And just outside the limits of Alexandria was Canopus, city of pleasure, the rival of Baiæ. There were also natural wonders to be seen, such as the Falls of Syene, and great structures like the pyramids and the colossal statue of Memnon. Upon the stones of these ancient monuments,

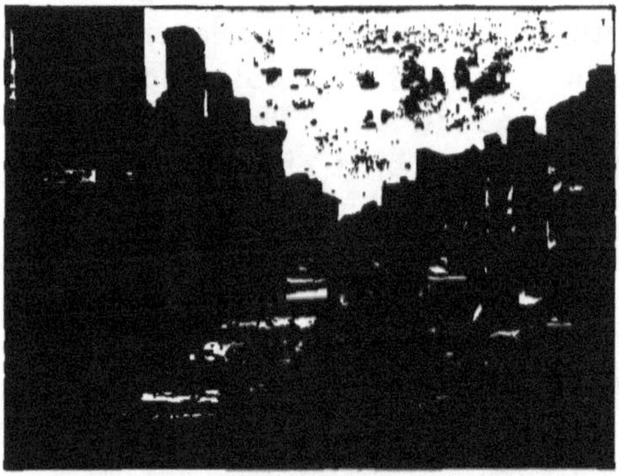

STREET OF FORTUNE, POMPEII.

Ancient monuments.

tourists almost always engraved their names, with the date of their visit. The legs of the statue of Memnon are covered with these inscriptions almost up to the knees. Innkeepers had not yet invented the travelers' registration book, and this was a very good substitute.

Travelers of moderate means, young men, people who enjoyed adventure and who could put up with discomfort, used to journey on horseback. But the rich and the delicate required a great caravan to accompany

The caravans of the rich.

them along the highways. Nero never had with him less than a thousand carriages; his mules, shod in silver, were driven by slaves dressed in a uniform of red tunics. Poppæa took along with her five hundred she-asses to furnish daily milk for her bath. And, aside from this imperial luxury, nothing was more magnificent than the train of a Roman optimate as he journeyed. A large body of domestics formed his retinue, carrying his favorite articles of furniture, his tableware, and in fact all the objects which he needed, or fancied, to render him unconscious, as it were, that he was not in his own house. The carriage which drew him, richly decorated, resting on springs to avoid jolting, and furnished with silk curtains, contained all kinds of comforts ; you could read or write in it, or even sleep there. Sleeping-cars are not wholly a modern invention ; the ancients had their sleeping coaches. In some of their carriages there were re-volving chairs, that the traveler might face whichever way he pleased without exerting himself, and in others there were contrivances for measuring the distance traversed and for indicating the time of day.

Sleeping coaches.

We shall have less difficulty in comprehending so many refinements, if we consider that the travelers could not count upon hotels or inns where they might refresh themselves after their fatigue. It was not always even in such watering-places as Baiæ, Canopus, and Edepsus that a tourist could find suitable hotels ; but outside of these cities, the most elementary pro-visions for the comfort of travelers were neglected. The hotel-keepers of Southern Europe have too faith-fully preserved these old traditions until the present day.

Hotels.

The masters of the poorest hotels did not fail, how-ever, to make fair promises. Look at all the signs— "The Great Eagle," "The Cock," "The Crane"— at all these places you are promised a good supper and a good bed.　Some innkeepers recommend their house by this alluring placard : "Equal to the capital."　On the door of a hotel at Lyons you might have read this naïve boast : "Here Mercury promises gain, Apollo health, Septimanus good cheer at table.　Whoever shall stop here will be well taken care of. Strangers, consider well where you lodge."

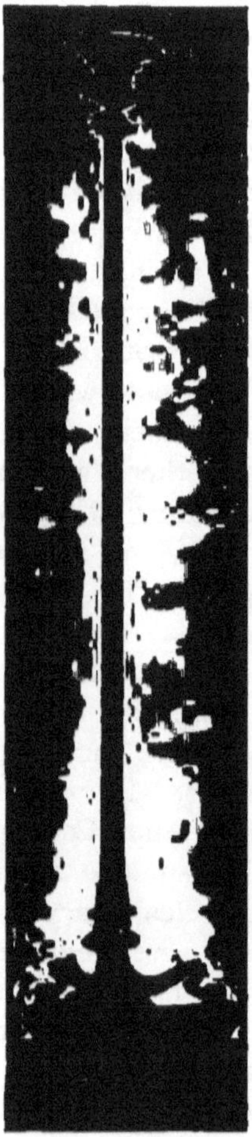

Very few travelers, however, allowed themselves to be deceived ; it was too well known that only low society was to be found in a hotel. An inn has been discovered at Pompeii in whose little cells, which served as bedrooms, some of the guests left their names.　They were people of the lower classes—a certain prætorian soldier on a furlough and some pantomimists who had come to the city for the purpose of giving an entertainment.　Often the patrons of these hotels were worse than plebeian, they were immoral.

No accustomed traveler would expect from hotel-keepers a scrupulous delicacy or considerateness. They undertook within their domains to do the work of the brigands outside ; they cheated, they adulterated the wine, stole the oats from the horses, and would gladly, had they dared, have made an item on their bill of the fleas that swarmed in their

An inn at Pompeii.

Hotel-keepers.

CANDELABRUM.

house.   We must not, then, be surprised that those who could afford it took such precautions as might render them independent of this questionable hospitality.

What especially excited the interest of travelers was the curiosities and the objects of art found usually in the temples.   Travelers used to stop to visit these buildings, which held the place then of our museums to-day.   But, although they contained much of value, there was absolute lack of classification.   Natural curiosities and objects of art were mixed together in bizarre confusion.   Beside images or celebrated statues, near the works of great artists, were displayed cocoanuts, stuffed crocodiles, huge serpents, and ants from India, enough bric-a-brac to excite the envy of a Jew second-hand dealer.   In these collections fancy was sometimes allowed very free play.   Varro saw in a temple of Sancus, a Sabine deity, the distaff and spindle of Tanaquil.   At Sparta the lance of Agesilaus was exhibited; at Platæa, a saber of Mardonius.   Sometimes the egg of Leda was shown, and also an amber cup offered by Helen to the Temple of Minerva, at Lindus.   Pausanias claimed that there was at Panope in Phocis some of the clay left from which Prometheus had molded man; and he gravely adds that this clay had the odor of human skin.

The collections of objects of interest in the temples.

There was a whole class of men who made it their business either to guide travelers to the interesting places, or to explain to them the sights which they beheld.   These ancient ciceroni were not less annoying sometimes than their modern successors.   It might happen occasionally that they were well-informed and possessed of good judgment, but this was the exception.   Usually they droned out with tiresome repetitions their explanations learned by heart and their

The ancient ciceroni.

marvelous anecdotes, invented to please the taste of the multitude. It is easy to imagine what torture such guides must have inflicted upon cultivated men visiting Athens or Olympia, and Plutarch in this connection tells an amusing anecdote in his essay "On Curiosity." A company of people were visiting the temple at Delphi, and they begged the guides to spare them all explanations in regard to the objects that they were to see. But the guides insisted upon fulfilling their usual office, and even went so far as to read all the inscriptions. And yet the least question that was addressed to them incidentally, or out of the usual order, confused them so that they were unable to continue for a time.

Such ignorance astonishes us when we consider that nothing interested the Romans in their travels more than historical associations. The little poem, "Ætna," which is attributed often to Lucilius Junior, contains explicit testimony on this point :

We traverse lands and seas, at the peril of our lives, in order to see magnificent temples, with their rich treasures, their marble statues, and sacred antiquities ; we eagerly inquire into the fables of ancient mythology, and make, as we travel, a visit to every nation. With what pleasure we behold the walls of Ogygian Thebes, and return in imagination into those early ages, wondering now at the stones which obeyed the voice of the singer and the music of his lyre, now at the altar whence arose in two distinct columns the smoke of the double sacrifice, now at the exploits of the seven heroes and the abyss which swallowed Amphiaraus. Again we are captivated by the Eurotas and the city of Lycurgus and the sacred troop following their chief to death. Then we visit Athens, proud of her singers, and of Minerva, her victorious goddess. Here it was that the perfidious Theseus forgot, upon his return, to hoist the white sail that was to have informed his father of his success. Was not Athens responsible for the tragic fate of Erigone, now a celebrated star? The story of Pandion's daughter, Philomela, who fills the woods with her

THE VATICAN LIBRARY.

song, and of her sister Procne, who, changed to a nightingale, builds her nest near the roofs, and of Tereus wandering in the lonely fields—these are also among the Athenian myths.

Lucilius shows that very many travelers were interested in works of art :

Works of art.

Yes, the paintings and the statues of Greece fascinate many people. Now it is Venus Anadyomene, with her dripping hair, or the terrible Colchian princess, with her young children playing at her feet, now the sacrifice of Iphigenia, or some work of Myron. This profusion of works in which so much art is manifested attracts many people, and you feel obliged to go to see them in spite of the perils of land and of sea.

But probably very few of those who followed the fashion by visiting artistic exhibitions really appreciated them. The majority agreed with Tacitus, who having once for all seen the picture or the statue that he came to see went away satisfied and never returned. Almost all were of the mind of Atticus, with whom Cicero makes us acquainted in his essay "On Laws":

Atticus.

Those places which are associated with men whom we love and admire produce a certain impression upon us. Even Athens, my favorite city, does not delight me so much by its Greek architecture and its precious masterpieces of the ancient artists as by the recollection that it arouses in me of the great men that have lived there, walked about its public squares conversing together, and who now lie buried there.

The Romans' appreciation of nature.

As to nature, the Romans had little appreciation of it. They liked best calmness in nature and wished to be calm themselves in order to enjoy it. While our tourists spare themselves no trouble or expense that they may contemplate the glaciers of the Alps, the precipices of the Pyrenees, or the desolate cliffs of Brittany, while our artists and authors try to cultivate our taste for the gloomy grandeur of the African deserts, the ancients were unmoved by all these spectacles which have been described as "beautiful horrors." They very rarely ascended mountains, and those of them who did accomplish such feats were not pleasure-seekers.

Those [says Strabo] who have climbed to the summit, covered with eternal snow, of Mount Argæus, near Mazaca in Cappadocia, report that on a clear day they can see from there two seas, the Euxine and the Bay of Issus. But there are very few that have dared to make the ascent.

The ancients took no delight in wild or romantic scenery. Everything that was confused, everything that expressed disorder, not only failed to charm them, but even shocked them. In morals they held the principle that there is nothing great that is not calm. And they applied the same principle in æsthetics. They surely preferred the Borghese Mars to the Gladiator of Agasias. Their architecture, with its careful proportions, where everything tends to rest and satisfy the eye, proceeds from the same idea ; their poetry also, with its regular harmony, is inspired by it. This taste for order and measure is exhibited again in their appreciation of natural beauties.

Vast plains, beautiful meadows, fertile fields, this [says M. Boissier] is what delights them. Lucretius can conceive of no greater pleasure, on those days when one has nothing to do, than "to lie down near a stream of running water under the leafage of a tall tree," and Virgil desires, as the supreme happiness, always to love the fruitful fields and the rivers which flow through the valleys. The foreground of a landscape which could charm a Roman is made up of meadows or harvests, some beautiful trees, and a lake or stream ; a pretty background might be formed by hills at the horizon, especially if their sides were cultivated and their summits wooded.

Let us add that a distant view of the sea would complete the picture ; for with the Romans "beautiful sites" and "maritime sites" were almost synonymous terms.

To enjoy such pictures there was no need of going outside of Italy. Did not the shores of Latium and the Gulf of Naples afford the Romans their favorite kinds of scenery? Where could nature, as it was then conceived, be enjoyed better than in the villa of Pollius Felix for example? Built upon the heights of Surrentum, it commanded from every side a beautiful view, overlooking Ischia, Capreæ, Procida, and the sea ; here the setting sun rested when the day declined, when the shadow of the mountains, with their crown of trees, lay upon the sea.

The Romans then who loved nature did not go abroad to enjoy its beauties ; they remained at home. They probably thought that the seclusion of a quiet retreat in some lovely country region helps one to enjoy more fully the beauties of the exterior world, and renders one more capable of feeling its profound sweetness and of comprehending its inalterable serenity. However this may be, life in the country held an important place in the existence of the Romans, and we should omit an important feature in this picture of their manners which we are trying to present to the reader if we should not describe the country villas and the life of those who inhabited them.

Enjoyment of rural life was much more common among the Romans than is sometimes supposed. Some, men of the old school, those who cherished the ancient traditions, loved the country because they liked farming ; but they did not form a very large class. Others, and doubtless their number also was small, loved it for the poetical emotions which it inspires.

NAPLES.

The rich and the powerful loved it because it permitted them to escape from the vexations and interruptions of city life. The poor loved it because there they found the air and the light which was denied them in their wretched dwellings in the narrow streets of Rome. All these classes could sympathize with Horace, when he exclaimed, "O rural landscape, when shall I behold thee?" Those who could not escape from the capital tried to produce a semblance of the country about their city houses by planting bushes and flowers.

Moreover, country life came to be something more than a luxury for those who enjoyed it; fashion was absolute in requiring her votaries to go to some summer resort during the hottest months of the year. A man who wished to hold a position in society could not afford to appear on the streets of Rome after a certain date of the summer season. If he respected himself he would leave before August for his villa or for the seaside. He would prefer to hide in his cellar rather than allow his presence in Rome to be known. So all of Italy, from the Gulf of Baiæ to the foot of the Alps, was dotted with elegant country houses.

The emperors set the example in building villas. Tiberius had his Capreæ; Nero loved to stay in his house at Sublaqueum, near the Anio, and Hadrian frequently came to his villa at Tibur, which, from the sixteenth century, has been studied by several archæologists, and of which M. Daumet has made a restoration.

When we examine the plan traced by this skilful architect, we are impressed with the difference which exists between this habitation and our princely country seats. Hadrian's villa occupies an immense extent. It is a Versailles on a large scale. We find there baths, thermæ, a hall for public readings, libraries, and an observatory tower. Thus far there is nothing to excite our surprise ; but we are astonished to find three theaters and a basilica, and our wonder increases when we learn that the emperor had caused to be reproduced in his villa imitations of the places which had most excited his interest during his travels of several years through all the provinces of his empire. We find a Lyceum, an Academy, a Pœcile (a celebrated portico at Athens), a prytaneum (in many Greek towns a public building sacred to Hestia, and containing the state hearth), a Canopus (city of Lower Egypt, a famous pleasure resort), a Vale of Tempe, and even, says Spartianus, "in order that nothing might be wanting, it occurred to him to make a reproduction of Hell there." We must suppose, however, that Hadrian had sufficient good sense and taste not to attempt to make these imitations literal ; they were doubtless very free. But, nevertheless, to execute them at all must have required the removal of enormous quantities of earth.

His imitations of foreign places.

Hadrian in all this was not original. The Romans, even in the country, were great builders. The natural conformation of the land seemed to have no charm for them. A site seemed to them beautiful in proportion to the pains which they had taken to remodel it according to their taste and their fancy. Notice how Statius admires the achievements of the workmen who constructed the villa of Pollius Felix :

Landscape gardening among the ancients.

There where a plain extends was formerly a mountain ; where now you walk under the shelter of a roof there used to be a frightful solitude ; where now large trees stand there was not even earth before. Truly the land has learned to bear the yoke. The palace advances and the mountain withdraws, obedient to the master's command.

Even in their love for nature the Romans exhibited their conquering disposition.

One peculiarity of Hadrian's villa, which arrests the attention of us moderns, is thus described by M. Boissier :

Lack of symmetry in Hadrian's villa.

The *ensemble* of these vast edifices escapes us. We admire their variety ; we find a remarkable fecundity of invention and resource in them, but we are astonished at not seeing more symmetry. . . . The architect seems to have added buildings one to the other as their want was felt, without troubling himself about the effect that might be produced by the whole.

This is quite contrary to all our ideas ; but as we have already had occasion to say, the Romans cared little about symmetry ; even their city houses were not symmetrical. The forum was only a confusion of temples, of trophies, and of basilicas. Five or six palaces encumbered the Palatine Hill. All the more in the country should we expect to find regularity of outline dispensed with.

The country homes of the Romans.

The general arrangements of Hadrian's villa are repeated in all the country houses of the wealthy Romans. The various buildings which we have enumerated, with the exception of those useful only to a prince or those which are purely fanciful creations, are found in the villas of which we find descriptions in Roman literature. Pliny has written at length about his two villas, the Tuscan and the Laurentine. Pliny's tastes were modest, as we know, but his reputation and his rank obliged him to live in style. His country seats, then, can furnish us an idea of an ordinary villa. Let us follow him as our guide over his Laurentine estate :

Pliny's Laurentine estate.

The courtyard.

My house is for use, not for show. You first enter a courtyard, plain and simple without being mean, and then pass into a colonnade in the shape of the letter D, the space

inclosed by which looks bright and cheerful. Here one has a
capital place of retreat in bad weather, for there are windows
all round it and it is sheltered by a projection on the roof.
Opposite the middle of the colonnade is a very pleasant inner
court, which leads into a handsome dining-room running out   Dining-room.
to the seashore. When the wind is in the southwest its walls
are gently washed by the waves which break at its foot. The
room has folding-doors, or windows as large as doors, and

POMPEII.

from these you might imagine you see three different seas.
From another point you look through the colonnade into the
court and see the mountains in the distance. To the left of
the dining-room, a little further from the sea, is a spacious
sitting-room, within that a smaller room, one side of which
gets the morning and the other the afternoon sun. This I
make my winter snuggery. Then comes a room the windows   Bedrooms
of which are so arranged that they secure the sun for us   and parlors.
during the whole day. In its walls is a bookcase for such
works as can never be read too often. Next to this is a bed-
room connected with it by a raised passage furnished with
pipes, which supply, at a wholesome temperature, and dis-
tribute to all parts of this room, the heat they receive. The

remainder of this side of the house is appropriated to the use of my slaves and freedmen, but yet most of the apartments in it are neat enough to entertain any of my friends who are inclined to be my guests.

In the opposite wing is a room ornamented in very elegant taste ; next to it lies another room which, though large for a parlor, makes but a moderate dining-room. It is warmed and lighted not only by the direct rays of the sun but also by their reflection from the sea. Beyond this is a bed-chamber and its ante-chamber, so high that it is cool in summer, and it is warm in winter, too, being sheltered on every side. Another apartment of the same sort is separated from this by a common wall. Thence you enter the grand, spacious cooling-room belonging to the baths, from whose opposite walls two round basins project, large enough to swim in. Adjoining this is the perfuming-room, then the sweating-room, and beyond that the furnace which conveys the heat to the baths ; two more little bathing-rooms which are fitted up in an elegant rather than costly manner join the latter room ; annexed to the little bathing-rooms is a warm bath of extraordinary workmanship, in which one may swim and have a view of the sea at the same time. Not far from there stands the tennis-court, which lies open to the warmth of the afternoon sun. Thence you ascend a sort of turret which contains two entire apartments below, the same number above, and also a dining-room which commands a very extensive prospect of the sea and coast, together with the beautiful villas that stand scattered upon it.

At the other end is a second turret containing a room which faces the rising and setting sun. Behind this is a large room for a repository, near to which is a gallery of curiosities and underneath a spacious dining-room, where the roaring of the sea even in a storm is but faintly heard ; it looks upon the garden and the *gestatio* [a promenade or driveway], which surrounds the garden. The *gestatio* is encompassed with a box-tree hedge, and where that is decayed with rosemary ; for the box in those parts which are sheltered by the buildings preserves its verdure perfectly well, but where by an open situation it lies exposed to the dashing of the sea-water, though at a great distance, it entirely withers. Between the garden and this *gestatio* runs a shady walk of vines, which is

Baths.

Tennis-court.

The *gestatio*.

so soft that you may walk barefoot upon it without any injury. The garden is chiefly planted with fig and mulberry trees, to which this soil is peculiarly favorable. Here is a dining-room, which, though it is at a distance from the sea, commands a prospect no less pleasant. Behind this room are two apartments, the windows of which look out on the entrance to the house, and to a well-stocked kitchen-garden.

You then enter a sort of cloister, which you might suppose built for public use. It has a range of windows on each side; in fair weather we open all of them; if it blows, we shut those on the exposed side and are perfectly sheltered. In front of this colonnade is a terrace, fragrant with the scent of violets and warmed by the reflection of the sun from the portico. We find this a very pleasant place in winter, and still more so in summer, for then it throws a shade on the terrace during the forenoon, while in the afternoon we can walk under its shade in the place of exercise, or in the adjoining part of the garden. The portico is the coolest when the sun's rays strike perpendicularly on its roof. By setting open the windows the soft western breezes have a free draught, and so the air is never close and oppressive. *A sort of cloister.*

On the upper end of the terrace and portico stands a detached building in the garden which I call my favorite, and in truth I am extremely fond of it as I built it myself. It contains a warm winter-room, one side of which looks upon the terrace, the other has a view of the sea, and both lie exposed to the sun. Through the folding-doors you see the opposite chamber and from the window is a prospect of the inclosed portico. On the side next the sea, and opposite the middle wall, stands a little closet, elegant and retired, which is separated from or thrown into the adjoining room by means of glass doors and a curtain. It contains a couch and two chairs. As you lie upon this couch, from the foot you have a view of the sea; if you look behind you, you see the neighboring villas, and from the head you have the woods in sight. These three views may be seen distinctly from so many different windows in the room, or blended together in one confused prospect. *The garden building.*

Adjoining to this is a bed-chamber which neither the voice of the servants, the murmur of the sea, nor even the roaring of a tempest can reach; neither lightning nor day itself can penetrate it unless you open the windows. This profound tranquillity is secured by a passage which divides the wall of this chamber from that of the garden, and thus by means of the empty space every noise is drowned. Annexed to this is a small stove-room which, by opening a little window, warms the bed-chamber to the degree of heat required. Beyond this lies a chamber and ante-chamber which has the sun, obliquely to be sure, from the time it rises till the afternoon. When I retire to this garden apartment I fancy myself a hundred miles from my own house, and take particular pleasure in it at the feast of the Saturnalia, when, by license of that season of joy, every other part of my villa resounds with the mirth of my domestics; thus I neither interrupt their diversions nor do they hinder my studies.

Amid the conveniences and attractions of the place, there is one drawback; we want running water. However, we have wells, or rather springs, at our command. Such is the extraordinary nature of the ground that in whatever part you dig, as soon as you have turned up the surface of the soil you meet with a spring of perfectly pure water, altogether free from any salt taste. The neighboring woods supply us with fuel in abundance, and all kinds of provisions may be had from Ostia. A man with few and simple wants might get all he required from the next village. In that little place there are three public baths, a very great convenience, in case my friends come in unexpectedly, and my bath is not ready heated and prepared. The whole coast is prettily studded with detached villas or rows of villas, which, whether you view them from the sea or shore, look like a collection of towns. The strand is sometimes, after a long calm, perfectly smooth, though in general, by the storms driving the waves upon it, it is rough and uneven. I cannot say that we have any very fine fish, but we get excellent soles and prawns. As to other kinds of provisions, my house is better off than those which are inland, especially as to milk, for the cattle come here in great numbers to seek water and shade. Tell me now, have I not just cause to bestow my time and my affection upon this delightful retreat? Surely you are unreasonably attached to the pleasures of the town if you have no inclination to take a view of it. I only wish that to its many charms there might be made the very considerable addition of your company to recommend it.   Farewell.

Much more modest was the villa of Suetonius Tranquillus.   This learned man had not grown rich by his writings ; yet he wished for a retreat where he might live at ease, and he requested his friend Pliny to secure for him a little piece of property which he thought

The villa of Tranquillus.

would suit his purpose.   Let us see how the amiable Pliny fulfils the commission :

My friend and guest, Tranquillus, has an inclination to purchase a small farm, of which, as I am informed, an acquaintance of yours intends to dispose. I beg you would endeavor he may get it upon reasonable terms; which will add to his satisfaction in the purchase. A dear bargain is always a disagreeable thing, particularly as it reflects upon the buyer's judgment. There are several circumstances attending this little villa, which (suppos-

Pliny's attempt to make a good bargain.

PORTRAIT STATUE. Vatican.

ing my friend has no objection to the price) are extremely suitable to his tastes and desires : the convenient distance from Rome, the goodness of the roads, the smallness of the building, and the very few acres of land around it, which are just enough to amuse him, without taking up his time.   To a man of Tranquillus's studious turn it is sufficient if he have but a small spot to relieve the mind and divert the eye, where he may saunter round his grounds, traverse his single walk, grow familiar with all his little vines, and count the trees in his shrubbery.   I mention these particulars to let you see how much he will be obliged to me, as I shall be to you, if you can help him to this convenient little box, at a price which he shall have no occasion to repent.   Farewell.

This house of Suetonius, which reminds us a little of Horace's, was very suitable for a literary man of moderate fortune. It might also have been purchased by some freedman in easy circumstances, or some small tradesman who had retired from business, after having earned enough to live on. It is the type of those dwellings which furnished a restful retreat for people of the middle class, for all those who in a later age might dream of the little white house with green blinds fondly imagined by J. J. Rousseau.

With us a country house suggests the idea of beautiful gardens and extensive grounds laid out with taste. What Boileau calls "the art of La Quintinie" (a French agriculturist) has been singularly developed in our modern civilization. This art since the time of Dufresny (French author and horticulturist) and his charming creations has been exercised by real masters. There was nothing like it among the Romans. The old paintings which contain representations of their gardens enable us to form a fairly correct idea of them. M. Boissier says :

These are always regular alleys, shut in by two walls of hornbeam, cutting each other at right angles. In the center a kind of round space is usually found, with a basin in which swans are swimming about. Every here and there little arbors of greenery have been arranged, formed of canes interlaced and covered with vines, at whose end a marble column or a statue is seen, with seats placed around to allow promenaders to rest for a moment.

These paintings remind one of the following saying of Quintilian, which naïvely expresses the taste of his age : "Is there anything finer than a *quincunx* so disposed that from whatever side one looks only straight alleys are perceived?"

The Romans were not satisfied with having their trees planted in regular lines ; the trees themselves had to be trimmed with precision, and even cut into geometrical forms. Furthermore—and this is the worst part of it—trees were tortured into all sorts of shapes, for Pliny says, "In my garden the box represents several animals looking at each other."

The trimming of trees.

To be just, however, we must admit that the Romans did not possess the means which we have at our command to-day for making gardens of varied beauty. The discovery of America has enriched Europe with a large number of strange or magnificent trees. Modern flora besides have assumed a variety and a splendor which the ancients never dreamed of. They were able, however, to enjoy the luxury of flowers ; Campania and Pæstum reaped a good revenue by furnishing the capital with flowers. During the winter they were raised in hot-houses or imported from Egypt. But this luxury consisted only in the abundance of flowers of a very few kinds, not in the variety and multiplicity of species. A flower bed was considered exceptionally fine if it contained some pretty clumps of lilies, of roses, or of violets, like Pliny's at his Tuscan villa. In short, the ancients were acquainted with but a very limited variety of flowers ; a list of the different kinds might be prepared from Meleager's "Garland," a poem in which the Alexandrine compares each celebrated poet to some flower. How much more copious are our horticultural catalogues !

Ancient and modern flora.

Walking in these poor gardens could not have been a very delightful recreation. How then did the Romans pass their time in the country? Pliny, writing to his friend Fuscus, informs us how he occupies himself at his villa at Tuscum :

`You want to know how I portion out my day in my summer villa at Tuscum? I get up just when I please; generally about sunrise, often earlier, but seldom later than this. I keep the shutters closed, as darkness and silence wonderfully promote meditation. Thus free and abstracted from those outward objects which dissipate attention, I am left to my own thoughts; nor suffer my mind to wander with my eyes, but keep my eyes in subjection to my mind, which, when they are not distracted by a multiplicity of external objects, see nothing but what the imagination represents to them. If I have any work in hand, this is the time I choose for thinking it out, word for word, even to the minutest accuracy of expression. In this way I compose more or less, according as the subject is more or less difficult, and I find myself able to retain it. I then call my secretary, and, opening the shutters, dictate to him what I have put into shape, after which I dismiss him, then call him in again, and again dismiss him. About ten or eleven o'clock (for I do not observe one fixed hour), according to the weather, I either walk upon my terrace or in the covered portico, and there I continue to meditate or dictate what remains upon the subject in which I am engaged. This completed, I get into my chariot, where I employ myself as before, when I was walking, or in my study; and find this change of scene refreshes and keeps up my attention. On my return home I take a little nap, then a walk, and after that repeat out loud and distinctly some Greek or Latin speech, not so much for the sake of strengthening my voice as my digestion; though indeed the voice at the same time is strengthened by this practice. I then take another walk, am anointed, do my exercises, and go into the bath. At supper, if I have only my wife or a few friends with me, some author is read to us; and after supper we are entertained either with music or an interlude. When this is finished I take my walk with my family, among whom I am not without some scholars. Thus we pass our evenings in varied conversation ; and the day, even when at the longest, steals imperceptibly away.

We see that Pliny's occupations are by no means rural. The story is that Diocletian used to cultivate his lettuce himself after he had laid down his scepter. But Pliny did not leave his pen to water his flower beds. And if he went hunting he took his writing tablets with him, as we learn from the following letter :

Diocletian and
his lettuce.

You will laugh (and you are quite welcome) when I tell you that your old acquaintance is turned sportsman, and has taken three noble boars. "What !" you exclaim, " Pliny !"—*Even he.* However, I indulged at the same time my beloved inactivity; and whilst I sat at my nets you would have found me, not with boar-spear or javelin, but pencil and tablet, by my side. I mused and wrote, being determined to return, if with my hands empty, at least with my memorandums full. Believe me, this way of studying is not to be despised ; it is wonderful how the mind is stirred and quickened into activity by brisk bodily exercise. There is something, too, in the solemnity of the venerable woods with which one is surrounded, together with that profound silence which is observed on these occasions, that forcibly disposes the mind to meditation. So for the future, let me advise you, whenever you hunt, to take your tablets along with you, as well as your basket and bottle ; for be assured you will find Minerva no less fond of traversing the hills than Diana. Farewell.

How Pliny
goes hunting.

People who were not so intellectually inclined as Pliny found sufficient amusement in those forms of recreation that are common to-day. The young and strong enjoyed horseback riding. Those who had grown heavy with age, or whom sickness had rendered weak, had themselves carried about outdoors in litters or sedan-chairs ; this took the place with the Romans of our carriage driving. In the gardens and parks of the villas there were walks, composed of sand and chalk,

Horseback
riding.

Hunting.

Fishing.

over which a litter could easily be carried without jar or jolt. Hunting had devotees more ardent than Pliny. To convince one's self of this, it is only necessary to read the third book of the "Georgics," in which Virgil gives instruction as to the choice of dogs suitable for running down the boar and the stag. As the villas were usually situated near a lake, a river, or the sea, fishing must have been a favorite amusement. Did not Ovid, who wrote for fashionable people, compose a poem entitled "Halieutica," or "Fishing," in which he compared terrestrial with aquatic animals? Does not this prove that fishing was, as we said, a popular sport?

Tennis.

Croquet was not known among the Romans, but they were familiar with the game of tennis, and had their champion players. Spurinna, who enjoyed, according to Pliny, the old age of a wise man, did not like to miss his game of tennis after his bath. We cannot regret that the silent whist had not yet been invented, but the

Chess and dice. Romans played chess and a game of dice.

To sum up, in their country houses, as well as upon their travels, the Romans remained faithful to the essentially practical genius of their race. When journeying they did not seek for adventures or for scenes that would arouse their poetic emotions. They loved historic sites, because they conceived of history as the school of life. When in the country they desired repose

Desire for repose and freedom. and freedom, outdoor life that exercises the muscles and renews the blood, life without business and without restraint which refreshes the mind and calms the soul.

> There leisure [said Pliny] is more complete, more sure, and consequently more sweet ; no ceremonial must be observed ; troublesome people do not intrude ; all is calm and peaceful ; and besides this profound repose, there is the healthfulness of the climate, the serenity of the sky, and the purity of the air.

CHAPTER X.

RETIREMENT FROM ACTIVE LIFE, DEATH, AND BURIAL.

UNDER the ancient republic the individual belonged to the city. The service of the state occupied the whole life of a Roman from his birth to his death. Cato, who, in the eyes of Cicero, was an ideal citizen, bore arms at the age of seventeen years, and when he was eighty-four years old, in the very year of his death, he impeached before the people Servius Sulpicius Galba.

But in the time of the Gracchi a great change began to appear in the manners of the Romans. The struggles between parties, the fruitless agitations stirred up by ambitious men, after having weakened the spring of civic activity, finally broke it. When politics fell into the hands of selfish and quarrelsome schemers, many good statesmen began to feel that it was not worth while to give one's whole life to the public, and so after a few years spent in serving their country, disgusted or weary, they would go into retirement. At first retirement from active life seemed excusable merely, but before long it was regarded as even praiseworthy. Pliny does not hesitate to congratulate his friend Pomponius Bassus upon having decided to seek that repose which he himself would have found very pleasant.

I had the great pleasure [he writes] of hearing from our common friends that you take your leisure and lay it out as a man of your good sense ought; living down in a charming part of the country and varying your amusements—sometimes driving, sometimes going out for a sail, holding frequent learned discussions and conferences, reading a good deal, and, in a word, daily increasing that fund of knowledge you already possess. This is to grow old in a way worthy of one who has discharged the highest offices both civil and military, and who gave himself up entirely to the service of the state while it became him to do so. Our morning and midday of life we owe to our country, but our declining age is due to ourselves.

This desire for retirement from active life, which under the expiring republic influenced Sulla to abdicate

TIBUR (MODERN TIVOLI).

and Lucullus to withdraw from the turbulent political contests of his time to enjoy the elegant luxury of his home, was under the empire very rapidly developed.

The character of the new *régime* favored its development. Absolute power tolerates political activity only when employed in its own service. All those who through family tradition or natural independence of spirit might have been disposed to take a firm but moderate stand against the government, understood that they would lose their pains, and they preferred to renounce the service of the state rather than enter into the emperor's servitude. As to the patricians, who owed it to their names to be uncompromising, their course was clear—to hold aloof, and maintain silence. Silence is a strong expression of protest ; and for them at this time no other expression of it was possible. *The course of the patricians.*

The new men, those who were not obliged by their birth to bear themselves as enemies of the imperial system, who hoped to be useful to the public, entered into active life but did not remain there long. If their ability was but mediocre, the emperor was soon tired of them. If it was superior, they became disgusted by the continual sacrifice of independence which they were obliged to make ; sometimes even they found cause to be deeply offended. We cannot doubt that Seneca entered public life with the noblest intentions, and that he truly possessed the capacity of a statesman, but in spite of his culpable weaknesses, he understood after some years that he was disliked by Nero, and that his safety lay in making himself forgotten. *The new men in political life.* *Seneca in political life.*

> If the state [he says in one of his treatises] is corrupt beyond the possibility of cure, if it is in the hands of wicked men, the wise man should not waste his time in useless efforts, nor spend his strength in vain.

He abandoned, therefore, his position at Nero's court, not without having begged his dismissal as a favor, for he feared that otherwise his departure might look like a form of opposition. He even desired to resign all the advantages attached to the possession of power, and offered his fortune to Nero. The emperor refused to accept it ; but Seneca, in order to escape attention, led thereafter the life of a poor man. *His withdrawal from court.*

Under certain emperors retirement was not only advisable but necessary. In the time of Caligula, of

Nero, and of Domitian there was a veritable reign of terror. Those who had the misfortune of living in these terrible years never felt that their heads were safe, and their hearts beat continually in the expectation of death.

But even under the emperors who were not monsters retirement from active life was a useful precaution for political men. This was well understood by Spurinna, whose sweet and lovely old age Pliny, in the following letter, describes for us :

I know not that I ever passed a pleasanter time than lately with Spurinna. There is indeed no man I shall so much wish to resemble in my own old age if I am permitted to grow old. Nothing can be finer than such a mode of life. For my part I like a well-ordered course of life, particularly in old men, just as I admire the regular order of the stars. Some amount of irregularity and even of confusion is not unbecoming in youth ; but everything should be regular and methodical with old men who are too late for labor and in whom ambition would be indecent. This regularity Spurinna strictly observes, and his occupations, trifling as they are (trifling, that is, were they not performed day by day continually), he repeats as it were in a circle.

At dawn he keeps his bed, at seven he asks for his slippers ; he then walks just three miles, exercising his mind at the same time with his limbs. If friends are by, he discourses seriously with them ; if not, he hears a book read ; and so he some-times does even when friends are present, if it be not disagree-able to them. He then seats himself, and more reading follows, or more conversation, which he likes better. By-and-by he mounts his carriage, taking with him his wife, a most admirable woman, or some friends—as myself, for instance, the other day. What a noble, what a charming tête-à-tête !—how much talk of ancient things ! what deeds, what men you hear of ! what noble precepts you imbibe, though indeed he refrains from all apparent teaching ! Returning from a seven-mile drive, he walks again one mile ; then sits down or reclines with a pen in his hand, for he composes lyrical pieces with elegance both in Greek and Latin. Very soft, sweet, and merry they are, and their charm is enhanced by the decorum of the author's own habits.

When the hour of the bath is announced—that is, at two in summer, at three in winter—he strips and takes a turn in the sun if there is no wind. Then he uses strong exercise for a considerable space at tennis, for this is the discipline with which he struggles against old age. After t h e bath he takes his place at the table, but puts off eating for a time, listening in the meanwhile to a little light and pleasant reading. All this time his friends are free to do as he does, or anything else they please. Dinner is then served, elegant and moderate, on plain but ancient silver. He uses Corinthian bronzes too, and admires them without being foolishly addicted

FALLS AT TIBUR (MODERN TIVOLI).

to them. Players are often introduced between the courses, that the pleasures of the mind may give a relish to those of the palate. He trenches a little on the night even in summer ; but no one finds the time tire, such are his kindness and urbanity throughout. Hence now, at the age of seventy-seven, he both hears and sees perfectly ; hence his frame is active and vigorous ; he has nothing but old age to remind him to take care of himself.

Such is the mode of life to which I look forward for myself, and on which I will enter with delight as soon as advancing

years allow me to effect a retreat. Meanwhile I am harassed
by a thousand troubles, in which Spurinna is my consolation,
as he has ever been my example. For he, too, as long as it
became him, discharged duties, bore offices, governed provinces ; and great was the labor by which he earned his relaxation.
I propose to myself the same course and the same end ; and I
give you my oath that I will pursue it. If some ill-timed ambition should carry me beyond this purpose, produce this letter
against me, and condemn me to repose whenever I can enjoy
it without being reproached for indolence. Farewell.

When the philosophers began to preach retirement,
they found the ground already prepared for their
instructions.   So the two doctrines, Epicurism and
Stoicism, were heeded, when they both counseled with
the same energy renouncement of worldly ambition.
Resignation and abstinence constituted, according to
these philosophies, the whole of wisdom.   The philosopher should withdraw from public life and should have
no other care than to establish in silence and calm the
peace of his soul.   Ambition, which had formerly been
regarded as a noble passion, fruitful of good results, was
condemned as the source of all evils.

In life [writes Lucretius] we have a Sisyphus before our eyes
who is bent on asking from the people the rods and cruel axes,
and always retires defeated and disappointed. For to ask for
power, which, empty as it is, is never given, and always in the
chase of it to undergo severe toil, this is forcing up hill with
much effort a stone which after all rolls back again from the
summit and seeks in headlong haste the levels of the plain.

And Seneca, the disciple of the Stoic philosopher
Cleanthes, echoes Lucretius, the disciple of Epicurus.
When he had abandoned his position of power, when he
had voluntarily become poor and obscure, he says :

This narrow way which I have found so late, and after so
many wanderings, I desire to show to others. I warn them—

**Pliny's pro-
posed course.**

**Resignation
and abstinence.**

**The teaching
of Lucretius.**

**Seneca's
warning.**

avoid what catches the eye of the vulgar, refuse the gifts of
chance ; when some unlooked-for advantage is thrown in your
way, before touching it pause, full of fear and suspicion.
Think of those allurements which are used to attract and snare
animals. "These are the gifts of fortune," you say. No, they
are her traps. If you wish to live in peace, distrust these
deceitful presents ; for when you think you have them, you
will find that you are caught. Whoever allows himself to be
attracted by them is fatally conducted to the abyss ; and a fall
is always the sequel to great prosperity.

These counsels were welcomed not only by those who
were engaged in politics, but also by that more frivolous
class of people whose activities were merely social.
Under the influence of a very refined civilization the
intensity and even the abundance of pleasures produces
weariness and disgust ; and those souls which possess
some nobility are filled with bitterness and ennui. So it
was under the Roman Empire. People were full of
desire without object and of vague aspirations, of
anxiety without cause, and of indefinable hope, and they
found a bitter enjoyment in the contemplation of their
misery, and a mysterious pleasure in seeking the key of
the enigma which tormented them. Such was the condition of that young Annæus Serenus, commander of
Nero's body-guard, rich, brilliant, crowned apparently
with all the gifts of nature and of fortune. He confided
his trouble to Seneca, and sought advice as follows :

> I beg of you, if you know any remedy for this malady, do
> not think that I am unworthy of owing my peace of mind to
> you. It is not the tempest which disquiets me, it is sea-
> sickness. Deliver me, then, from this evil, whatever it is, and
> aid a wretch who suffers in sight of the shore.

And Seneca, who took an interest in this noble but
weak young man, and sympathized with him in his
anguish, gave him much kind counsel, all of the same

import.   He advised him to live for himself, to seek a retreat where he might enjoy that " happy condition in which the soul tastes an inalterable joy, and maintains itself in a peaceful state, free from exaltation or depression."

We are tempted to believe that melancholy had become fashionable, that it was stylish to be disillusioned and disappointed, as at the commencement of our century it was common to play the part of Werther or René, and that to treat this supposed malady with the favorite remedy of the philosophers, retirement from active life, was a proof of good taste and supreme elegance.

In the houses of the wealthy a singular custom had been established. In the midst of all the many far-sought forms of luxury, a retreat was reserved called the "poor man's chamber."

ROMAN PRIEST.   Vatican.

Here one so disposed might retire for a day now and then, to eat out of earthen dishes and sleep upon a straw bed.   Doubtless this was mere play, and perhaps even a last refinement of voluptuousness, to enable one to renew his capacity for enjoyment by the contrast of a day's privations. But can we not see even in such fantasies a proof that the custom of retiring from active life was becoming more general from day to day?

In reading Pliny's letters we find several examples of rich and cultivated men who withdrew early from public life, or never allowed themselves to be drawn into it. One day he met in the country one of these sensible men. Pliny, whose life had been so easily successful, and whose amiable optimism had attached him to the world, was doubtless somewhat astonished that any one should be willing to conceal himself from fame and from the eyes of men ; he was obliged, however, to recognize the fact that this taste for repose and security had become very prevalent.

O the numbers [he wrote] of learned men modesty conceals, or love of retirement withdraws from public fame ! And yet when we are going to speak or recite in public it is the judgment only of professed critics we stand in awe of ; whereas those who cultivate learning quietly and to themselves have in so far a higher claim to regard in that they pay a tribute of silent reverence to whatever is great in works of genius—an observation which I give you upon experience. Terentius Junior, having gone through the military duties suitable to a person of equestrian rank, and discharged with great integrity the post of receiver-general of the revenues of Narbonensian Gaul, retired to his estate, preferring the enjoyment of uninterrupted tranquillity to those honors that awaited his services. He invited me lately to his house, where, looking upon him only as a worthy head of a family and an industrious farmer, I started such topics as I imagined him to be most versed in. But he soon turned the conversation, entering with considerable display of learning upon subjects of literature. With what purity and delicacy did he express himself in Latin and Greek ! For he is such a master of both that whichever he speaks seems to be the language he particularly excels in. How extensive and varied is his reading !   How tenacious his memory !   You would not imagine him the inhabitant of an ignorant country village, but of polite Athens herself.   In short, his conversation has increased my anxiety about my works and taught me to revere the judgment of these retired country gentlemen as much as that of more known and distinguished *literati.*   Let me persuade you to consider them in the same light ; for, believe me, upon a careful observation, you will find that as in the army the best soldiers, so in literature the best scholars are often concealed under the most uncouth appearances.   Farewell.

The best scholars often concealed.

The poets of this time, Martial and Statius, were preeminently parlor versifiers.   We find in them no note which suggests the beautiful stanza of La Fontaine :

The poetry of Martial and Statius.

> Ah, country fields, in me a secret pain
>   Is wakened by your solitude and calm.
> Your cool and shade to weary heart and brain
>   Are like a fragrant balm.

And yet it is probable that many of the poets dreamed of a peaceful asylum, a retreat sacred to the Muses. Was not Tacitus expressing a poet's sentiment when he wrote this beautiful passage in his "Dialogue on Oratory" ?

The delight of Tacitus in the calm of nature.

As to the woods and groves and that retirement which Aper denounced, they bring such delight to me that I count among the chief enjoyments of poetry the fact that it is composed not in the midst of bustle, or with a suitor sitting before one's door, or amid the wretchedness and tears of prisoners, but that the soul withdraws herself to abodes of purity and innocence and enjoys her holy resting-place. . . .   For myself, as Virgil says, let "the sweet Muses" lead me to their sacred retreats, and to their fountains far away from anxieties and cares, and the necessity of doing every day something repugnant to my heart.   Let me no longer tremblingly experience the madness and perils of the forum, and the pallors of fame.   Let me not be aroused by a tumult of morning visitors, or a freedman's panting haste, or, anxious about the future, have to make a will to secure my wealth. Let me not possess more than what I can leave to whom I please, whenever the day appointed by my own fates shall come ; and let the statue over my tomb be not gloomy and scowling, but bright and laurel-crowned.

But even the poets who had no natural liking for retirement were sure sooner or later to feel the need of it. At this age of the empire literary life was very burdensome. The public had become as difficult to please as a sultan weary of life. It demanded to be served with dishes always new and appetizing. The optimates who played the part of Mæcenases only patronized those writers whom they found compliant and obedient to their whims. What man ever exhibited more subserviency than Statius? What constantly enforced restraint saddened the life of this beggar-poet !

Furthermore, rivalries were singularly active. Authors attacked each other unmercifully ; they tore each other to pieces. How, living in such an atmosphere, could one

The tribulations of authors.

ALTAR AT OSTIA.

fail to experience weariness at first, and soon exhaustion? Those who were able, therefore, escaped from this misery ; they went, as Juvenal says, to find in the country "some lizard's hole" where they might vegetate. Even Martial, whose tastes were never rural, whose poetry seldom expresses love of the country or of solitude, went to Spain, and, in the little village of Bilbilis,

Their attempts to find repose.

tried to rest from the artificial life he had led at Rome. In the following epigram he describes his experience :

Whilst you, my Juvenal, are perhaps wandering restless in the noisy Subura, or pacing the hill of the goddess Diana, whilst your *toga*, in which you perspire at the thresholds of your influential friends, is fanning you as you go, and the greater and lesser Cælian Hills fatigue you in your wanderings, my own Bilbilis, revisited after many winters, has received me, and made me a country gentleman—Bilbilis, proud of its gold and its iron ! Here we indolently cultivate with agreeable labor Boterduna and Platea ; these are the somewhat rude names of Celtiberian localities. I enjoy profound and extraordinary sleep, which is frequently unbroken, even at nine in the morning ; and I am now indemnifying myself fully for all the interruptions to sleep that I endured for thirty years. The *toga* here is unknown, but the nearest dress is given me, when I ask for it, from an old press. When I rise, a hearth heaped up with faggots from a neighboring oak grove welcomes me ; a hearth which the bailiff's wife crowns with many a pot. Then comes the housemaid, such a one as you would envy me. A close-shorn bailiff issues the orders to my boy attendants, and begs that they may be obliged to lay aside their long hair [in order to be ranked among full-grown men, and do men's work]. Thus I delight to live, and thus I hope to die.

Martial in the country.

We must admit that this enthusiasm did not last long. The poet soon conceived a dislike for the stupid provincials. He longed for Rome and thus confessed it to his friend Priscus :

I know that I owe some apology for my obstinate three years' indolence ; though, indeed, it could by no apology have been excused, even amid the engagements of the city, engagements in which we more easily succeed in making ourselves appear troublesome than serviceable to our friends ; and much less is it defensible in this country solitude, where, unless a person studies even to excess, his retreat is at once without consolation and without excuse. Listen, then, to my reasons ; among which the first and principal is this, that I miss the audience to which I had grown accustomed at Rome,

His longing for Rome.

and seem like an advocate pleading in a strange court ; for if there be anything pleasing in my books it is due to my auditors. That penetration of judgment, that fertility of invention, the libraries, the theaters, the social meetings, in which pleasure does not perceive that it is studying—everything, in a word, which we left behind us in satiety, we regret as though utterly deserted. Add to this the back-biting of the provincials, envy usurping the place of criticism, and one or two ill-disposed persons, who, in a small society, are a host—circumstances under which it is difficult to be always

A SHRINE IN A ROMAN PRIVATE HOUSE.

in the best of humors. Do not wonder, then, that I have abandoned in disgust occupations in which I used to employ myself with delight.

Martial was not fitted to be happy as a citizen of a small town, that is certain. Nevertheless he also, in his turn, felt the need of retiring.

Various were the reasons which led people to live in retirement. Many a man who did not have to fear political reverses, whose heart was free from sorrow, who was satisfied with an obscure career, and aspired to nothing more brilliant, went away to live forgotten and forgetful in some corner. Some yielded to the desire for an easy existence without care and without business ; others, ruined, did not wish to exhibit the spectacle of their misery ; many whom sickness rendered incapable of work and unfit to enjoy pleasures sought to obtain a cure, or at least to learn patience,

Various reasons for retirement from active life.

from solitude. This last class was the most numerous.

Beginning from the empire, sickness plays an important part in social life. Excesses of all sorts, the overcrowding of the population which was constantly increasing at Rome, the changes introduced in the matter of food, and bad hygienic habits were certainly enough to injure the public health. Perhaps, also, people had become less brave in the endurance of illness and more wrapped up in themselves. At any rate, infirmities to which the men of a previous generation seemed to pay no attention, which did not interrupt their activity until their strength gave way completely, exercised, at the time of which we are writing, an important influence upon the career of a Roman.

The increase of ill-health resulted in (was caused by, perhaps some cynics would say) the multiplication of physicians.

Medicine was a science of late development at Rome. The earlier physicians were usually Greek ; very few were Roman. They made money fast, but were not held in high esteem. Pliny the Naturalist has expressed his complaints against the physicians of his time in the following interesting passage, which Molière must have read :

Medicine is the only art which the Romans will not consent to practice, in spite of all the profit that it yields. Besides, those who cannot speak Greek have no prestige, not even with those who do not understand this language. Patients have less faith in prescriptions when they understand them. So physicians enjoy the privilege of being believed on their mere word, when they claim that they are qualified in their profession, and yet there is no case in which misrepresentation is more dangerous. . . . . Furthermore, there is no law to punish their ignorance ; we have not an example of a physician who has suffered capital punishment for his mistakes. It is at our risk

and peril that they learn their business, and it is in killing us
that they acquire experience. No one but a physician can kill
a man with impunity; moreover, the reproach does not rest
upon the physician; people accuse the intemperance of the
patient, and the dead are always to blame. . . . As avari-
cious as they are ignorant, the physicians will dispute about the
price of their visits at the bed of
the dying patient.

Yet Pliny the Elder did
not succeed in inspiring his
nephew with his horror of
physicians and their art.
When Pliny the Younger was
ill, he observed carefully the
directions of the doctors and
was patient and docile, and,
when restored to health, he
did not find fault with those
who had cured him. On the
contrary, he advises his
friends to make it easy, by
their confiding submission, for
the physicians to perform
their task. Read the following letter of Pliny's:

This obstinate illness of yours
alarms me; and though I know
how extremely temperate you
are, yet I fear lest your disease
should get the better of your

*Pliny's faith
in doctors.*

ÆSCULAPIUS.   Museum of Naples.

moderation. Let me entreat you, then, to resist it with a determined abstemiousness—a remedy, be assured, of all others
the most laudable as well as the most salutary. Human
nature itself admits the practicability of what I recommend; it
is a rule at least which I always enjoin my family to observe
with respect to myself. "I hope," I say to them, "that should
I be attacked with any disorder, I shall desire nothing of which

*His advice
to a friend.*

I ought either to be ashamed or have reason to repent ; however, if my distemper should prevail over my resolution, I forbid that anything be given me but by the consent of my physicians ; and I shall resent your compliance with me in things improper as much as another man would their refusal."

I once had a most violent fever ; when the fit was a little abated and I had been anointed, my physician offered me something to drink ; I held out my hand, desiring he would first feel my pulse, and upon his not seeming quite satisfied, I instantly returned the cup, though it was just at my lips. Afterward, when I was preparing to go into the bath, twenty days from the first attack of my illness, perceiving the physicians whispering together, I inquired what they were saying. They replied they were of opinion I may possibly bathe with safety, however that they were not without some suspicion of risk. "What need is there," said I, "of my taking a bath at all ?" And so, with perfect calmness and tranquillity, I gave up a pleasure I was upon the point of enjoying, and abstained from the bath as serenely and composedly as though I were going into it. I mention this, not only by way of enforcing my advice by example, but also that this letter may be a sort of tie upon me to persevere in the same resolute abstinence for the future. Farewell.

We must suppose that Pliny, whose views usually coincide with those of the majority of his contemporaries, expressed upon physicians the prevailing opinion of his epoch.

But often, in spite of the good-will of the patient, his malady baffled the physician ; often recourse was had in vain to all the known treatments, cold baths prescribed by Charmis, warm baths ordered by Æsculapius, *régime* of wine recommended by Cleophantus, or *régime* of water advised by Antonius Musa ; in vain were the drug stores spoiled of their medicines ; the malady was obstinate and refused to yield. Some patients, under such circumstances, were hopeful and refused to give up. Others were resigned to the inevitable and tried to see the bright side of their fate. It is for such that Pliny wrote this charming letter, which might be entitled "The Eulogy of Sickness" :

The lingering disorder of a friend of mine gave me occasion lately to reflect that we are never so good as when oppressed with illness. Where is the sick man who is either solicited by avarice or inflamed with lust? At such a season he is neither a slave of love nor the fool of ambition ; wealth he utterly disregards, and is content with ever so small a portion of it, as being upon the point of leaving even that little. It is *then* he recollects there are gods and that he himself is but a man ; no mortal is then the object of his envy, his admiration, or his contempt ; and the tales of slander neither raise his attention nor feed his curiosity ; his dreams are only of baths and fountains. These are the supreme objects of his cares and wishes, while he resolves, if he should recover, to pass the remainder of his days in ease and tranquillity, that is, to live innocently and happily. I may therefore lay down to you and myself a short rule, which the philosophers have endeavored to inculcate at the expense of many words, and even many volumes ; that "we should try to realize in health those resolutions we form in sickness." Farewell.

Pliny's "Eulogy of Sickness."

Excellent words, and helpful to those whose sufferings are not too sharp ; but to those unfortunate invalids bound to a bed of pain, for whom the future held no prospect but a series of agonies, what comfort could such words bring? None, assuredly ; in such hopeless cases, where all the known remedies had been tried and had failed, the last recourse was to that infallible and supreme remedy, death.

Hopeless cases.

Atticus, who had been sick for a long while, sent for his son-in-law Agrippa, and his friends L. Cornelius Balbus and Sextus Peducœus. When they arrived, he spoke to them as follows :

Atticus.

There is no need of my reminding you what care I have taken to restore my health, for you know already. Since then

I have done my best to preserve myself for you ; it remains for me now to think of myself. I wished to let you know. Yes, I am going to cease nourishing my malady. For all the food that I have taken these last few days has only prolonged my life to increase my pain. I beg of you, then, to approve of my resolution and do nothing to shake it.

They implored him to change his purpose, but he would not listen to them ; he refused to take any nourishment and died after two days.

Silius Italicus. The poet Silius Italicus, who, after having been an informer under Nero, had succeeded in winning back public esteem, and in his villa at Naples was leading a quiet life, surrounded by affection and respect, suffered from an incurable abscess ; he did not hesitate to commit suicide.

Corellius Rufus. Corellius Rufus chose the same method of putting an end to his malady. Let Pliny relate to us the sad circumstances :

I have suffered the heaviest loss ; if that word be sufficiently strong to express the misfortune which has deprived me of so excellent a man. Corellius Rufus is dead ; and dead, too, by his own act. A circumstance of great aggravation to my affliction ; as that sort of death which we cannot impute either to the course of nature, or the hand of Providence, is, of all others, the most to be lamented. It affords some consolation in the loss of those friends whom disease snatches from us that they fall by the general destiny of mankind ; but those who destroy themselves leave us under the inconsolable reflection that they had it in their power to have lived longer. It is true, **His induce-** Corellius had many inducements to be fond of life ; a blame- **ments to live.** less conscience, high reputation, and great dignity of character, besides a daughter, a wife, a grandson, and sisters ; and, amidst these numerous pledges of happiness, faithful friends. Still, it must be owned he had the highest motive (which to a wise man will always have the force of destiny) urging him to this resolution. He had long been tortured by so tedious and painful a complaint that even these inducements to living on, considerable as they are, were overbalanced by the reasons on the other side.

In his thirty-third year (as I have frequently heard him say) he was seized with the gout in his feet. This was hereditary; *His painful malady.* for diseases, as well as possessions, are sometimes handed down by a sort of inheritance. A life of sobriety and continence had enabled him to conquer and keep down the disease while he was still young; latterly, as it grew upon him with advancing years, he had to bear it manfully, suffering meanwhile the most incredible and undeserved agonies; for the gout was now not only in his feet, but had spread itself over his whole body. I remember, in Domitian's reign, paying *Pliny's visit to Rufus.* him a visit at his villa, near Rome. As soon as I entered his chamber, his servants went out; for it was his rule never to allow them to be in the room when any intimate friend was with him; nay, even his own wife, though she could have kept any secret, used to go too. Casting his eyes round the room, "Why," he exclaimed, " do you suppose I endure life so long under these cruel agonies? It is with the hope that I may out- *Outliving a tyrant.* live, at least for one day, that villain."

Had his bodily strength been equal to his resolution, he would have carried his desire into practical effect. God heard and answered his prayer; and when he felt that he should now die a free, unenslaved Roman, he broke through those other great, but now less forcible, attachments to the world. His malady increased; and, as it now grew too violent to admit of any relief from temperance, he resolutely determined to put an end to its uninterrupted attacks, by an effort of heroism. He had refused all sustenance during four days, when his wife Hispulla sent our common friend Geminius to me, with the *The resolution of Rufus.* melancholy news that Corellius was resolved to die; and that neither her own entreaties nor her daughter's could move him from his purpose; I was the only person left who could reconcile him to life. I ran to his house with the utmost precipitation. As I approached it, I met a second messenger from Hispulla, Julius Atticus, who informed me there was nothing to be hoped for now, even from me, as he seemed more hardened than ever in his purpose. He had said, indeed, to his physician, who pressed him to take some nourishment, " 'Tis resolved," an expression which, as it raised my admiration of the greatness of his soul, so it does my grief for the loss of him.

And no one thought of blaming such conduct. Titius Aristo, being seriously ill, begged his friends to find out from the physicians whether there was any hope for him. He thought he owed it to his friends to neglect no means of saving himself ; but if recovery was impossible, he was resolved to take his own life.

Tomb at Pompeii.

This [says Pliny] I consider more than usually difficult and praiseworthy. For to rush upon death with impetuosity and ardor is common to many ; but to deliberate about it, and discuss the arguments for it and against it, and live and die accordingly, is worthy of a great mind.

What must we conclude from these examples, chosen from thousands, if not that death, for the men of this age, was not so terrible as it appears to many in the present time?

The two great systems of philosophy, which attempted

to teach the ancients concerning the fate of the soul after death, offered them no consolation perhaps, but on the other hand suggested no horrible possibilities.

Epicurism affirmed boldly that there was no future life. Natural law gives us birth, natural law causes us to die. It has drawn us out of nothing and it sends us back to nothing. After having loved and suffered, we shall cease to love and suffer. We shall return to mix with the elements which have given us life, and shall thus in our turn give life to other beings ; we shall become mere chemical ingredients in the great laboratory of nature.

> Death [says Lucretius] does not extinguish things in such a way as to destroy the bodies of matter, but only breaks up the union amongst them, and then joins anew the different elements with others.

As to the Stoics, they do not deny absolutely the immortality of the soul, but they do not believe in the persistence of personality. According to them, when the human being dies, the soul is absorbed into the universal soul.

But why was it that these Romans, so unconcerned about the future after death, placed so much importance upon their funerals and their burials?

In the earliest times the Romans believed that a remnant of life persisted beyond the tomb, that the body and the soul were still capable of suffering, and that the withholding of certain funeral rites might result in eternal woe to the dead. This general belief became later a superstition from which even those who made a profession of Epicurism were not free. The poet Lucretius, with passionate irony, protested against such inconsistency :

> When you see a man bemoaning his hard case, that after

The protest of Lucretius.

death he shall either rot with his body laid in the grave or be devoured by flames or the jaws of wild beasts, you may be sure that his ring betrays a flaw and that there lurks in his heart a secret goad, though he himself declare that he does not believe that any sense will remain to him after death. He does not, methinks, really grant the conclusion which he professes to grant nor the principle on which he so professes, nor does he take and force himself root and branch out of life, but all unconsciously imagines something of self to survive.

The formality of funeral rites.

But in the time of the Antonines, this superstition had disappeared among cultivated men. Yet the formality of funeral rites was by no means diminished, and in this there is nothing surprising. Those who desired that funeral honors should be paid to them were not influenced by religious faith ; they were simply conforming to custom. The ancient religion no longer existed except in its forms ; but the Romans, who were a formalistic people, would have been shocked at the idea of abandoning time-honored ceremonies.

Arrived at the end of our task, it only remains for us to accompany to their final resting-place these Romans whose daily life we have attempted to follow.

Preparations for burial.

When some member of a family was on the point of death the nearest relative stood by him and closed his eyes. Then as soon as life was extinct those who surrounded his bed called upon him several times by his name, crying loudly *vale* (adieu). His body, washed and anointed, was laid, dressed in a white *toga*, upon a couch in the atrium, the feet turned toward the street. A branch of cypress was placed outside the door of the house, to warn the *pontifex maximus*, who would incur pollution by entering where a dead body lay. At the same time notice of the death was sent to the Temple of Libitina, the goddess of corpses and funerals, and the *Libitinarii* (undertakers) came to take charge of the funeral.

Among the wealthy and those of rank the obsequies were performed with much pomp. The atrium was filled with visitors, the men wearing the *pænula* (a traveling cloak) and the women the *ricinium* (a sort of mantle with a hood attached to it). Hired female mourners were present to sing dirges over the dead. The procession was marshaled by the master of ceremonies, the *designator.* First came the musicians, then the hired mourners, next dancers and *mimi.* The *archimimus* imitated the appearance, bearing, and language of the deceased. Next in order were men who represented the dead man's ancestors; they wore as masks the *imagines* (images) of the ancestors, and were dressed in their official costume. These mock ancestors rode upon

The funeral procession.

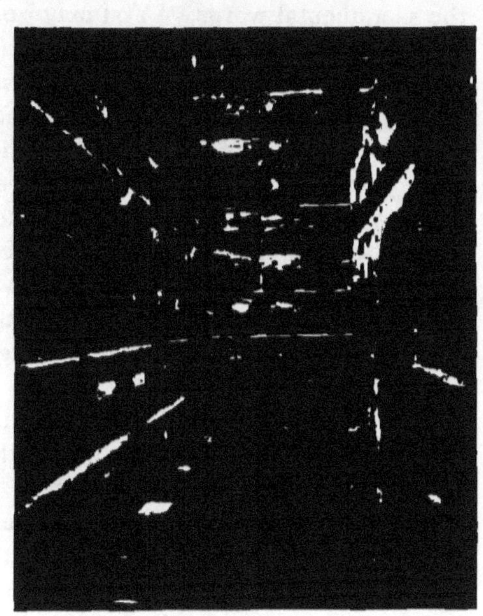

COLUMBARIUM AT ROME.

chariots and were followed by the body. The procession was closed by friends and relatives. When the funeral pyre was reached, which was required by law to be sixty feet from any building, the bier was placed upon it, and the procession moved solemnly around it,

At the pyre.

the faces turned toward the east, and the friends of the dead threw offerings upon the pyre, perfumes, and tokens of love. After this gladiators fought to the death ; and when the combat was finished for want of combatants, the son or nearest relative, with averted face, applied a torch to the pyre. The bones and ashes were gathered into a brass urn, to be placed in the family sepulcher. Finally, the *designator* purified those present by a sprinkling of pure water, and pronounced the sacramental words, "You may go."

A poor man's funeral was much simpler. There were no hired mourners, no master of ceremonies, no dirges, no magnificent funeral pyre. His body was inclosed in a sort of coffin, and was carried to the public subterranean burial-place near the Esquiline Hill, called the grave-pits (*puticulæ*). Nothing indicated the place where he took his eternal sleep ; he could not, like the rich entombed along the Flaminian Way, receive the blessings of the passers-by, whose attention was invited by such inscriptions as "Stop, traveler," or "Look, traveler."

But beginning with the first century of the Christian era, societies were formed among the poor, with the object of giving to their members a suitable burial. Those who, by paying the required dues, joined a society of this sort had the assurance that instead of being buried after death in public ground, their ashes would be placed in the *columbarium* (a chamber with niches for receiving urns of ashes) where their associates reposed.

CHAPTER XI.

PLINY'S CORRESPONDENCE.

PLINY THE YOUNGER is the author whom we have oftenest quoted in the course of this work. Let us explain why we have given such weight to his testimony upon the private life of his contemporaries. Why is Pliny's testimony valuable?

In the first place, what opportunity had Pliny for knowing the truth in this interesting matter? Let us consider the circumstances in which he was placed, his social relations, and his character.

We learn from an inscription that has been preserved for us that Pliny occupied in succession all the magistracies from the lowest to the highest, that he held one after another, in regular order, all the military, financial, and political offices, beginning his career as superintendent of the public road work in Rome, and finally attaining the administration of a great province, Bithynia. His active public life. Whatever love Pliny may profess for literature, he was not merely a man of the school and the study. He mixed in public affairs ; he did not depend upon books for his knowledge of life ; he was not without experience of the world. We cannot deny that he loved a studious retreat, a calm life, occupied mostly with intellectual pleasures ; but we must recognize the fact that he was compelled to live a practical life, that he could not give all his days to poetry and eloquence, and that he did not view his contemporaries only from the platform of the lecture hall.

He had among his friends Silius Italicus, Martial, and

many other poets and men of letters, whose names alone survive to-day, and of whom, as he tells us, there were many in his time. But let us not suppose that his social relations were limited to this narrow circle of literary men. He associated also with statesmen and men of the world ; they were his peers ; with them he was in his natural element. In spite of his devotion to the Muses, he perhaps even thought he was lowering himself when he sought the companionship of Martial, that needy poet, and of his other friends or rivals who led what we might call to-day a bohemian life.

But Pliny was perfectly at home with his friend Spurinna, that wise old man who knew well how to live and better how to die ; or again with Virginius Rufus, a truly noble soul, who under Nero had refused the empire offered him by his legions, and who, by a glorious anachronism, made the manners of the republic flourish again under the empire. These great personages had witnessed the dawn of Cæsarism ; like all aged people, they loved to recall the past and to dwell upon their reminiscences ; and they often drew, for those who were wise enough to listen, useful comparisons between the former time and the present time. Must not Pliny have profited by his acquaintance with them? Junius

Mauricus, the brother of Rusticus Arulenus, a heroic outlaw, Corellius Rufus, who had experienced the tyranny of Domitian, and who in spite of his calamities did not wish for death, because he wanted to survive the monster Domitian, Erucius Clarus, advocate eloquent and skilful, honoring his profession by his honesty, his courage, and his modesty, Titius Aristo, an eminent scholar, Maximus, a literary optimate, governor of Achaia—such are the men, either lawyers, politicians, or scholars, who formed the true society of Pliny. They were all men of serious purpose, cultured, distinguished by fortune, honors, and character, and they looked upon the combat of life from the point of view of those who have entered into the conflict.

It is to such men that he applies for advice when he is placed in a delicate or difficult dilemma, which concerns his conscience or his safety. Let us quote Pliny's letter to his friend Voconius Romanus :

Did you ever see a man more cowed, more down in the mouth, than Regulus since the death of Domitian? His crimes under Domitian were quite as bad as those under Nero, but they were less easy of detection. He began to fear I was angry with him, and so indeed I was. He had done his best to imperil Rusticus Arulenus ; he openly rejoiced at his death, and even published a book in which he abused him, and called him "an ape of Stoic philosophers." He made such a savage attack on Herennius Senecio that Metius Carus said to him : "What have you to do with my victims? Did I ever attack Crassus or Camerinus?" These were men whom Regulus accused and ruined in Nero's reign. He thought I was indignant at all this ; and so, when he gave a reading to a select circle out of the book he had published, he did not invite me.

He remembered, too, what a savage attack he had once made on me in the Court of the Hundred. I was counsel for Arrionilla, a case which I had undertaken at the request of Arulenus. I had Regulus against me. In one part of the case I laid much stress on an opinion given by Modestus, an excellent man, who was then by Domitian's order in banishment. Up jumps Regulus, and says to me, "Pray, what view do you take of the character of Modestus?" It would, you see, have been very dangerous to me to have replied, "I think well of him"; it would have been an infamous thing to have said the contrary. Well, I really believe that Providence helped me out of the scrape. "I will answer your question," I replied, "if this is the matter on which the court is about to pronounce judgment." He could say nothing. I was praised and congratulated for having avoided compromising my credit by a safe but discreditable answer, and for having escaped the snare of such an invidious question.

He was thoroughly frightened, and rushes up to Cæcilius Celer and Fabius Justus and begs them to reconcile us. This was not enough for him; he goes off to Spurinna, and with that cringing manner which he always has when he is frightened, he says to him, "Pray, go and call on Pliny the very first thing in the morning (be sure you do this, for I can't endure my anxiety any longer), and do your best to prevail on him not to be angry with me." I had risen early; there comes a message from Spurinna to this effect, "I am coming to see you." I sent back word, "I am myself coming to you." Well, we met on the way in Livia's portico; Spurinna explains the wishes of Regulus, and adds his own entreaties, as you would expect from a very good man on behalf of one wholly unlike himself. I replied to him: "You will yourself clearly perceive what message you think had best be sent back to Regulus; you ought not to be misled by me. I am waiting the return of Mauricus (he had not yet come back from exile); I can't give you an answer either way, because I mean to do whatever he decides on, for he ought to be my leader in this matter, and I ought to be simply his follower."

A few days afterward Regulus met me at one of the prætor's levees; he kept close to me and begged me to give him a private interview. He then told me he was afraid that a remark he had once made in the Court of the Hundred still rankled in my mind. The remark, he said, was made when he was replying as counsel to myself, and to Satrius Rufus, and was this: "Satrius Rufus, who does not attempt to rival Cicero, and who is content with the eloquence of our own day." My answer to him was: "I see now that you meant it ill-naturedly, because you admit it yourself; but your remark might have been taken as intended to be complimentary. I do try to rival Cicero and I am not content with the eloquence of our own day. It is, I think, the height of folly not to propose to one's self the best pattern for imitation. But how comes it you remember this circumstance so distinctly and have forgotten the occasion in court when you asked me what was my opinion of the loyalty of Modestus?" Pale as he always looks, he turned as pale as death, and stammered out that he asked the question, not to hurt me, but to hurt Modestus. Note the fellow's vindictive cruelty; he actually confessed to himself that he wished to do an injury to one in exile. He added an admirable reason for his conduct. "Modestus," he said, " in a letter written by him which was read out before Domitian, used the following expression: 'Regulus, of all two-footed creatures the wickedest.'" And Modestus was perfectly right. This ended our conversation. I did not wish to go further in the matter, or to tie my hands in any way, till Mauricus had returned. I am very well aware that Regulus is a formidable person. He is rich, influential, courted by many, feared by many, and to be feared often does more for a man than to be loved.

The formidable power of Regulus.

But, after all, even the tyranny of fear may be broken ; for a man's bad credit is as shifty as himself. However, to repeat, I am waiting until Mauricus comes back. He is a man of sound judgment and great sagacity, formed upon long experience, and one who, from his observations of the past, well knows how to judge of the future. I shall talk the matter over with him, and consider myself justified either in pursuing or dropping this affair, as he shall advise. Meanwhile I thought I owed this account to our mutual friendship, which gives you an undoubted right to know not only about all my actions, but about all my plans as well. Farewell.

Such was Pliny's genial nature that he enjoyed the society of young people and ladies. Saturninus used to submit to him confidentially the literary efforts of his young and charming wife ; Fuscus Salinator and Numidius Quadratus, two talented young men who had just been admitted to the bar, firm friends, chose Pliny as model and master. Pliny could not refrain from expressing his pleasure at this :

Pliny's enjoyment in the society of young people and ladies.

O what a happy day [he wrote to Maximus] I lately spent ! I was called by the prefect [mayor] of Rome, to assist him in a certain case, and had the pleasure of hearing two excellent young men, Fuscus Salinator and Numidius Quadratus, plead on the opposite sides ; their weight is equal, and each of them will one day, I am persuaded, prove an ornament not only to the present age, but to literature itself. They evinced upon this occasion an admirable probity, supported by inflexible courage ; their dress was decent, their elocution distinct, their

Fuscus Salinator and Numidius Quadratus.

tones were manly, their memory retentive, their genius elevated, and guided by an equal solidity of judgment. I took
infinite pleasure in observing them display these noble qualities ; particularly as I had the satisfaction to see that, while
they looked upon me as their guide and model, they appeared
to the audience as my imitators and rivals. It was a day, I
cannot but repeat it again, which afforded me the most exqui-
site happiness and which I shall ever distinguish by the fairest

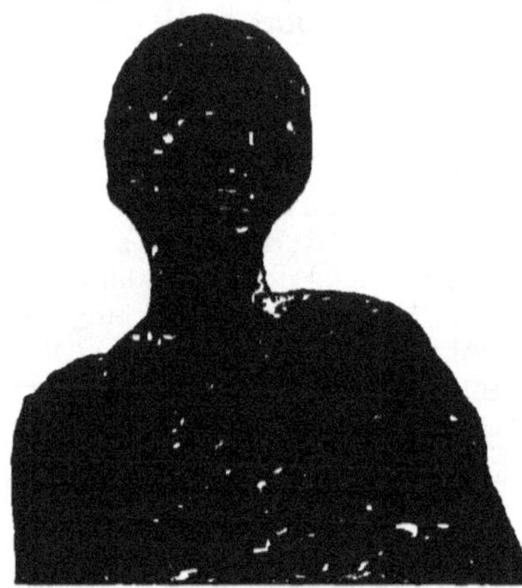

A ROMAN WOMAN.

mark. For what, in-
deed, could be either
more pleasing to me on
the public account than
to observe two such
noble youths building
their fame and glory
upon the polite arts ; or
more desirable upon my
own than to be marked
out as a worthy example
to them in their pursuits
of virtue ? May the
gods still grant me the
continuance of that
pleasure ! And I im-
plore the same gods,
you are my witness, to
make all these who think me deserving of imitation far better
than I am. Farewell.

Pliny was received as an intimate friend in the family
of Thrasea, where we find so many noble and lovely
women, and he certainly knew what he was talking
about when he praised Fannia, the heroic wife of Helvidius, in the following letter :

The illness of my friend Fannia gives me great concern.
She contracted it during her attendance on Junia, one of the
vestal virgins, engaging in this good office at first voluntarily,
Junia being her relation, and afterward being appointed to it
by an order from the college of priests ; for these virgins, when
excessive ill-health renders it necessary to remove them from

the Temple of Vesta, are always delivered over to the care and custody of some venerable matron. It was owing to her assiduity in the execution of this charge that she contracted her present dangerous disorder, which is a continual fever, attended with a cough which increases daily. She is extremely emaciated, and every part of her seems in a total decay except her spirits ; those indeed she fully keeps up, and in a way altogether worthy the wife of Helvidius and the daughter of Thrasea. In all other respects there is such a falling away that I am more than apprehensive upon her account ; I am deeply afflicted.

Fannia's illness.

I grieve, my friend, that so excellent a woman is going to be removed from the eyes of the world, which will never perhaps again behold her equal. So pure she is, so pious, so wise and prudent, so brave and steadfast ! Twice she followed her husband into exile, and the third time she was banished herself upon this account. For Senecio, when arraigned for writing the life of Helvidius, having said in his defense that he composed that work at the request of Fannia, Metius Carus, with a stern and threatening air, asked her whether she had made that request, and she replied, "I made it." Did she supply him likewise with materials for the purpose? "I did." Was her mother privy to this transaction? "She was not." In short, throughout her whole examination, not a word escaped her which betrayed the smallest fear. On the contrary, she had preserved a copy of those very books which the senate, overawed by the tyranny of the times, had ordered to be suppressed, and at the same time the effects of the author to be confiscated, and carried with her into exile the very cause of her exile.

Her heroism.

How pleasing she is, how courteous, and, what is granted to few, no less lovable than worthy of all esteem and admiration ! Will she hereafter be pointed out as a model to all wives, and perhaps be esteemed worthy of being set forth as an example of fortitude even to our sex ; since, while we still have the pleasure of seeing her, and conversing with her, we contemplate her with the same admiration as those heroines who are celebrated in ancient story? For myself, I confess I cannot but tremble for this illustrious house, which seems shaken to its very foundations and ready to fall ; for though she will leave descendants behind her, yet what a height of virtue must they attain, what glorious deeds must they perform, ere the world

A model for all wives.

will be persuaded that she was not the last of her family.

It is an additional affliction and anguish to me that by her death I seem to lose her mother a second time ; that worthy mother (and what can I say higher in her praise ?) of so noble a woman ! who, as she was restored to me in her daughter, so she will now again be taken from me, and the loss of Fannia will thus pierce my heart at once with a fresh, and at the same time reopened, wound. I so truly loved and honored them both that I know not which I loved the best ; a point they desired might ever remain undetermined. In their prosperity and their adversity I did them every kindness in my power, and was their comforter in exile as well as their avenger at their return. But I have not yet paid them what I owe, and am so much the more solicitous for the recovery of this lady, that I may have time to discharge my debt to her. Such is the anxiety and sorrow under which I write

Pliny's devotion to Fannia and her mother.

A Vestal Virgin. Rome.

this letter ! But if some divine power should happily turn it into joy, I shall not complain of the alarms I now suffer. Farewell.

Pliny's wide horizon.

Pliny shows by his friendships that he had interests outside of literature. His horizon, his field of observation were wide.

Why, then, should he not have been well acquainted with the manners of the higher classes of his time ? If he is not a good authority on this subject, should we not

be compelled to suppose, when we take into consideration his opportunities, that his intelligence was deficient?
Now those who admire Pliny the least cannot go so far
as to hold this view; the most that they can say is that
his intelligence was only average. But was he easily
prejudiced? Was he a man of whims? By no means;
to convince one's self of the contrary, it is only necessary
to read him.

We are forced, however, to admit that he had a gen-
eral tendency toward optimism; and this fact may affect His optimism.
the value of his testimony to a certain degree. The
reign of Domitian produced little effect upon his mind.
He perhaps shuddered at the recollection of it, as if it
had been a terrible accident; but the horrors of the
epoch did not leave in his soul that bitterness and melancholy which characterize the pages of Tacitus, his
contemporary and friend. The reigns of Nerva and
Trajan undid as far as possible the evil that Domitian
had done; the good people who had been banished from
Rome met, on their way back as they were returning
from the land of exile, the informers who had caused
their banishment. Social life, interrupted by the reign
of terror, began again, more brilliant than ever. The
people rejoiced in the shadow of legality, and in the
appearance of liberty.

This was enough to satisfy Pliny. Life had always
smiled upon him, and he smiled upon life. At eighteen His un-
years of age he inherited his uncle's wealth and name; troubled life.
there were no obstacles in his career; he passed without
any struggle through the successive degrees of rank; he
experienced no reverses of fortune, no family sorrows;
true, he was twice a widower, but Calpurnia, his third
wife, loved and admired him; the joys which children
bring were denied him, but then he was not obliged to

suffer the anguish and the disappointment so frequently the lot of a father.   We find no evidence that Pliny ever formed a deep friendship, like that of Cicero's for Brutus, or Montaigne's for Boétie ; his correspondence with Tacitus reminds us of that of Racine's with Boileau.   It was cold and polite, full of respect, but without a trace of spontaneous affection.   But, on the other hand, Pliny never felt the bitterness of a false friendship.

Pliny not a man of deep friendships.

How could one who had so many reasons for counting himself happy, or at least so little to complain of, be disposed to find fault with people about him?   How could Pliny help acquiring a habit of ready kindness, when life was so kind to him?   And, in fact, he seems to have been one of those people of whom Quintilian makes fun because they consider it good social tact to exchange compliments upon every occasion.   Pliny was too much inclined to praise his friends with excess.   He was criticised for this by one of his acquaintances, to whom he made the following gracious reply :

A SACRIFICE.

Pliny's urbanity.

You tell me certain persons have blamed me in your company, as being upon all occasions too lavish in the praise I give my friends.   I not only acknowledge the charge, but glory in it ; for can there be a nobler error than an overflowing benevolence? But still, who are these, let me ask, that are better acquainted with my friends than I am myself? Yet grant there are any such, why will they deny me the satisfaction of so pleasing a mistake? For supposing my friends not to deserve the highest encomiums I give them, yet I am happy in believing they do. Let them recommend, then, this malignant zeal to those, and their number is not inconsiderable, who imagine they show their judgment when they indulge their censure upon their friends. As for myself, they will never be able to persuade me I can be guilty of an excess in friendship. Farewell.

His praise of his friends.

The one thing lacking in Pliny's life was sorrow. No one knows himself well, and no one can know others, if he has been petted by fortune, and if he has never suffered. So, while Pliny's social relations presented him with a good opportunity for observing the manners of high life in his time, his character was not such as to enable him to interpret profoundly all that he saw. He preferred to dwell upon the noble and lovely aspects of society. He did not aim to analyze motives, knowing well that he would not have succeeded in such an attempt, and having no taste in that direction besides. He had no desire to encroach upon the domain of his friend Tacitus.

Pliny's inexperience of sorrow.

He is not an analyzer of motives.

We shall not find, then, in Pliny's writings those lightning flashes, swift and penetrating, which reveal the most hidden recesses in the soul of a man. Nor, on the other hand, shall we have to make any allowance, in drawing our conclusions from Pliny's testimony, for the tendency to which moralists are liable of unfair suspicion in judging men. For so great is the pleasure in discovering the secret motives for actions that one is tempted to imagine them where they do not exist. After all, there is more justice and justness in the good-will of a Pliny than in the rage of a Juvenal. The exaggeration in the praises bestowed by Pliny upon his friends, in

Pliny's good-will juster than Juvenal's bitterness.

which the polished complaisance of the man appears, leads us not so far from the truth as the exaggeration of Juvenal's invectives.

Satisfied with the world in which he lived, Pliny did not try to go outside of it. Charmed by the brilliant society of the patricians, he did not condescend to notice the plebeians. He did not care to penetrate into the tavern of a Syrophœnician, and to mix with sailors, sharpers, fugitive slaves, coffin-makers, and mendicant priests of Cybele. In high society he tried to see only the pleasant aspects ; and in society as a whole he considered only the upper class. Wretched clients, half-starved parasites, shabbily clothed poets, people engaged in questionable occupations, all this miserable crowd had no existence for him. Whoever desires to become acquainted with it must go to Juvenal, not forgetting, however, to be on his guard against being misled by the satirist's severity. When Juvenal depicts for us this strange world, does he not indulge too freely an artist's fancy for the picturesque? Does he not take a certain pleasure in representing glaring wretchedness because his palette was rich in crude colors? Has he not made the shadow too black upon certain portraits and certain pictures? Pliny has said very little of any slaves but his own, and yet I am inclined to believe that what he has told us of their condition contains more general truth on the subject of slavery than we are able to gather from Juvenal's satires.

In short, our author was not able and did not try to learn the whole truth, but, with the exception of some exaggerations in his eulogies, he has told us nothing but the truth. We should not conclude from his panegyric addressed to Trajan that Pliny was a flatterer. The tone of this piece of rhetoric is doubtless artificial and false ; but the sentiment is sincere. Moreover, at the time when Pliny wrote there was no longer any danger in saying only what one thought. Trajan imposed adulation upon no one.

Nor was there any special merit in saying only what one thought. Anxious to repair the evils effected by Domitian, to inspire with a sense of freedom those who had been exasperated by oppression, the new emperor thought it his best policy to grant some liberty to the orators and writers. Juvenal and Tacitus at this time uttered certain proud sentiments which caused them to be taken, wrongly perhaps, for republicans. Pliny could therefore without danger praise and blame friends and enemies ; he did not need to consider their standing at court.

Besides all these reasons for giving him our confidence, there is another still more decisive. His letters were not sent to his friends to be kept by them in their portfolios ; in writing them their author manifestly had in mind their publication.

Since the success of Cicero's letters, correspondence had become a distinct species of literature. Books were written consisting of letters on various subjects. Fashion approved of this, and Pliny in spite of his seriousness paid his court to fashion. It was, then, much less to his correspondents than to the public that he addressed his missives. This is very apparent to one who considers the fact that no private details are given in the letters. What he writes to his wife, whom he appears however to have loved dearly, is vague and abstract :

You write that you are no little troubled by my absence, and find your only solace in making my books take my place and setting them where I ought to be. I am glad that you miss me ; I am glad that you find some rest in these alleviations. For my part, I read and reread your letters, taking them up in my hands many times, as though they were newly come ; but this only stirs in me a keener longing for you. What sweetness must there be in the talk of one whose letters contain so much that pleases ! Write, nevertheless, as often as you can, though this, while it delights, still tortures me.

Cicero wrote in a different tone to his Terentia. This was because he did not meditate his letters, but wrote them wherever and whenever he could. "I take," said he to his brother, "the first pen that I find, and use it as if it was good" ; for the messengers "are ready to start, with their traveling hats on ; they say that their companions are waiting at the door."

Pliny requires more leisure.

Your earnest request [he says to Sabinus] that I would write to you very frequent and very long letters is extremely agreeable to me. If I have forborne to do so, it has been partly because you were busy and I did not like to disturb you ; and partly from some very cold and uninteresting affairs of my own, which engage my thoughts, and at the same time weary me.

We perceive in the writer of this letter the man who is not willing to let anything escape from his pen that is not carefully composed. He would never have put to his correspondents the following questions which Cicero asked his :

What do you think of my letters? Do you not think that I write to you in a commonplace style? But one cannot always maintain the same tone. A letter cannot be expected to resemble a plea, or a political speech. . . . In letters we ought to use every-day expressions.

Pliny certainly understood that the epistolary style should not be stilted, but he did not admit that it should be conversational ; he claimed that it should be, if not ornate, at least elegant. So his careful compo-

sition is everywhere shown in his letters. An insignificant note is embellished with quotations and studied
phrases. It suggests the idea of a jewel in a casket
worth more than itself.

You tell me in your letter [Pliny says to Suetonius] that you
are extremely alarmed by a dream, apprehending that it fore-
bodes some ill success to you in the case you have undertaken
to defend, and therefore desire that I would get it adjourned
for a few days, or at least to the next. This will be no easy
matter, but I will try,

" For dreams descend from Jove."

Meanwhile it is very material for you to recollect whether your
dreams generally represent things as they afterward fall out, or
quite the reverse. But if I may judge of yours by one that
happened to myself, this dream that alarms you so seems to
portend that you will acquit yourself with great success. I had
promised to stand counsel for Junius Pastor ; when I fancied in
my sleep that my mother-in-law came to me, and, throwing
herself at my feet, earnestly entreated me not to plead. I was
at that time a very young man ; and the case was to be argued
in the four centumviral courts ; my adversaries were some of
the most important personages in Rome, and particular favorites of Cæsar [Domitian] ; any of which circumstances were
sufficient after such an inauspicious dream to have discouraged
me. Notwithstanding this, I engaged in the cause, reflecting
that,

" Without a sign, his sword the brave man draws,
And asks no omen but his country's cause,"

for I looked upon the promise I had given to be as sacred to
me as my country, or, if that were possible, more so. The
event happened as I wished ; and it was that very case which
first procured me the favorable attention of the public, and
threw open to me the gates of fame. Consider, then, whether
your dream, like this one I have related, may not pre-signify
success. But, after all, perhaps you will think it safer to pursue
this cautious maxim : "Never do a thing concerning the recti-
tude of which you are in doubt " ; if so, write me word. In
the interval I will consider of some excuse, and will so plead

The dream of
Suetonius.

Pliny's dream.

Its signification.

Pliny's advice
to Suetonius.

your cause that you may be able to plead it yourself any day
you like best. In this respect, you are in a better situation than
I was ; the court of the centumvirs, where I was to plead,
admits of no adjournment ; whereas, in that where your case is
to be heard, though no easy matter to procure one, still, however, it is possible. Farewell.

The fact that Pliny had the public in mind when he
wrote his letters is shown by the choice of subjects, and
by their treatment.

Pliny's subjects.

Do not expect Pliny to chat in his letters, or allow
his pen any freedom. He will, it is true, consent to
speak of trifles, but only for the sake of clothing them
in graceful language, and of introducing some striking
phrase. With him no unrestrained and charming gossip, such as the reader enjoys in the letters of the lovely
Marquise de Sévigné. When he is on the point of

His studied
style.

being natural, he struggles against the temptation and
resists it, a fact which the following letter illustrates :

It is a rule which we should upon all occasions, both private
and public, most religiously observe, "to be inexorable toward
ourselves, while we treat the rest of the world with tenderness,
not excepting even those who forgive none but themselves " ;
remembering always what the humane, and *therefore*, as well
as upon other accounts *great* Thrasea used frequently to say :
" He who hates vice hates mankind." You ask, perhaps, who
has provoked me to write in this strain. Well, a person lately
—but of that when we meet—though upon second thoughts not
even then, lest in condemning and exposing *his* conduct I
should act counter to that maxim I particularly recommend.

Glance through a collection of Pliny's letters, and you
will readily perceive that the author did not try to make
his pages the echo of the rumors that he heard, the
mirror of the events which passed before him. The
arrangement of subjects is ingeniously varied. They
succeed each other with a diversity skilfully calculated

to pique and awaken the attention. Whatever Pliny may say, the order of his letters is chronologic, and by no means abandoned to mere chance ; a certain subject suggested a certain subject ; here, an antithesis was necessary, there, a comparison. The letters of recommendation, of congratulation, of condolence are purposely made to alternate with descriptions, or discourses on moral or literary subjects. Do not, then, believe Pliny when he writes to his friend Septicius :

Chronologic order in Pliny's letters.

> You have frequently pressed me to make a select collection of my letters, if there really be any deserving of a special preference, and give them to the public. I have selected them accordingly, not indeed in their proper order of time, for I was not compiling a history, but just as each came to hand. And now I have only to wish that you may have no reason to repent of your advice, nor I of my compliance ; in that case, I may probably inquire after the rest, which at present lie neglected, and preserve those I shall hereafter write. Farewell.

An artist's coquetry.

This is an artist's coquetry—nothing more. The erudition of Tillemont and of Mommsen has proved that the chronologic order is preserved in the arrangement of the letters, with the exception of the first book.

So we must not hope to find in Pliny that abandon, that amiable carelessness, which is the charm of the correspondence of Cicero, of Madame de Sévigné, or of Voltaire. This attraction is lacking in our author. But should the historian regret the fact? M. Boissier has well shown the danger of receiving unreservedly the testimony of the great Roman orator :

> In his judgments upon events or men, he often passes within a few days from one extreme to the other. In a letter dated the last of October, Cicero speaks of Cato as an excellent friend and declares himself well satisfied with his conduct upon a certain occasion. At the beginning of November, Cicero accuses Cato of having been shamefully malevolent upon the same

Cicero's inconsistencies.

occasion.　This inconsistency is explained by the fact that Cicero relies for his judgments upon his impressions ; and in a mobile soul like his impressions succeed each other quickly ; they are vivid, but very different at different times.

This appreciation may be applied with equal appropriateness to the letters of Madame de Sévigné and to those of Voltaire.

No rash judgments in Pliny's letters.

We have no such rash judgments to fear in Pliny's case.　He intends to publish his letters, and to publish them during his lifetime.　He will not, then, give us his first impressions ; whatever he shall tell us will always be weighed and considered.　What a disgrace if his contemporaries should discover error or falsehood in his statements !　His optimism may lead him to exaggerate the good, but his regard for the reader will always prevent him from fabricating anything.

To sum up, if the information which Pliny furnishes us has not the detailed precision of Cicero's confidences, it is valuable at least for its certainty and its seriousness.　He has not expressed, nor did he try to express, the whole truth ; but, we repeat it, he has said nothing that was not true.　His testimony needs to be completed, but not rectified.